Date Due

FEB 2 3 2002

Cover photographs used with permission:

Bob Edwards: *Glenbow Museum Library & Archives Department*
Ruth Lowe: *Tom Sandler*
Grant MacEwan: *MacEwan/Foran Collection*
Mona Parsons: *Andria Hill*
Jacques Plante: *Roland Forget, La Presse, Montreal*
Nell Shipman: *Northwest Museum of Arts & Culture*
Jay Silverheels: *Photo from world wide web*

◄ THE ►

CANADIANS

Biographies of a Nation

Volume II

Patrick Watson

McArthur & Company
Toronto

National Library of Canada Cataloguing in Publication Data

    Watson, Patrick, 1929 –
      Canadians: biographies of a nation

    Companion volume to the television series,
      Canadians: biographies of a nation

    Includes bibliographical references.
    ISBN 1-55278-170-4 (V.1) – ISBN 1-55278-240-9 (V.2)

1. Canada - Biography. 2. Canadians: biographies of a nation
(Television program). 1. Title

    FC25.W37 2000   971'.009'9   C00-931507-1

Design & Composition: *Mad Dog Design Inc.*
Cover & Photo f/x: *Mad Dog Design Inc.*
Original cover concept: *Carol Powers*
Printed in Canada by *Transcontinental Printing Inc.*

McArthur & Company,
322 King Street West, Suite 402,
Toronto, ON, M5V 1J2

The publisher would like to acknowledge the financial support of
the Government of Canada through the Book Publishing Industry
Development Program (BPIDP) and the Canada Council for our
publishing activities. The publisher further wishes to acknowledge the
financial support of the Ontario Arts Council for our publishing program.

10 9 8 7 6 5 4 3 2 1

Contents

THE CANADIANS
BIOGRAPHIES OF A NATION
Volume II

Both the television series and these books, based on that
series, have been gratifyingly successful. The series, opening under the title *Faces of Canada* when History Television
began to cablecast five years ago, was lucky to reach a few
thousand people as the fledgling specialty service first
opened its windows in a world crowded with competing
channels. From the beginning, audiences demonstrated an
appetite for stories about Canada and the people who have
given her the character and the texture of her life. By the
end of the fourth broadcast season, these one-hour classical biographical documentaries were reaching more than
half a million viewers weekly, in a wide demographic
curve across the country. Audience surveys, word-of-
mouth, mail, and people who stopped me in the street let
us know that this is a loyal audience who regularly seek
out these programs in the cluttered landscape that is the
contemporary Canadian television scene.

By the end of this coming season (beginning broadcast in April 2002), we will have completed sixty-six of
these hours, and a satisfying number of them have been
earning international awards at film and television festi-
vals. Teachers and others can order videocassettes of the
documentaries from www.history.ca or by phone at
(416) 486-1227. As of this writing, Great North Productions

of Edmonton has just completed the pilot of what we hope to become a complete collection of six- to seven-minute video digests of these programs to be made available to teachers across Canada for classroom use.

Volume I of what will probably become a series of books based on the television series was delivered to bookstores in January 2001 and by that August was already in its fourth printing. If Canadian readers continue to show such fascination with the rascals and heroes who make up these pages, there will certainly be a Volume III, and . . . who knows? In any case, the old supposition that Canadians are dull and not interested in their history has effectively been retired. The dramatized series *Canada: A People's History* has been one of the most successful in recent CBC Television history, and the continued growth of History Television's audiences suggests that these two broadcasting services are having a synergetic effect on the palpably growing hunger for our own stories.

I would be remiss not to acknowledge the vision of Norm Bolen and Sydney Suissa at History Television, the encouragement of Michael Levine and publisher Kim McArthur who conceived the books, the support of the Historica Foundation, the diligence and creativity of the producers, writers, and directors (acknowledged at each chapter's end), the clarity and energy of Executive Producer Patricia Phillips (who is very much the Hands-On chief of the television project), and the editorial guidance of Caroline Furey Bamford.

Patrick Watson
October 2001

Part One

MONA PARSONS
THE ROLE OF A LIFETIME

Imagine a *Heritage Minute* produced from the following script.[1] While the Mona Parsons story seems too close to a romantic movie script to be anything more than a highly contrived version of what really happened, it is in fact, except for a great deal of compression as required by the format, very close to the true story of a truly extraordinary Nova Scotian woman.

◆　◆　◆

MONA PARSONS
A Heritage Minute

(1) EXT. DUTCH COUNTRYSIDE. DAY. The aftermath of war. In the distance, puffs of smoke and the rumble of gunfire. Two fighter aircraft scream overhead. Jeeps and walking soldiers proceed away from the camera. Coming towards us, a small platoon of sad, exhausted German prisoners is being herded along the road by Canadian soldiers. SUPER: *THE DUTCH/GERMAN BORDER, 1945*

MONA, an emaciated, slightly dazed forty-five-year-old

---

1. This is an actual script that, as of October 2001, was in the queue for production in the *HISTOR!CA* heritage project. Continuing the work begun in 1988 by Charles Bronfman's CRB Foundation, the *Heritage Minutes* are a series of (as of this date) almost seventy "micro-movies": dramatic slightly fictionalized films of sixty seconds' duration that are seen on more than a thousand movie screens across Canada when first released, and then given as gifts to every television broadcaster and cable service in Canada.

woman, is being escorted by a young Canadian
SERGEANT, towards the camera, as three or four OFFI-
CERS come into frame from the opposite direction.

MONA

I'm telling you it IS true! I've been in a Nazi prison camp for
four years. Look at me! I'm half starved! I . . .

Clearly seen in the foreground as the OFFICERS meet
MONA and the SERGEANT is an officer's shoulder patch
or other insignia: The Nova Scotia Highlanders.

LIEUTENANT

What's going on here, Sergeant?

SERGEANT (cont.)

Claims she's a Canadian, sir.

SERGEANT (cont.)

(sotto voce) *I think she's a German spy, sir.*

LIEUTENANT

What's your name, lady?

MONA

Mona Parsons, sir.

FOSTER, an older officer, with general's shoulder mark-
ings, pushes forward.

FOSTER

Mona Parsons!! From Wolfville? Mona! It's me! Harry
Foster. My God, what's happened to you?

MONA

(still dazed)

Well . . . you see . . . I . . .

DISSOLVE TO

(2) INT. NAZI COURT MARTIAL. HOLLAND, 1941. DAY. A Nazi flag, a mix of uniformed and civilian officials. MONA in the dock. The dialogue is in German, with subtitles. SUPER: *AMSTERDAM, 1941*

The judge is a uniformed officer, monocled, dignified, a scar on his cheek.

JUDGE

(in German)

. . . and you are convicted of hiding enemy airmen in your Amsterdam home, and aiding their escape to Britain. The penalty for treason is death by firing squad.

MONA

(under her breath)

Firing squad!

JUDGE, PROSECUTOR, UNIFORMED GUARDS and others watch her with cool cynicism; they expect her to break down. Instead, after a cool beat, she bows courteously to the court, speaks with real dignity.

MONA

Meine Herren: Guten Morgen.

The JUDGE, others, are surprised, impressed.

(3) EXT. AMSTERDAM STREET. DAY. Two soldiers escort MONA to a vehicle. The JUDGE is standing near it in a leather trench coat, attended by two junior OFFICERS. He bows courteously as she is brought to the vehicle.

JUDGE
(in German)
Dear Lady: you have great courage. I recommend you appeal the sentence. You may use my name.

They lock eyes.

(4) INT. A WOLFVILLE LIVING ROOM. DAY. As the camera gently prospects the room, plants, piano, many photos of Mona, at several ages, including at the piano, we hear, with the accompaniment of appropriate music:

NARRATOR
Mona Parsons and her Dutch husband had saved dozens of downed Allied airmen. Escaping from a German prison in 1945, she walked several hundred kilometres across Germany to Holland. Widowed, she came home to Wolfville, married again, and died in 1976.

During this narration we DISSOLVE TO

(5) EXT. WOLFVILLE CEMETERY. DAY. Mona Parsons' actual tombstone. The inscription reads simply: Mona Louise Parsons, 1901–1976, Wife of Major General Harry Foster CBE DSO.

END

◆　◆　◆

The story came to this writer's attention almost by accident. A short article about Mona had appeared in *The Beaver*, a small historical monthly published by The Bay, in the October/November edition of 1998. I had barely skimmed that edition, being preoccupied with a documentary in production at the time, and had left it in the out-basket. Caroline Bamford, my wife, business partner, and the in-house editor at our small concern, put the magazine back on my desk a few days later with an imperious note scrawled on it in black marker-pen:

"Heritage Minute in Here: Page 16!"

I re-read the piece.

The author, actress Andria Hill, was a graduate student at Acadia University, in Wolfville, Nova Scotia. She was doing research for a Master's thesis on the history of the Acadia Ladies' Seminary in Wolfville, an institution that had, early in the century, a very active theatre program. She came across a brief note saying that one of the 1920 graduates of that program had been found safe in Holland at the end of World War II after spending nearly four years in Nazi prisons. Andria Hill set off on a quest.

Her research began in Middleton, Nova Scotia, in the heart of the Annapolis Valley, where Mona Louise Parsons was born at 370 Main Street, on February 17th, 1901. Her father Norval was the eponymous head of Parsons and Elliott Home Furnishings on Commercial Street, just around the corner from the family home. Mona was the youngest of Norval and his wife Mary Parsons' three children, with older brothers Ross and Quinn. The business was prosperous, as was the town of Middleton, in the years leading up to the Great War. Norval was a patriot as well as a successful merchant. He wore the uniform of an officer in the local militia, and his photos show a confident, genial man with a sense of position and of the obligations of that position. This morality he seems to have communicated to his adored youngest child, Mona.

A class photograph at the new MacDonald Consolidated school, taken in 1910, shows an already graceful, womanly Mona, glancing at the camera with what might have been a shy look, but knowing what we know about her as she matured may well have been an early example of her skill as an actress.

The turn of the year, from 1910 to 1911, was expected by the Parsons family to be the opening of another decade of prosperity. But disaster struck a month after Christmas. Downtown Middleton — like many Nova Scotia towns built almost entirely of wood — caught fire on January 26th. Parsons Elliott Home Furnishings was completely destroyed, along with most of the downtown area, and photographs of the smouldering town a day later show it almost flattened.

Norval Parsons was not only a successful merchant but also a prudent one, and the insurance on the furniture business allowed him to move the family sixty kilometres up the tracks to Wolfville, where he decided to become a stockbroker, having done pretty well in the market during his home furnishing days. Wolfville was already a lively university town. There was some old money. The colonial sense of class and position was still alive and well in those pre-war days, and we have to suppose that Lieutenant Colonel Norval Parsons did not find that aspect of the community's social life difficult to live with.

Norval and his sons would go off to war in 1914, and survive it (Norval coming home with the crown and pip of a lieutenant colonel on his epaulettes), and while they were away the little girl transformed into a tall, lithe, elegant young woman with a modestly theatrical manner and a bewitchingly sultry voice. After graduation, she studied voice in Boston, and then taught drama in Arkansas between visits home. By 1929, she knew she wanted a career on stage and that she should go where the theatre was the centre of the universe instead of a casual amusement for the better families of a small provincial town. When Mona announced her intention of going to New York to try her luck on the stage there, her mother Mary was not pleased. Mona and Mary had spent the war closely together while the men were away in the army, and Mary found the prospect of losing her great companion difficult to contemplate. But Norval was enchanted: his daughter on the stage? In New York! He quietly let Mona know that it was all right with him. Anything that was all right with Norval, it seems, was all right with Mona too. So off she went.

New York in the 1920s presents a series of old black-and-white newsreel and movie images that keep turning up in historical documentaries and studies of the social evolution of the United States, almost like icons. It was a euphoric time for a while after the horrors of The War To

End All Wars had died down, and the world was at peace and would always be at peace for the rest of time, as everyone knew. The prosperity that had boomed with America's wartime production of armaments kept on booming. In 1920 the "manufacturing, sale, or transportation" of alcoholic beverages had been made illegal by the Eighteenth Amendment to the Constitution. This ill-conceived and destructive legislation, supported by the *Volstead Act*, which added a powerful enforcement mechanism and was intended to strike the fear of the law into drinkers and merchants of drink, in fact so dramatically produced the opposite of what its promoters had intended that a best-selling novel a few years later was based entirely — and quite credibly — on the premise that the anti-alcohol movement had been started and funded by the distillers.

What happened was that flouting the law by drinking became a kind of national sport. Respect for the law and its officers was a laughing matter. Thousands of people died from drinking cheap bootleg liquor. Distillers in Canada and the United states became rich while no alcohol-based tax revenue flowed into the national coffers. For hundreds of thousands of Americans organized crime became glamorous and flourished as never before.

New York was peppered with illicit drinking spots called speakeasies. Disdain for the law was reflected in widespread public dismissal of proprieties of all kinds. Dress became flamboyant. Sexual adventuring was open and glamorized. The automobile, still in its youth and still competing with horses (and their droppings) in the streets of all North American cities, grew exponentially as a favourite location for sexual adventure and a favoured mechanism for showing off flamboyant clothes and wild behaviour. This was the New York where Mona Parsons came to make her mark on the stage.

It did not go well — at least, not in the way she had expected. Instead of stardom in the latest Noel Coward or Sherwood Anderson play on Broadway, she auditioned for a bread-and-butter job as a chorus girl in the Ziegfeld Follies. This was a series of stage reviews produced by the flamboyant Florenz Ziegfeld in imitation of Paris's famous *Folies Bergères*. They were splashy, naughty, expensive, popular: a stage reflection of the genially outrageous tone of the age. The chorus-line dancers were trained to a mechanical perfection, and cast for their legs and their faces almost as much as for their dancing abilities. It is probable that many of the girls dancing alongside Mona Louise Parsons thought they had reached some kind of professional pinnacle to be doing the high kick in the Follies, but not Mona. She liked the glamour and the attention, all right; there was no shortage of lively dates and brilliant parties. The pay was adequate. But the artistic rewards were not what she had come to New York to find.

Remember, this is a woman in her late twenties to whom the universe has been very good. She carries herself with a combination of regality, confidence, and grace that bring people to a dead stop just to watch her pass. When her eyes light on yours as she sweeps the room, you hope that she really sees what a fine and desirable person you are; you can't help a surge of something like desire. There is a combination of appraisal, delight, and quizzicality in that glance from which you cannot look away.

There are people who love the camera and people whom the camera loves: Mona Parsons was both. Had she grown up in the early days of television she would have set new benchmarks, perhaps as an actor, but more likely as a program host. We know from the thousands of photos and the few moments of home movie footage that you could not take your eyes off her, and from what her friends said and wrote we know that her voice held you in thrall.

But New York is New York: the best and the brightest in the world of theatre still come there for the main chance, and many end up working in drug stores or offices — or head for home. The competition is so vast and the decisions of casting directors and producers so whimsical and ultimately private that there simply is no guarantee that rockets will ignite as designed. Mona Parsons kept on pounding the streets auditioning for serious roles and for a while she kept on hoping. But what happened next suggests that the New York exhilaration had exhausted itself. While she seems to have fallen in love with Manhattan like so many who come to try it out and end up staying forever, after a while that dream of triumph on the stage began to seem more like a fantasy than a strategy.

It is probably not necessary to say that up to this point there is nothing in the Mona Parsons story that in any conceivable way points to her finding herself in the dock in a Nazi court in Amsterdam, accused of the capital crime of treason, just a little more than ten years down the road. What did happen next was a call from home: Mary Parsons had been felled by a stroke. She was calling for Mona. She needed constant care. Mona gave her notice to the Ziegfeld people, gathered her stuff together, said good-bye to her pals, and took the train for Canada. It was just a few days before her 29th birthday, February 17th. A day after that birthday Mary Parsons had a second stroke and died.

It is at this point that Mona Parsons makes one of the relatively few conventional decisions of these first few decades of her life. It seems that the sudden death of her mother led her to stand back and reconsider the romantic role of the New York star of stage (and screen?), and to conclude that it was either less glamorous or less possible than she had hoped. Probably influenced by her father's practical business and career outlook, in the midst of an economic depression that left millions starving and walking the streets, she knew that she had better find something to do that was solid, predictable, useful, not likely to be made less viable by the depression. She chose something that — at a time when careers were very limited for independent-minded women — was seen as normal: nursing.

We next find her in New Jersey, at the Jersey City Medical Center. When she finished training there she made use of family contacts and landed a job with a Nova-Scotian expatriate, Dr. Ross Faulkner, who had a fashionable clinic in Manhattan, on Park Avenue. So there she was, professionally established in a city she adored, well placed to find a husband should she choose to do that, among the medical professionals or the fashionable clientele of Dr. Faulkner's clinic. And if it had not been for a phone call from her brother Ross, it seems likely that she would have done exactly that.

Ross had come to know a wealthy Dutchman named Willem Leonhardt, who was travelling in North America to develop outlets for his family's plumbing fixture business. He was coming to New York and needed someone who knew the town well, and was socially gifted, to show him around. At first, when she learned that Willem was divorced from a woman who had born a son he had not fathered, Mona hesitated to respond to the millionaire's playful charm and his obvious infatuation with the willowy, throaty-voiced, dark-eyed beauty from Nova Scotia. But the relationship blossomed pretty rapidly, all the same. In the summer of 1937 the two of them went to Wolfville to visit Norval (who had remarried), and then got on a liner bound for Holland. She had agreed to marry him.

Mona was a hit in Holland. Willem Leonhardt's nephew Kristoph told Andria Hill when the author arrived in Amsterdam to track down that part of Mona's story that when he first met the compellingly beautiful Mona he said to himself, "My God! My uncle is marrying an American film star!"

Willem was the centre of a lively social circle. Mona had to start from scratch learning Nederlands, not the easiest of the Germanic languages, but despite that handicap she played her new hostess role like a trooper, and soon won over the initially suspicious Leonhardt parents (after all, their son was a millionaire, so of course they would be suspicious). And — ironically as it would turn out — she also won over Willem's close friend the horse breeder Piet Houtapell and his very young wife Pam.

The documentary film of Mona's story is rich with

photographs of that period, most in black and white but some in a faded colour that still seems very immediate and present almost sixty-five years later. There are photos of the family gatherings, of the smiling faces of Piet and Pam Houtapell, with their arms around Mona and Willem, of the wedding with its luxurious outdoor reception, Mona reigning queenlike and confident over the legions of the Amsterdam upper crust who came to celebrate Willem's latest. Mona's brother Ross is in those pictures too, with his wife Mary. The champagne bottles and the wedding cake and the mountains of food and the extravagant dresses, the monocles, the top hats, the Amsterdam *savoir-faire*, the nonchalance, the luxury, all recorded by the omnipresent camera.

As was much of the honeymoon that followed. Six months of it, in the swellest resort spots of Europe. Money was not a problem for Willem Leonhardt. They drove fast cars, lounged on yachts and danced in glamorous ball-rooms. If they were conscious of the rumblings from Germany, it did not show. When they got back to Holland early in 1938 they found a piece of land at Laren about half an hour from downtown Amsterdam, and built a house there, and called it *Ingleside*. They hired staff, and planted hedges and gardens which are still there and were pho-tographed by Andria Hill when she went to see *Ingleside* for her book on Mona.

Willem was away in Amsterdam a lot, commuting in a series of expensive cars. Soon *Ingleside* and its glamorous couple were the talk of the town. Willem had a pale oak August Förster grand piano specially built for her. She would play classical favourites for her guests and preside over those glittering evenings as if she were a stage queen, in gorgeous costume and careful makeup. It was a role, and by God she was going to play it really well.

Before long, she would be caught up in the role that would bring her the biggest challenge of her acting career. The Second World War was moving in on them.

The Germans crossed into Holland in the small hours of the morning, and in five days, despite a brave but ill-prepared resistance by the tiny army of Holland, it was all over. Some of the survivors will tell you now that the defences had been concentrated on the coast for so long, because of the historic rivalry and difficulties with England, that they were not ready for invasion from the East. As unlikely as that seems (since the war had been raging for eight months when the Germans crossed the border) wherever the Dutch had concentrated their defences there would be, by May 10th, 1940, no way for that small country to stop the *Blitzkrieg*.[2]

The historian Hans DeVries who helped guide us through the Holland part of the Mona Parsons story says that for many people life went on much as it had, at least for the first few months of the German occupation. "The Germans sort of pussy-footed their way in," De Vries said, describing their early attempts to relax and even make friends with their new Dutch "citizens." But by late 1941 the colour of that occupation had changed. Rigid rationing had been introduced, there was a nine o'clock curfew. A resistance movement had been organized. Arrests were fre-

2. *Blitzkrieg* literally means "lightning war."

quent, and so were executions. People disappeared. The pretence of normalcy was gone.

Now as the war gathered momentum the traffic of warplanes across the English Channel, in both directions, became heavier week by week. In 1941 the Battle of Britain began with the nightly pounding of London and other industrial targets, the flattening of the city of Coventry, the brilliant defence by teenage pilots in Spitfires and Hurricanes that would lead Winston Churchill to say that "Never in the field of human conflict was so much owed by so many to so few." But it was not just Britain that felt the rain of bombs. She was vigorously retaliating against Germany, and morning after morning, as the exhausted and often wounded bomber crews returned over Holland from their raids deep into German territory, pilots sometimes decided that they were out of luck, or fuel, or altitude, and decided to bail out over land rather than over the dark seas where they would never be found alive. Dutch citizens began to take them in.

This was perfect for the brilliant, wealthy socialite proprietors of *Ingleside*. They built a secret room up under the eaves. Downed Allied pilots and crews, protected by the farmers who found them hiding by the dikes or windmills, could be brought to the Leonhardt house for their few nights of hiding before transport could be arranged to Leiden, on the coast, and thence by fishing boat to waiting British submarines. This was a great adventure for Mona and Willem, a cool adventure, a feeling of invulnerability in face of the risk of death, of pulling it off under the noses of the hated enemy, of Nothing Can Happen To Us, we're the Leonhardts. There was a kind of cell of conspirators, trusted old friends mostly, deeply pleased with themselves to be — in the midst of the seeming impotence of an occupied people — to be actually *doing something*.

However, one of the trusted friends at the Leiden end of the underground railroad was in fact a Nazi informer. The *Ingleside* safe house had been used only four times before the Leiden cell was infected. In September 1941, Willem and Mona gave shelter to two allied airmen, Richard Pape and William Moir, for an unprecedented six days — unable to move them because of the increasingly tight net of Nazi intelligence. A couple of days later, when Pape and Moir arrived at Leiden, the Nazis moved. Now *Ingleside* was on their map. An architect named Dirk Brouwer was arrested and shot. He had brought fliers to *Ingleside*. Mona and Willem thought that if they fled it would be evidence of guilt, but if they stayed they would be sitting victims.

Willem was well known as a fishing enthusiast; so, assuming that only the male members of the cell would be of interest to the Germans, they decided that Mona would continue to entertain at *Ingleside*, as usual, and just say — if they came after him — that Willem was on a fishing trip, she didn't know when he would be back. When two Gestapo agents appeared at her door she invited them in and offered them drinks.[3] They were not fooled. Before long she was in Weteringschane Prison in Amsterdam, awaiting trial.

In a way, you already know the rest. But it is a story that keeps unfolding its amazing chapters. The Gestapo

---

3. *Gestapo*: a contraction of *Geheimestaatspolizei* meaning "state secret police."

were holding Mona as bait to help catch Willem. It took three months. Then they caught him; December 21st, 1941. On December 22nd Mona's cell door opened, and she was told to dress; she was going to trial.

It would be a military court. Military courts did not convict women. But they convicted Mona. The trial was in a ballroom where Mona had often danced the night away, at the Carlton Hotel, in Amsterdam. Mona's comprehension of German was not very good, but she did understand the phrases *Todestraffe*, and *Exekutionskommando*, "death sentence," and "firing squad." She blanched but stayed erect. She offered a cool, dignified bow to the court. She said, in the best German she could muster, "*Meine Herren: Guten Morgen*," and walked with dignity between her escorts towards the waiting van.

The judge must have been a man of character. He had clearly been struck by her courage and dignity. He crossed the court and stopped the escorts. He complimented her, and recommended that she appeal, and said he would forward the appeal to the highest-ranking officer in Holland, with a recommendation of clemency.

The first of the many prisons Mona would live in for the next few years was at Krefeld, in the German Rhineland. She was put to knitting socks for soldiers, and concealed a painful blister knot in each sole. They found her out. Eventually she was moved to a prison at Vechta, in Northern Germany south of Bremen, and thrust into solitary confinement. But after a while she was put back to work again, this time in the kitchen, as a cleaner, and here is where the next part of the story begins.

A young Dutch Baroness was also in a solitary cell in the Vechta prison, having shown her German captors that she was an incorrigible escape artist. Somehow the two women got to know each other, and Mona began to smuggle a few potatoes, in her apron pocket, to the hungry twenty-two-year-old aristocrat. The Baroness Wendelien van Boetzelaer. Now that she had an ally, the Baroness began to devise another escape plan. Interviewed in Amsterdam for our television program, she told us that not only were they very hungry in Vechta, but that there was no heat on that top floor where the solitary cells were, and that, oddly, the prison governess took sufficient pity on the two women to respond to their pleas for some warm clothes to help them survive the winter of 1944. This, Wendelien pointed out to Mona, would give them cover for their prison drabs when the opportunity came for them to slip away. She was sure, she said, that such an opportunity would come. When it did it was spectacular and dramatic.

To help them keep up their morale, Wendelien told us, "[W]e exchanged recipes, which was a great thing in the camps because everybody was so hungry. And Mona was fond of delicious recipes. Also she had a great repertoire of songs . . . military songs, happy songs, naughty songs, whatever." Before long there was an opportunity that would shut the songs down, but get them out of Vechta.

Vechta had an airfield and rail yards. The two prisons, one for women and one for men, flanked the runway. The Allies, in the early months of 1945, were systematically destroying airfields and rail facilities all over Germany, and one day they hit Vechta. The first bomb missed the runway and blew the men's prison to fragments, killing hundreds of inmates. Wendelien still does not understand why she had been allowed to come down to the ground floor that day, but she was there and watched with horror as the other prison building burst into flames and began to collapse. Suddenly the head of the women's prison ordered her charges out into the yard, under guard, in case her building was going to be a target for the Allied bombs as well.

"All these German women threw themselves on the floor shouting 'Ich will nicht sterben!' (I don't want to die!)" Wendelien recounts, at seventy-nine, still crinkling with what looks exactly like mischievous delight at the memory. "So Mona and I . . . we took each other by the hand and we [just walked] out. No one even looked at us. All these guards were [distracted] by the bombs . . . and we just ran along the airfield. So. On and on we ran."

Vechta is some 160 km from the Dutch border. So "on and on" would be the condition of life for the forty-four-year-old Canadian and the twenty-two-year-old Dutch girl for quite a few days. Eighteen kilometres the first day. They had nothing to eat. They drank water out of ditches. They shivered in the cold, even under their extra clothes. As night came down they came to a farm where the barn was well separated from the house. There were lights in the house but the barn was dark. Exhausted, they took the chance, slipped into the dark old building, found some straw, bundled themselves up under it, and slept.

In the morning they were starving, and decided to take the chance. They walked boldly up to the farmhouse.

"Of course Mona didn't speak . . . German,"Wendelien told us.

And we were supposed to be Germans. We were not supposed to be an English (sic) woman and a Dutch woman evading from prison. So my German happened to be quite good, but Mona absolutely had to keep her mouth shut. So we had to pretend that she was a little . . . ga ga. A little, you know, addled. Which she was very good at! Because she was an actress. She had trained as an actress. She was fantastic. They were sorry for that condition, they were sorry for me! And she played that up so naturally that even I thought she was not quite well in the head!

It took them two weeks. They did farm chores in exchange for food. As they came closer to the Dutch border they began to find people they felt they could trust. At a village near the border with Holland they took the risk of confiding in the mayor, who gave them false papers. And from then on, billeted in different homes, they did not see each other again until they met for dinner — at *Ingleside* — a year after the war.

The first troops across the border in the sector that Mona and Wendelien had found themselves in were Poles. Right behind the Poles were the Canadians. Battalion commanders were very careful about German civilians trying to cross the border. They had been warned that the Germans might use women as decoys or subversives, plant booby-trap bombs on them or give them weapons they could use to kill senior officers they got close to. So when Mona was picked up walking out of Germany, despite her fluent English and exhausted appearance, they were not going to take any chances. The first encounter in was not precisely the way we depict it in the *Heritage Minute* script; that is dramatic licence. But the encounter with the North Novies in a later interrogation was every bit as dramatic in its essence.

The Nova Scotia Highlanders are headquartered in Amherst and have been since the unit was formed to fight in the Great War, in 1914. Captain Robbins Elliott, a Highlanders veteran, was a young logistics officer at the time, and knew a young soldier who was the third or fourth to question her.

"And she said, 'I am a Canadian.' And he said, 'If you are a Canadian where are you from?' And she said 'My name is Mona Parsons and I come from a little tiny village in Nova Scotia called Wolfville.' And apparently he nearly dropped the box he was holding. He said, 'Dear God! My name is Clarence Leonard. I'm from Halifax, and you've just encountered the North Nova Scotia Highlanders!'"

The unit surgeon was Kelly MacLean. Mona had acted on the Acadia stage with him. And there were two other friends from her Acadia days: Captains Vincent White and Ralph Shaw. She also met an old childhood chum, Harry Foster, now a major general. Mona's amazing story got her a ride home to *Ingleside*, and a good long rest among friends.

There was no sign of Willem. Young Captain Robbins Elliott, whom she had met with the North Novies, came and visited her at Ingleside. So did Lie Van Oldenburg, a neighbour who had managed to grab some of her possessions when she was arrested, and keep them out of the hands of the Germans who had taken over her house for an officers' billet, and left schnapps glass stains all over the oak surface of the beautiful August Förster, which was, miraculously, still there and still playable. There was no sign of Willem.

In fact he was alive but not well. The three years of starvation and brutal prison conditions had worsened an inherited kidney disease, and when American forces liberated his concentration camp they put him into hospital for ten weeks, during which time he was able to get word to Mona. Relieved that he would be coming home after all, Mona sought the healing touch of plants and flowers, and began to restore her gardens. When Willem did get home, finally, he sold his part of the family business to his brother, and — between bouts of hospitalization and immobility — he and Mona travelled, at first in Europe, and then to Canada. Mona's brother Ross organized a Nova Scotia–style fishing trip for Willem, and Mona tried to persuade him to stay in Canada. But as his body and spirit deteriorated, he wanted to be home and with doctors and surrounding he knew and trusted.

Now Mona who had always suffered from lung problems and bronchitis began to have more frequent and more serious bouts of illness. Willem sent her to the Birchel Benner Clinic in Switzerland, and while she was resting there in 1953 she got the news that he was permanently bedridden. When she got home to *Ingleside*, she was surprised to find that Piet Houtapell's young wife Pam had taken over as the principal caregiver. This made Mona a little uneasy, and for good reason. When Willem died in

April 1956, she discovered that he had left one-quarter of his estate to Pam, and that they had been carrying on a secret affair for years.

Then, in the midst of that devastating news, the estranged son from Willem's first marriage, a man who was not even Willem's natural son, launched legal action to claim three-quarters of the remaining estate. The legal battle continued until 1961. By that time there was little left of the estate, and Mona had lost. That struggle finished Holland for Mona, for all time. She took what was left, including her beloved August Förster piano, and headed back to Canada.

When she had first come back to Nova Scotia in 1957, she stayed in Halifax's elegant Lord Nelson Hotel, and then moved to a flat at 56 Inglis Street. Norval was dead; her two brothers Ross and Gwynne, and her stepmother Alma, were the only family left. One day she ran into her old chum, Major General Harry Foster, retired, and as they chatted about that extraordinary encounter on the Dutch/German border more than a decade before, a sense of the affection that grows out of shared adventure and adversity grew up between them, and in 1959 they were married. It was a good, comfortable marriage. They lived for a while in the Chester Basin in a tranquil house at Lobster Point. Friends came to visit, and life was good for a while, until Harry was diagnosed with a cancer, and died just five years after their wedding. Now Mona said it was time to go home to Wolfville.

The August Förster piano is still there, you can go and see it if you make friends with its new owner. Mona kept it in Wolfville for a few years, and invited young people to come and play it. She took a course or two at the university, went to the theatre, developed a reputation for amiable eccentricity, managed to cope with the encroachments of old age, and, oddly, did not say much about her wartime adventures. After a while, to pay for the extra health care she needed, she began to sell her possessions, including the piano with its schnapps-stained lid, and to give away her silverware to friends. She refused to have it refinished; it had memories. She let her friends know about the family plot at the Willowbank Cemetery, just off Ridge Road in Wolfville, and wrote to her old comrade Wendelien that, "At least when it's my turn to go they won't have to cart me from anywhere."

And among her things, when she died in November of 1976, they discovered two certificates of commendation for her contribution to the Allied War Effort. One is signed by British Air Chief Marshall Lord Arthur Tedder. The second bears the signature of the Supreme Commander of the Allied Forces in Europe, and later President of the United States, Dwight D. Eisenhower. Her photograph is on the wall of Branch 74, of the Royal Canadian Legion in Wolfville, just behind the dyke that keeps Wolfville from being flooded by the giant tides of the Bay of Fundy. If you get invited to the Legion on one of the great anniversaries, D-Day, say, (the invasion of Normandy) or VE-Day (the end of the war in Europe), you'll probably be with the grizzled old veterans there when they stand and raise their glasses to that photograph, and call out a toast "To Mona Parsons, a brave and beautiful lady."

But if you stroll over to Willowbank, to the Parsons Family Plot, you will not find on the fine big stone that marks her place anything that even hints at the courage and fortitude and wartime experience of this valiant and luminous woman. The marker says simply:

MONA LOUISE PARSONS
1901–1976

WIFE OF MAJOR GENERAL HARRY FOSTER
CBE DSO

◆ ◆ ◆

The original documentary was produced and directed by F. Whitman Trecartin. It was written by Andria Hill and F. Whitman Trecartin, and photographed by Les Krizsan, CSC.

ADDITIONAL READING:
 Andria Hill: *Biography of Mona Parsons*

Part Two

JOSHUA SLOCUM
A New World Columbus

The great challenge to the biographer, whether on film or video or in print, is first of all to find an imaginative way into not only the narrative line of his subject's life, the list of events and people and places, but also into that life's texture, its buzz, its little manners and asides and apparently trivial details. A writer trying to put together a meaningful account of the life of someone who has been dead for a hundred years should read not only whatever documents have survived, and pore over photographs, he should also walk the streets and touch, if he can, the physical objects that were touched by his subject: the books, clothes, furniture, the cups, and plates. To be true to the subject, if that subject climbed a mountain, the biographer should climb it too. If it is a painter we are dealing with, the biographer should at least know the smell and texture of wet paint, and the feel of its going onto canvas; if a magician, the writer who takes the trouble to find out what it is like to perform some sleight of hand will get further into that magician's mind than the writer who only sees a performance.

Filmmaker Peter Rowe, himself an experienced single-handed deepwater sailor, set out to make this documentary on the life of Joshua Slocum. He found he was in the company of many other sailors who, in trying to reproduce the Fundyman's extraordinary feat of sailing alone around the world, had to become partial biographers themselves.

Some of these sailor/disciples provided our writer-director with the very kind of physical texture I am talking about. Many of the sailors who set out to emulate the Slocum circumnavigation have chosen to do so in replicas of Slocum's own vessel, the *Spray*, a decaying wreck that Slocum found at Fairhaven Massachusetts and rebuilt, plank by plank, until she was a totally new boat. Director Peter Rowe concluded that the *Spray* has been copied more than any other vessel in the history of sailing, perhaps as many as eight hundred times. Burl Ives had a *Spray* and when it began to decline and fail, another would-be Slocum imitator named David Dunn not only acquired the famous folksinger's replica, but also followed the pattern of Slocum's own reconstruction of his *Spray*, building a steam box to bend the new planks in, and replacing everything that needed to be replaced. Many others have started from scratch, using the drawings and descriptions that the pioneering circumnavigator published in his classic of narrative writing, *Sailing Alone Around the World*. David Dunn is an Idaho schoolteacher who dropped his career for a complex ten-year project on the ancient mariner. He told us,

We are going to recreate Slocum's voyage in its entirety. Again, we'll enter and exit the ports at the same time Slocum did. Our vessel is the largest copy of the Spray *ever made. We have totally rebuilt her and systems are set up as an expedition vessel. And then teams of teachers will join me in teams of three. They will teach via satellite into the Internet and the lessons will be distributed around the world.*

We will meet and hear from several other Slocum pilgrims and emulators, but it is time to step back and review some of those narrative signposts of place and people and events upon which the texture of a life story is arranged.

Joshua Slocum was born on the shores of Nova Scotia's famous Bay of Fundy, on (he wrote) "a cold spot on coldest North Mountain, on a cold February 20, 1844." He was the fifth child of John Slocum, of a loyalist New England family. John Slocum was a not very successful farmer, and by his son's account a tyrannical father. In 1852 he gave up the failing farm and moved the family out to Brier Island where he started a boot factory. Joshua was set to work there when he still just a boy. Pew 13 in the Westport Baptist Church is marked with a plaque to show where the Slocum family worshipped every Sunday. The building that housed the boot factory is still there too. The ferry that takes you out to the island bears the name *JOSHUA SLOCUM* on the plate across the wheelhouse, both fore and aft, the young boot-maker and later master mariner being the island's most famous son, perhaps its only famous son.

He used to muse about the sea as he watched the sails pass outside the boot shop window. When he cobbled together a miniature clipper ship out of scraps of wood and canvas — almost certainly a meticulous model given what we know of his skills at make-and-mend when he finally did go to sea — the father saw the little vessel as a sign of frivolity. "The handiwork of the devil," he said — and smashed it under foot. That was probably the moment when young Joshua saw unequivocally that he did not belong in that boot shop with that man. He soon ran away to sea, first as a cook on a schooner, and then as an ordinary seaman on a *deal drogher* sailing for Liverpool. *Deal* is a very old word for slices of timber (nine inches wide, three inches thick, at least six feet long) rough sawn from a log. *Drogher* (or *droger*) is a not very complimentary word, originally for slow and awkward coastal vessels in the West Indies. Later the word was applied to the rough craft that sailed the millions of tons of Nova Scotia pine and spruce that for a couple of centuries constituted the colony's principal export to Britain.

Young Slocum had only a few years in school, but books and words caught him young, and there is a natural cadence to his writing, never more winning than when he is dealing with the passion that guided his life.

The wonderful sea charmed me from the first. I was born in the breezes, and I studied the sea as perhaps few have, neglecting all else.

That study rewarded him well. Almost entirely self-taught, he rapidly acquired the complex mathematical skills needed to navigate by sun, stars, and compass. He impressed his superiors with his confident handling of rope and canvas, the repairing of broken spars, and his command of the respect of others. Throughout the 1860s and the 1870s he sailed the Atlantic, the Caribbean, the Pacific, and the South China Sea. He also tried boat building, fishing, and for a season, hunting sea otters off the coast of British Columbia. By 1869 he had won command of his first ship, a coasting schooner. He was twenty-five years old.

Two years later he was commanding a barque bound for Australia. The barque, with its main and foremast billowing with classic square sails, a cloud of triangular jibs and staysails forward and a mizzenmast aft, also fore-and-aft rigged, was *the* ship for the merchant skipper of the period. Sail had less than a quarter century left before steam overtook it as the motive force of maritime commerce. But to be in command of a transoceanic barque at the age of twenty-seven was to have arrived.

Ashore at a dance in Sydney he met the beautiful, confident Virginia Albertina Walker. As captain of a vessel he had private quarters and the right to bring his wife along on voyages. Within weeks Virginia was Mrs. Joshua Slocum, and had gone to sea with her new husband. This courageous woman would, in her tragically short life, bear all of her children at sea, often with only her husband to help. She would save his life during a mutiny, much later, coming on deck with a pistol at the crucial moment. And she would leave him bereft when she died, during a voyage, after only thirteen years of marriage.

But before that blow to the young skipper's life, he rapidly climbed about as high as it was possible to climb. The *Northern Light*, his next command, was said by many to be the finest American merchant vessel afloat. Her owners had been impressed by the young Nova Scotian with the reputation for firm command, sure navigation, and rapid crossings. The command of the *Northern Light* was not all they had to offer: they gave him shares in the ownership of the magnificent ship. He fitted out the captain's cabin so that Virginia could live in comfortable elegance. Before long he owned the ship outright. He had been five times around the world, had skippered some of the finest ships afloat, and now was part owner of the best of them all. He was just forty years old.

But there was not much time for him to enjoy it. Things began to sour, rapidly, but it is hard to discern exactly why. On a sixth voyage around the world, the captain with the reputation for firm and successful command found himself faced with mutiny, his wife having to take up a weapon to help him. He regained control and put the mutineers in irons. Later a mate whom Slocum had imprisoned brought criminal charges against him, the principals were able to confiscate Slocum's shares in the ship. So he had lost the *Northern Light*. He took over a smaller vessel, the *Aquidneck*, running to Argentina and Bolivia. It was on *Aquidneck*, anchored off Buenos Aires, that he lost his beloved Virginia.

His second marriage, to a distant cousin, was a disaster. He took *Aquidneck* to Brazil with a cargo of poorly stowed pianos that were destroyed in a storm. Disease was rife on the ship, and when she was wrecked, finally, off the coast of Brazil, and Slocum had paid off the crew, he was left with almost no money, a very unhappy wife and two sons, and no way to get home.

It was at that point that Joshua Slocum seems to have begun to look at himself in a new light. He was, at first, appalled at the loss of his ship.

I'll wager that since man first took to the oceans, there have been literally millions of ships sunk on the edges or the bottom of the seas, but hefty precedent doesn't make you feel any better when you hear that terrible sound of keel striking bottom, or feel the awful sensation as your ship cuts her way, not through water, but into granite.

He looked at the wreck. He still owned it, what was left of it. He had experience as a boat builder. He had two sons to help him. We do not know enough of what was going through his mind to tell exactly how the notion came to him, but somehow he decided to build a seagoing canoe, the *Liberdade*, and take his young family home to New England in it. And he did that. The vessel was thirty-six feet long, rigged with slat-ribbed sails, like a Chinese junk. The *Liberdade* voyage, 5,800 miles from Brazil to Washington, DC, was quite remarkable just as a feat of seamanship. When they reached American waters Slocum decided to take the little craft north through the swamps and wetlands of the Carolinas, thus becoming one of the first blue water boats to navigate what is now called the intracoastal waterway. Slocum would later turn that adventure into his first book, *The Voyage of the Liberdade*.

This book has also generated at least one imitator. More than a century later, one of the many Slocum followers, who had also lost his own ship (to a storm in the Irish Sea) decided that his next challenge should be to reproduce that part of the great old Captain's life as well, and he too built a *Liberdade*. He also wrote a book about it, and sailed it across oceans to relive the experience of his hero. This was a Welshman named David Sinnett Jones. His career as a professional racing driver had been wrecked when he lost a lung to cancer. His first boat, a replica of Slocum's *Spray*, lay at the bottom of the Irish Sea. Like Slocum on a beach in Brazil, David Sinnett Jones set about to rebuild his life.

I said to Suzanne, "That's what I should do, if I can get
sponsorship to build Liberdade, because I'm shipwrecked,

*so I haven't got a ship. So this is what I should do, the
same as Joshua did. He built the Liberdade when he was
shipwrecked in southern Brazil."*

So he built a replica, the first ever, of the thirty-six-foot
sailing canoe that Slocum had built with his family on the
Brazilian beach. This seventy-one year old with one lung
sailed his *Liberdade* alone from Wales to Brazil, then recre-
ated Slocum's route, sailing from Paranagua to Martha's
Vineyard.

Slocum's new wife, after the terrors of the shipwreck
and the terrors of the Liberdade voyage, would never sail
again. She took the children by rail to live with her inland
relatives. Slocum's marriage was crumbling, and so, it
seemed, was his life at sea. Steamships, "filthy, stinking
steamships" he called them, were replacing the great
winged sailing ships. When the Brooklyn Bridge was built
in the 1880s it was made too low for the tall ships to pass
beneath. Electric trams were replacing horses. Railways
were replacing ships on the coastal runs. Slocum tried con-
tracting himself out to that disagreeable new coal-fired
world. He undertook to deliver a warship, the *Destroyer*, to
a civil war–torn Brazil. The wrong faction — from
Slocum's point of interest — intercepted him and sank the
Destroyer. The contract was not fulfilled; so the backers did
not pay their captain, and he slunk home broke in pocket
and broken in his soul. Within five years Slocum had lost
virtually everything: his wife, his home, his money, his
family, and his profession. He had run aground.

One day he heard that the great Herman Melville was
coming to a Massachusetts hall to read from a new novel.

Melville, Robert Louis Stevenson, and a few others had found the decline of the age of sail a literary goldmine. As the world began to feel the disappearance of a great commercial and cultural set of images, some novelists discovered the poetic and fictional power of accounts of a vanishing craft. Slocum went to hear Melville. The novel was *Typee*. Always a great reader, and with one fairly successful book already in print, he began to think that perhaps the prime task of the next part of his life would be to translate into print his own adventures across the oceans and among the islands that so beckoned readers' imaginations away from the dark Satanic mills. If there was going to be no more need for traditional sailing captains in command of great vessels with great crews, what about making a major voyage in a smaller boat, and then, like Melville and Stevenson turning the adventure into literature, and making the voyage pay by telling others about it.

But he *would* need a ship. In a Boston shipyard a chance meeting with an old whaler would put his life back on course. Captain Eben Pierce was a whaling captain who had made his fortune (and contributed to the reduction of the world's whale population) by inventing the power harpoon. He listened to the tale of Captain Slocum's declining fortunes. "You want a ship?" he asked. "Come down to Fairhaven. I'll give you a ship."

The ship Pierce was offering was a rotting, 100-year-old oyster smack sitting in a field with a tree growing through it. Slocum sat on a log and stared at the derelict. It was called the *Spray*. The name was attractive, and so were its lines. Despite the smell of rotting wood and the sunlight filtering between the shrunken planks, there was something about the thirty-nine-foot sloop. She was broad of beam, fourteen feet, squat, clinker built, a broad flat transom, good cabin space below. To the Captain's eye she just felt right.

Like his follower David Dunn, Joshua Slocum built a steam box and began to rip the old planks off the frame of the derelict. As sunlight penetrated the dank interior, with the removal of each plank the oak framing began to look pretty questionable too. From the amused farmers in the neighbourhood Slocum got permission to cut a few oak trees. Always at ease with wood and cutting tools, he seems to have found himself exactly where he wanted to be, and while another builder might have been dismayed at the unfolding revelation of decay, Slocum, realizing that he would finish with an entirely new ship, with nothing left of the original *Spray*, wrote of the enterprise with relish.

But why call it *Spray*, when it was done, if it were to be an entirely new boat? The old master mariner knew his marine insurance regulations. Lloyds of London had set it down quite explicitly, in the case of a vessel named the *Jane*. "A vessel repaired all out of the old, until she is entirely new, is still the *Jane*." And, wrote Slocum later, the reality was that even he could not say with precision "at what point the old died or the new took birth." Another Slocum disciple, Len Pearson, helped us with our biographical need for texture by describing his own restoration of a derelict *Spray* in British Columbia 120 years later. Except for the local references and a few phrases unlikely to have been used by Slocum himself, in Pearson's account you can almost hear the voice of his nineteenth-century mentor:

It was a lot of work and a pretty rough looking project, but the bare essentials were there in aces, and it was very, very good. I did a lot of scrounging. Most of the teak came from old steamer doors from an abandoned shipyard. And I chased old demolition companies around to scrounge the best material out of the houses that were being torn down in Victoria back in the 70s. So every piece of wood on this boat has a history.

Len Pearson would spend years on his replica. Joshua Slocum finished his reborn *Spray* in thirteen months. He took odd jobs as a fitter on whalers, and probably was able to "scrounge" some bits and pieces from those ships as well as feed himself and pay for the few articles he actually bought. He claimed that the total cost was $553.62, which would put it in the $50,000 range in today's money, modest enough for a boat built of prime oak frames and beams, and planked with 1 1/2-inch-thick Georgia pine. He fitted her out with comfortable bunks and a good set of bookshelves — for he never went to sea without a library if he could help it — and confidently launched the *Spray* in the spring of 1894.

Now it was time to test her mettle. Joshua Slocum came from a world of Nova Scotia fishermen; fishing could bring a reliable livelihood in those days if you owned your own boat and knew what you were doing. He deferred some of the below-decks finishing and took *Spray* out off the coast of New England. There he fished her for a year. He was able to put a little cash aside, but more importantly he got the feel of the craft in which he now *knew*, with almost religious certainty, that he was going to sail alone around the world and be the first person in history to do so. To his delight he discovered that once he had set the sails to their optimum for any course, off or into the wind, he could lash down the wheel and *Spray* would hold whatever course he had set for her, until the wind changed. This reduced the burdens of the day for the single-handed fisherman, of course; but on the voyage he was about to undertake it would save his life by allowing him to keep well-rested below as the stout little sloop ploughed through the oceans all night long with no one at the wheel.

I have called her a sloop — a single-masted fore-and-aft rigged boat with a four-sided mainsail topped by a wooden gaff running out at an angle from the mast, and one or two triangular sails, jibs, forward of the mast, varying in size depending on the strength and direction of the wind. The mainsail could be shortened by reefing. It carried two lines of reef points, short cords embedded in the canvas a foot or two apart in a line parallel to the boom (the wooden spar at the foot of the sail). There are two halyards, lines fastened to the gaff, and used to haul up the sail till it was trim and straight along the luff (the line of sail parallel to the mast). By slacking off the halyards the sailor can bind those reef points around the boom thus reducing the size of the sail by the amount of canvas tucked in under the reef points. Slocum always called the *Spray* a sloop too, although many of the drawings in his book, and many photographs of *Spray* replicas show a small second mast mounted on a tiny half-moon shaped ledge fastened to the flat stern (the transom). A sailboat with a second mast stepped abaft the wheel or tiller is properly called a yawl, and when the *Spray* was so rigged (Slocum called this short mast a jigger) she was technically a yawl. Sailors are tiresomely punctilious about language in this respect. "But I called her a sloop all the same," he wrote in *Sailing Alone Around the World*, "the jigger being merely a temporary affair."

Although the world voyage would officially begin at that Fairhaven launch point (on April 24, 1895), and conclude there three years, two months, and three days later, Slocum had a few ports of call to make before he left the sight of land. He stopped off in Boston. There he met a vivacious and optimistic young heiress, Mabel Wagnall of the giant Funk and Wagnall publishing empire. Whatever the relationship became, Mabel Wagnall told Slocum that she had no reservations or qualms about his improbable adventure, and that she would help with the book he intended to write about it. Others might tell him he was crazy; Mabel Wagnall was an enthusiast. She was one of the pioneer promoters of the artificial language Esperanto, and her archives contain a lot of documentation on the development of that movement. She became personally involved in some of the company's projects, such as the life of Franz Liszt by Carl Lachmund whose archives contain the author's letters to Mabel. When she looked at the lean, grizzled, fifty-one-year-old Bluenoser from the Bay of Fundy, she saw that mariner's look of infinite horizons that we can still see in his portrait by the famous Civil War photographer Matthew Brady. She listened to his story, and she told him to follow his dream. "The *Spray* will come back," she said flatly, and that was that.

He headed north for Nova Scotia. Phil Shea, in his nineties now, lives on Brier Island in a Westport not that much changed since its famous navigator dropped in that time for a last visit. Shea's great aunt had told him stories about the Captain's having an eye for the ladies. Her father didn't like that very much, and disappointed her by saying no when Joshua invited her to come out on the *Spray* for a sail around Brier Island. He did succeed in hosting some other young ladies for a few such trips, and then headed for Halifax and the open sea. In Westport our documentary crew found a letter of Slocum's that contradicts the traditional accounts of the Slocum circumnavigation, which all give Yarmouth as the departure point. In this letter, mailed from Gibraltar a few months later, Slocum says he had a score to settle in Halifax, but changed his mind at the last minute, sailed around George's Island, and headed out into the Atlantic.

The first day out, he reported, he trawled a line astern and caught "one cod, two haddock and one hake." He had a barrel of good potatoes and lots of butter. Was the butter tinned? How could it keep? He does not say. There are dozens of provocative little puzzles like that in his book. His sister gave him a big fruitcake before he left Westport. He writes that it lasted forty-two days! One newspaper account of his return to Fairhaven years later says this:

> *Fairhaven Star, July 9, 1898*
> **Voyage Around the World**
> Captain Joshua Slocum, the intrepid navigator, who in April, 1895, started from Boston in

the 33 foot yawl *Spray* on a trip around the world, dropped anchor above the bridge, within a short distance from the spot where the *Spray* was built, Sunday. Captain Slocum has sailed something like 46,000 miles since leaving Boston, and during the entire trip he was entirely alone. The captain came to Fairhaven for a little rest, to put the *Spray* back in condition, and renew his acquaintance with his many friends in Fairhaven. The hold of the *Spray* is filled with all kinds of curiosities gathered from various parts of the world. Judging from the books of newspaper clippings in the captain's possession, he is considered an excellent lecturer and has been honored by high officials everywhere. He has a stereopticon and 300 excellent slides which he uses to illustrate his lectures. Captain Slocum said he intends to remain around here a few days and will then go cruising with his wife and son. He intends to go to London before long. Among the mementos brought home by Captain Slocum is a big bamboo stick given him by the widow of Robert Louis Stevenson. The bamboo was grown by the novelist. Captain Slocum also received several books from the library of the late novelist.

This takes us some distance ahead of our story, but I insert it here because it is characteristic of those textual puzzles. Slocum himself writes of giving lectures with the "stereopticon" in Australia. A stereopticon was a pair of "magic lanterns" projecting superimposed images taken from different positions to produce the illusion of three dimensions, and usually viewed with spectacles of different colours to filter out one image for each eye. Did Slocum carry a supply of such spectacles? Were they standard issue in lecture halls? Where did he get the slides, and what did they represent? Slocum makes no mention of his carrying a camera with him. Making the double image photography needed for these stereoscopic images is not a casual affair and requires a special and rather challenging setup. Given the Captain's curiosity about everything, and his delight in the details of his daily round, it is not believable that he would have been taking these demanding photographs but not writing about the process. So what did the slides depict, that he could lecture knowingly about? Were they slides he acquired at different ports-of-call? We will probably never know. We will probably never know whether the ship that reported his patched together mainsail in the Pacific, after Tierra del Fuego storms had blown the original to shreds, and said that "Captain Slocum was evidently using a patented sail of some very modern design" was Slocum's invention, or just an exception to his later statement that in his entire voyage across the Pacific he did not see another ship.

I insert this observation here, because the tale that follows is full of wonders. Joshua Slocum was a sailor. Sailors tell stories. There is probably a good deal of invention in Slocum's. But there is also no doubt that the broad lines of his great adventure are what he claimed them to be. He can have appeared in the ports he appeared in only by actually traversing the seas he said he traversed. There is ample written evidence of his being where he said he was on the dates he reported. The modern reader of his engaging account of that adventure cannot help pausing from time to time over some of the details, but this writer will not much pause on them further, having given this caution, as the story unfolds.

He was lonely at first. For a while he called out commands to an imaginary crew, but gave it up because "my voice sounded hollow." He regretted that the press of commerce upon the passing steamers — much as he detested them — had done away with the tradition of ships "speaking" to each other. "No poetry-enshrined freighters on the sea now," he wrote, ". . . it is a prosy life when we have no time to bid one another good-morning."

His first landfall on the east side of the Atlantic, as it is for many a sport sailor today, was the Azores. Like hundreds who follow in his wake he painted on the seawall his name and the date and the ship's name as a memento of his visit; it has been carefully preserved. He attended services for the appropriate guardian saints and angels. Somebody gave him some plums and white cheese, and a day or two out of the Azores he ate them and then developed painful cramps that sent him below in agony. He awoke after a troubled night to find a bearded figure in fifteenth-century garb beaming down at him from the wheel above the aft companionway. This person identified himself as a pilot on Columbus's ship the *Pinta*, and, according to Slocum, assured the sick man that the ship was in good hands. He was chewing black twist tobacco, somewhat anachronistically, and, writes Slocum, the apparition again turned up several times further along in the voyage, at times when the Captain was feeling out of sorts.

He sailed north to the Straits of Gibraltar where he was welcomed by the British Navy, who knew he was coming, towed him in, drydocked and checked out the hull of the *Spray*, entertained him royally, warned him about the danger of pirates if he proceeded east through the Mediterranean to the 171-kilometre-long Suez Canal, which had opened for business more than twenty years earlier, and sent him on his way back out into the Atlantic. He boasted that he beat everything across the Atlantic, both ways, except steamers. He was appropriately proud of his navigation by dead reckoning. Dead reckoning usually requires not only a compass, but also an accurate timepiece and a way of measuring your daily run. Slocum ran a "patent log," a kind of four-bladed propellerlike rotor towed astern and reading out on a counter. But his timekeeping was not state-of-the-art.

My old chronometer, which was a good one, had been long in disuse. I tried to get it cleaned and rated, but they wanted $15 for it. $15! They may as well have asked for the moon. I travelled with nothing until I got to Nova Scotia, but once I got to Yarmouth, I got my famous tin clock, the only timepiece I carried on the whole voyage. The price of it was a dollar and a half, but on account of the face being smashed, the merchant let me have it for a dollar.

He had long ago mastered the now largely forgotten lunar method of determining latitude and longitude, a fairly accurate but laborious system that does not depend on a timepiece. Whatever the method, his landfalls were sure and his crossings rapid. Taking the advice of the British Navy he headed back across the Atlantic towards South America. He describes a near encounter with a felucca, off the African coast, which may or may not have been a pirate vessel but from which he was saved by a freak wave sweeping over the approaching marauder. He grounded on the coast of Uruguay and was nearly drowned (like most Nova Scotia fishermen of the time he did not swim), and later had to struggle to retrieve both the *Spray* and its tender from Gauchos who hitched horses to them and tried to tow them inshore. But later, news of his adventure always preceding him, he ran into old mariner friends who gave him money ("an advance" he called it) and in Montevideo the British steamship agents drydocked the ship, overhauled it for him at their own expense, and gave him 20 pounds sterling to help him on his way.

Leaving Brazil, he rigged the jigger, wanting the increased directional stability of the balanced rig when he entered the legendarily difficult waters of the Magellan straits at the very southern tip of the continent. This was the most challenging part of the whole amazing voyage. Nobody had tried it alone before, and few have since. To get a feeling for this mysteriously beautiful and difficult passage, director Peter Rowe contacted Larry Tyler, a British filmmaker and singlehanded sailor, who took a camera with him through the straits, and talked to it, against the background of looming mountains and luminous snowstorms. In the documentary we see one of these video diary entries at a moment of uncharacteristic calm, for those waters.

*The three most important voyagers who came down here,
the first was Magellan. He discovered the straits and they
have been named after him. And secondly was Sir Francis
Drake, who sailed through the straits from the Atlantic
through to the Pacific in sixteen days without any chart.
And thirdly, and probably the most remarkable in terms of
seamanship, would be Joshua Slocum.*

Following in the wake of Joshua Slocum on the Spray*,
the Dove and I, we sailed a similar route from Montevideo
to Buenos Aires and then from Buenos Aires out into the
sea, encountering the same kind of conditions that he had,
horrible head winds. And we beat out two days and two
nights with nasty, sharp seas. The whole place is like a
graveyard to ships. Then once we were out at sea, we headed south down the Patagonian coast, a wild and forbid-
ding country. The winds just howl and howl and howl.
Today you could say it's the calm before the storm. It's one
of these dead, dead calm days, hardly any wind. We're
hardly making any headway. But within an hour we could
start having a snowstorm. In the evening it could be hail-
ing or heavy, heavy rain. It's a very dramatic and wild
corner of the earth. It's a challenge for sailing boats to
come down here nowadays. But think of it a hundred years
ago when Joshua Slocum was here. It was even more of a
challenge. A most remarkable man.*

As Tyler talks of the snow, he cut in for us shots of the
soaring ridge above his passage, with wings of snow
sweeping over it almost as if they were alive. We see the
hailstones bouncing off his deck, and the whipping spray
rising off the turbulent water like animated beings as the

convoluted passage sends twisted ropes of aerial turbulence whistling along its dramatic corridors. Slocum was blown out of the straits and then back into them. Some say he did part of his navigation by echoes off the land at night. David Dunn, planning his own GPS- and Internet-guided passage told us, as he contemplated his approach to a section of the straits called the Milky Way,

that it is considered to be the most treacherous water on the earth. The story goes is that only two vessels have ever, in that time anyway, have ever made it through the Milky Way. One was the Beagle *with Darwin and a full crew, and they made it during the daytime. And Slocum made it through the Milky Way by himself, tacking by sound at night. It just — it boggles my mind to think about it. But I believe five attempts to get it through. I remember one time he lost forty days he said, and he said he just turned the boat around and whistled a new tune and started to tack it all over again.*

The passage took Slocum several weeks. Nothing in his account of it suggests that he even approached the threshold of despair. He wrote, in *Sailing Alone*:

It's a fact that in Magellan, I let pass many ducks that would have made a good stew, for in this lonesome, wild strait, I really had no mind to take the life of any living thing.

And then he was out. A last burst of steady but powerful wind brought him clear of the west coast. The winds continued favourable all the way across the Pacific, bringing him by Juan Fernandez Island where Alexander Selkirk's marooning gave Daniel Dafoe the story that would become *Robinson Crusoe*. Slocum climbed to Selkirk's cave, pronounced himself moved, and sailed on. He didn't stop again until Samoa, where, as noted above in the Fairhaven Star, he visited the widow of one his literary mentors and heroes, Robert Louis Stevenson, and slept in Stevenson's house. Then it was on to Australia.

How did he pass the time? Reading, much of it. He fished. Often flying fish would crash into the sails at night and fall on the deck; he would feast on them in the morning. Old friends and new admirers in his many stops made sure he went away with fresh provisions. When the day's chores were done and his belly full, he stretched out on the bunk below, his back comfortably propped on pillows against the bulkhead under the bookcase, and he read his Hackluyt's *Voyages*, his Drake, and his Hawkins. He wrote his diary. He made sure he was well rested except when storms forbade it. Much of the time he let the *Spray*, with its extraordinary directional stability, steer itself, the wheel lashed down, often finishing the day (according to his never diffident account of his navigational skills and the *Spray*'s steady heading) within a mile or two of his predicted day's run.

Much of the power of this spellbinding book is Joshua Slocum's account of putting the *Spray* back into operating condition after she had been damaged in a storm. Rescuing broken spars before they were swept overboard, getting out his sailor's palm[4] and heavy needle, and (and here is a part of the story that is difficult to grasp in an age where the loss of a few seconds drives professional people to the

4. The sailor's palm is a kind of open leather glove. Fixed into its palm is a large pitted lead dome like the working end of a giant thimble. This allows the craftsman to push a heavy needle and thick, tarred twine through a thick piece of sailcloth or canvas.

point of rage, never mind the loss of days) Slocum would spend two or three days, or a week, rebuilding a sail out of scraps of cloth that a storm had left him with when the previous sail disintegrated in an explosive gust. Nothing seemed to discourage him. Irritated as some readers may be at the self-congratulatory tone, if that was the state of mind that kept him at it, we have to end up in thrall to his skill and his determination.

In Australia he hauled the boat out for repairs and began to give lectures with the stereopticon we have already met. Mariners like David Sinnett Jones are still continuing the tradition, in Sinnett Jones's case telling his tale and retelling Slocum's in the same village hall where Slocum himself had spoken a hundred years earlier.

From Australia, with a new set of sails given to him in Sydney, he sailed to Cocos Keeling Island in the Indian Ocean, a passage of 2,700 miles, in twenty-three days, of which, Slocum says, he spent less than three hours at the wheel. Many scoffed at this claim, indeed, scoffed at his entire voyage. They didn't believe he could sail alone, that the boat would steer itself; but the modern replicas, built as exactly to the old *Spray* plans as their obsessed Slocum acolytes can make them, demonstrate the same true tracking.

He met President Kruger in South Africa and argued with him about Kruger's fundamentalist conviction that the earth was flat. In the South Atlantic, east of the African coast, he visited St. Helena where Napoleon Bonaparte had lived out his last dreary years of exile. They gave him a goat at St. Helena, so that he could have some fresh meat on the upcoming third Atlantic crossing of the voyage. The goat got into the charts and ate the Caribbean. Slocum knew the Caribbean as well as he knew the deck of the *Spray*, and didn't even bother trying to find a replacement chart when he made his landfall after a three-week crossing. And then it was a straight run up a familiar coastline, easing into Harbour in Massachusetts where many had assumed him long dead. June 27th, 1898. Three years, two months, three days.

What next?

What does a fifty-four-year-old former merchant captain do, who has achieved something no other sailor in the history of the world has ever achieved, but has nothing much to show for it but memories? He writes a book. Mabel Wagnall helped him get it published. His return to his home port had been overshadowed by the Spanish-American War, but when *Sailing Alone Around the World* appeared it was immediately admired and has been reprinted and translated hundreds of times since. Two years later, and by now a celebrity though still impecunious, he took the *Spray* up the new Erie Canal to Buffalo for an extraordinary exposition. Director Peter Rowe uncovered some very early motion picture footage of that now somewhat-nondescript bustling upstate New York border city, which had been fantastically transformed in 1901. He wrote these words for me to narrate over the last few minutes of the documentary, and this is exactly how they are heard in that film.

In 1901, Joshua Slocum, late of Brier Island, Nova Scotia, was invited to bring his boat to Buffalo, New York, to the great Pan American Exposition, the biggest ever held. He towed the Spray *by horse up the Erie Canal. The canal, built and expanded throughout the nineteenth century, played a vital role in opening up the mid-west of America. Now again Slocum cut a new swath, being one of the very first non-commercial boats to use the canal in the way it is used today — a passage for adventurers between the Great Lakes and the Atlantic, and then the South Seas.*

As can still be seen in this early motion picture tour shot by Thomas Edison, the Exposition was a fantastical recreation of Venetian canals, and along their sides electric towers and Eskimo villages, and Slocum's Spray. *While Slocum was moored in Buffalo, he printed and sold a small souvenir pamphlet describing his voyage, with an auto-graphed piece cut from the tattered mainsail he'd used until Australia. For a Slocum aficionado to find a copy today and touch the sail that took Slocum around the world is a rare and almost awesome moment.*

Slocum traded yarns here with Buffalo Bill Cody who'd brought his Wild West show to the Exposition. In September, President William McKinley visited the Exposition, boarded the Spray, *and signed Slocum's log-book. An hour later McKinley was shot to death by an anarchist. Slocum was at the swearing-in of the new pres-ident, Theodore Roosevelt, and became a good friend of the energetic and adventurous new chief.*

The Exposition is long gone, but this lake and the very wall that Slocum tied to are still there. He left Buffalo for Martha's Vineyard, mooring the Spray *here in this har-bour, just like this replica a hundred years later. Martha's Vineyard is a place of grand yachts, grand hotels, and grand houses. Slocum is still remembered today, though with one of the world's most overgrown and neglected memorials.*

In Slocum's day the Vineyard was a sleepy farming and fishing community. Slocum tried his hand at growing hops. But it was a dismal attempt to "toss in the anchor." It didn't work. Within a year he was back at sea, sailing for the Bahamas, Jamaica, and the Caymans.

But now the Spray *was beginning to look as weather-beaten as her skipper. In 1908 he told President Roosevelt of his plan to sail to Venezuela, up the Orinoco and on to the headwaters of the Amazon. He took off into a November gale and was never seen again. He may have foundered in that gale. He may have fallen overboard. Perhaps the old girl sprung a plank. But most likely, one of his hated steamships had finally caught up with him.*

His most recent biographer, Anne Spencer, has found evidence identifying a particular Caribbean mail steamer as the ship that ran old Slocum down. Whatever really happened, it seems appropriate that the old seadog who loved the sea and did so much to share that love with the world, should still be in and of it.

Less appropriate to those who love his memory is the dry language of the Dukes County court official statement: "The court finds that Joshua Slocum disappeared, absconded, and absented himself on the 14th day of November, A.D., 1909, disappearing under the following circumstances. He sailed from Tisbury, Massachusetts in the sloop Spray *of nine tons burden and has never been seen since, and therefore the court declares that the aforementioned be declared lost at sea and legally dead."*

There is not another story quite like it. No one who
has gone down to the sea in ships, in ships that are moved
through the waves by the wind filling out one sail or twenty sails, can fail to be taken by it, to be in some measure in
love with the *idea* of this man and his adventure. Hard-
minded sceptics may flinch a bit at some of the tall tales,
although even the tallest of them are probably somewhere
rooted in fact. He loved to tell how a certain Captain Pedro
Samblich gave him a box of tacks to sprinkle on the deck at
night if he had to sleep moored or anchored during the
Patagonian passage (the Straits of Magellan), in territory
where there were tribal peoples with a reputation for local
piracy. Slocum says the tacks saved his life several times.
His revelling in that story will make some readers uncomfortable. In the long run it does not matter. Whatever the
cultural and moral currents he carried out of his childhood
in Westport, Brier Island, Nova Scotia, first among them
were courage, patience, indomitable confidence.

And a love of his element. Give him the last word:
*The sea is in its grandest mood. You must then know the
sea, and know that you know it, and remember that it was
meant to be sailed upon.*

Note: In May of 2001 this documentary television biography, in competition in Houston, Texas, with more than a
thousand other documentaries from around the world,
was awarded the Gold Special Jury Award at the 34th
Annual Houston International Film Festival.

◆ ◆ ◆

The original documentary was written and directed by Peter Rowe, with producer F. Whitman Trecartin. It was photographed by Fred MacDonald, Peter Rowe, and Larry Tyler, and edited by Michael Vernon.

ADDITIONAL READING:

Joshua Slocum: *The Voyage of the Liberdade*
Anne Spencer: *Sailing Alone Around the World*

On the web: *www.mcallen.lib.tx.us/orgs/SLOCUM.htm* will put you in touch with David Sinnett Jones' web site, and with Commodore Ted Jones, who runs the internationally active Joshua Slocum Society. You can also send, via this site, for plans of the *Spray* and of the *Liberdade,* and download photographs of both vessels and of Captain Slocum. Just entering the name of Joshua Slocum in any good search engine will bring up plenty of sites to explore.

Part Three

JACQUES PLANTE
THE MAN BEHIND THE MASK

*"There are good goalies and there are important goalies —
and he was an important goalie."* —Ken Dryden

*"Will I ever see a goalie who will play better than Plante
did? I have my doubts."* —Red Fisher

He was the eldest of eleven children, born Joseph Jacques
Omer Plante, in a farmhouse near Mt. Carmel Quebec, on
January 17th, 1929. His sister Thérèse said that while it was
a family typical of the times and the region, where every-
one helped out with every aspect of the household econo-
my and there was never enough money, that her brother
Jacques was unquestionably the leader, right from the start.
"First in everything," she said. "And we followed him."

Soon after Jacques' birth, their father abandoned the
farm and went to work as a machinist at the aluminum
company in Shawinigan. He held onto his job despite the
wreckage of the economy in the stock market crash when
Jacques was nine months old. His sister thinks that Jacques
began to play hockey (without skates — who could afford
skates?) when he was three years old, and that his mother
taught him to knit at about the same time, toques, hockey
socks. "You're going to learn because I can't knit for everyone," the mother would say. "He was very fast and he
never dropped a stitch," according to his sister. Writer-
director Andy Thompson, who said he made this docu-

mentary because he had grown up in Montreal in the 1950s when "Plante was the greatest goalie ever, playing for the greatest team ever. And besides, he was my mother's favourite player, probably because of the knitting."

He must have decided that he was a goalie pretty early on because people remember him haunting the doors of the arena — he seldom had the ten cents you needed to go in and skate — and saying to the other boys as they arrived, "If you need a goalie for your team, I'm ready to play." They took him up on it fairly often; the crease was not a popular position in those days. Even Jacques did not especially want it, not at first; but it was a way of getting to play when you had no money. More importantly, while he had started as a defenseman, he found that his asthma left him on the boards after a few minutes of play. Since he just could not sustain continual high-speed skating, he settled for net-tending. Most would agree that Jacques Plante's asthma led to a better game.

By the age of twelve he was obsessed. When they sent him to bed before the hockey broadcasts started on Saturday night, he would slip into Thérèse's room. The room above was rented to a man who played his radio loud enough that if young Jacques stood on the bureau with his ear near the ceiling he could follow the game.

Hockey was his life. Before he hung up his skates he would play almost fifty thousand minutes on the ice in more than eight hundred games, with a remarkable goals-against average of 2.34, and a shared record (with Clint Benedict) for playoff shutouts (15), that would hold until 2001 when Patrick Roy pulled ahead of them. His first paid game was back at that Shawinigan arena where, by the time he was fifteen, he was playing for the factory team. When his father found out he was not being paid he insisted he do something about it. Jacques approached the coach in his typically straightforward way. The coach said, All right, fifty cents a game, but don't tell the other boys.

In the National League he would play for the Edmonton Oilers, the California Golden Seals, the Boston Bruins, the New York Rangers, the Saint Louis Blues, the Toronto Maple Leafs and, of course, the team that he had set his heart on from childhood and for whom he was playing in 1959 when he changed the look of professional hockey forever: *Les Canadiens de Montréal*, "the Habs." He earned the Vezina trophy for best NHL goaltender seven times (once shared with Glenn Hall), played on several All-Star teams, and was inducted into the Hockey Hall of Fame in 1978.

In 1947 he finished high school and signed up with the Quebec Citadels. Up to that time the goaltender always stayed in his net and did his best to stop the pucks that were fired at him. Jacques Plante's first important innovation changed that. He decided that it was perfectly acceptable, and within the rules as established, for the goalie to do a little traffic management *before* the puck was fired, and that meant coming out of the net. People said, "It's impossible! Goalies don't leave the net." But Plante left the net. He said that he surveyed what was going on during one game, and realized he had a group of incompetents out in front of him.

Ahead of me were four defensemen with assorted flaws.
One couldn't skate backwards. One couldn't shoot the

puck up to the blue line. One of the other two could only turn one way. Somebody had to clear loose pucks, and I began to do the job myself. It worked so well that I kept right on doing it. Right up to the NHL.

By the end of the 1948 season he was the man to beat, and one man who played against him, Dickie Moore, says he was assigned to swing his stick in front of Plante's face to try to make him blink. The whole league was still perplexed at the way he was coming out of the net to clean up the mess just in front of the crease, and they said that years later the great Toe Blake would still grit his teeth with anxiety when the masked man left the gaping net back there behind him as he came down the ice to create order out of disorder.

Despite his demonstrated talent, breaking into the National League proved difficult for Jacques Plante. The Montréal Canadiens, his dream destination, had bought up the rights to a substantial number of strong players, and already had a goalie, Bill Durnan, who some said was the best in the league. Durnan was not about to be replaced by some teenaged newcomer. In May of 1949 the Montréal Royals took Plante on and that same year he got married to Jacqueline Gagné. Dickie Moore, the man who used to swing his stick in his face, was a teammate on the Royals. Moore says that another difference with Jacques, right from the start was that "he played the game like a first baseman, with his glove. I would say — even in today's hockey — no one — no one catches the puck like Jacques Plante did."

In 1951 his first son Michel was born, and he bought a home movie camera. Those films show a man whose family life was becoming as vital a part of his life as hockey had been until then. Hockey was also beginning to acknowledge that this was a pretty outstanding player. Bill Durnan retired and was replaced by Gerry McNeill. McNeill broke his jaw in a Toronto game on November 1st, 1952, and coach Dick Irvin brought Plante in for what he was told would be a three-game tryout, starting against the New York Rangers. McNeill said his chagrin at having to be replaced was somewhat tempered by the new kid's spectacular ability.

I thought he was very good. You know, I keep saying that to myself today. I needed a good goalkeeper to replace me. . . . If it was a guy that wasn't so good, I wouldn't feel so good.

Jacques still wore one of those toques his mother had taught him to knit; it had become a trademark. In his first practice sessions the coach assumed that he just wore it for fun; it certainly was not part of the uniform. But Dickie Moore was there.

We would try to pull it off with our sticks sometimes, from behind the net. But I mean he went through hell to wear that toque. I was there when the coach says, "You don't play if you wear it!" And that's hard. For a kid that's coming out of nowhere and be strong enough to say, "I want to wear it!" . . . You have to be proud of him for standing up for his rights.

It made Dick Irvin very nervous, that toque. First of all it would bring ridicule, some on Plante for wearing it and some onto the coach for not being able to control his rookie. Plante said — perhaps with a touch of the tongue in the cheek — that it was for his health.

When I was young we played on outdoor skating rinks, and because it was cold we had to wear toques to cover our ears. When I began to play on indoor rinks, that weren't heated, it was cold. I'm asthmatic and I didn't want to catch a cold. So I kept my toque. Well, I kept right on up until those three games that I played in '52 with the Canadiens. I was preparing to go play, but my toque — my toques (I always had two or three) had disappeared. I asked the coach, "What's going on?" And he says, "I don't know. They disappeared."

That sartorial argument he would lose. But not the next one.

In the meantime he beat the Rangers 4 to 1 in that first game for Montréal, tied the next, and then beat Toronto 3 to 1. Pretty good for a rookie, everyone said, and a couple of months later Montréal signed him for $9,100 a year and sent him to their farm club, the Buffalo Bisons, to get him worked up. The local press began to call him Jake the Snake.

The Bisons did not make it into the American Hockey League finals that spring, but if that bothered Plante the bother did not last. Irvin brought him back to the Canadiens as a back up for Gerry McNeill in the Stanley Cup Playoffs. On April 3rd, 1953, it is said that there were shock waves when Dick Irvin sent Plante out instead of McNeill, when Chicago was leading 3 games to 2. It was 7 p.m. at the hotel, just as they were leaving for the Chicago Stadium for the sixth game. With no warning,

Dick Irvin calls me. He says, "Jacques, you are going to be the goalie tonight." I had no idea . . . since Jerry McNeill was in good health and all that. So I started to tremble. In

the dressing room. I tried to lace up my skates, but it was impossible. I couldn't do it. Maurice Richard came to see me and said, "Jacques, in a game like this one, everyone's nervous." And he held out his hand, like that, and it was shaking too.

But Plante got over the shakes, scored a shutout in that game, and three days later led his team to a 4 to 1 victory in the playoffs. They were off to the finals. He won one and lost one against Boston, but the Habs took the championship, and so in that spring of 1923 when he was twenty-four years old Jacques Plante's name was, for the first time, incised into the ever-expanding metallic rounds of the Stanley Cup.

McNeill admits to letting Irvin know that he, the *real* goalie, was not very happy about being arbitrarily replaced by Plante, and the new kid was sent back to the Bisons for the '53 to '54 season. Then, when Irvin put him out as first-string goaltender at the start of the '54 to '55, McNeill said to hell with it, and retired. "I wasn't the type that could handle that," he says. Towards the end of that season Jacqueline gave birth to a second son, Richard, and Jacques was leading the Canadiens into the Stanley Cup finals again, when St. Patrick's Day arrived and all hell broke loose in Montréal.

In a game in Boston on March 13th a nasty brawl had broken out. When the smoke cleared, NHL Commissioner Clarence Campbell announced that the luminous Maurice "The Rocket" Richard, some say the greatest player ever, had been suspended for the rest of the season because of his role in the fights. In Montréal the fans were outraged.

When Campbell came into the Forum on the night of March 17th he was physically attacked, a tear gas bomb went off, the game was forfeited to Detroit, the building was cleared, and a major riot began to spread along Ste Catherine Street. There were hundreds of arrests. Maurice Richard was not allowed back on the ice that season, and Detroit took the cup.

This is all part of the mythology of hockey in this country. Today, with the Forum no longer there and the great Rocket and Jake the Snake both gone too, the details of the story have faded somewhat, but the entire era is vividly recalled by someone who started the next season as a new young sportswriter at the *Montréal Star*, Red Fisher.

I first saw him when I started covering the Canadiens in 1955, '56. He was different. He was a splendid goaltender. He's certainly the best goaltender that I ever saw and I've seen a few over the years. But, I got to tell you this about Jacques Plante: he played for Toe Blake for eight years, and Toe Blake hated Jacques Plante.

I mean really hated the guy because Toe liked to be in control, that's what made him a great coach. He controlled the players; he told them what to do. But, he just couldn't move Plante around the way he did the other players. And I'm talking about guys like the two Richards and Béliveau and Geoffrion and Moore. But I still remember him telling me, in the five years that the Canadiens won the Stanley Cup, Jacques Plante was the best goaltender he's ever seen. You have to know Toe Blake to understand how great an admission that is because when Toe Blake didn't like somebody everything was bad about the guy. So when he says

Jacques Plante was the best he's ever seen, for those five years, you know it's coming from the right guy. . . . I've never met anybody who studied the game as much, who knew more about the game, who knew more about the job that he had to do, who was more proud of the job he did.

With Toe Blake at the helm, the Canadiens would go on to become perhaps the finest hockey team in the history of the league (and some say in the history of hockey). They won five Stanley Cups in a row. Dickie Moore says Plante had a lot to do with that.

Jacques was a big instrumental player; he kept us in the game. Like, I can go and talk about Boston, it's like yesterday, when they'd hold us in our zone for ten minutes — ten Minutes! And Jacques Plante would keep us in the game, and wouldn't let them score. We needed that goaltending and he was the guy that did the job. He used to sleep thinking hockey. He would wake up playing the game. I mean this guy — believe me! — knew hockey inside out. He studied every hockey player that played against him. He knew if they slapshot or if they deeked or what have you. He knew all their shifts on the ice.

Sometimes a teammate would feel that Jacques was doing more than sharing his knowledge, when he pronounced upon an aspect of the game that was not exactly within his field of expertise. Jean Beliveau said that he once got a bit irritated when Plante started instructing him on *his* part of the game, and told Plante a bit sharply, "You take care of your net and I'll take care of the face-off." Others will recall that he was a bit slow to put his hand in his pocket when it was time to pay for the drinks, or for being more of a loner than is the norm in a sports team. But in the end the affection and respect that both opponents and allies had for him is the dominant theme of all the interviews that were given to the producers of our documentary. His son Michel confirmed that his father was something of a solitary figure

even at home when he wasn't playing with us, or when there was nobody around him, he liked to be on his own. He would read all kinds of books, listen to classical music, taking pictures of birds and filming some birds. The bird that he had was a singing bird. It was making life in the house, it was maybe creating for him a different scene — a different environment — then to concentrate always on hockey.

In the late 1950s, as the new curved sticks made it possible to scoop up the puck more decisively than the old straight sticks and gave the slapshot its murderous potential, a man named Bill Burchmore suggested that Plante wear a fibreglass mask in practice. He offered to mould one to the shape of his face. Michel Plante says that Burchmore came to the Plante house and that the two men worked on it together on the basement workbench. Toe Blake tolerated the mask in practice, but then there came that turning point game in New York in November 1959 when Plante and Blake nearly came to a parting of the ways. Red Fisher said,

I was in New York, the night he first put it on. Andy Bathgate of the Rangers comes down and lets go a short backhand, and I thought it was deliberate, right into Plante's face. And there was a cut from the corner of his mouth that ran right up through his nostril. I was the only

guy in there with him. And he's standing in front of the mirror and he's spreading the cut apart and it looks pretty ugly and even he agrees that he and it look pretty damn ugly. And then he went over to the table, where the doctor waited. He stitched him up — no anaesthetic. A whole pile of stitches. And then he came out of the clinic, skated across the ice, and then went to the Canadiens' dressing room and put on the mask.

Toe Blake threatened to fire him if he went out on the ice wearing that mask. Blake swore it would hurt his game, make it hard for him to see what he had to see. Plante insisted, the other players thought it was a blessing, and young fans today have never seen a league game with a barefaced goalie. Jacques said that playing catcher in baseball had helped him think about the value of the face-protector.

I had been a catcher in baseball as well as a goalie in lacrosse and in both those sports I wore a mask. And in hockey I was perhaps more unlucky. My nose was broken four times, the two bones in my cheek got broken, my jaw twice, and so on. So, I said to myself, for crying out loud if I was going to be injured as often as this, I had better protect myself. We had a good club; we kept winning and in '59 when I began to wear the mask, in the spring of that year, we won the Stanley Cup in eight consecutive games. So, no one could say that the mask prevented me from playing well. So, thanks to the Canadiens and their strength, the mask was introduced early and eventually the mask was accepted.

But the courage of standing up to a bullying, powerful coach was what the world admired as much as the innovation. And as it turns out, Blake was wrong about the mask's detracting from the goalie's alertness. Another eminent goalie, Ken Dryden, says that the mask in fact helps do the job.

Playing goal is always at least an unconscious compromise between safety and effectiveness. And part of that compromise is if you get hit in the head it hurts or worse. And so you try to keep your head as far away from the action as you possibly can. Now if you're wearing a mask you don't need to do it quite as much. So you know the impact doesn't stop with safety, it bleeds over — nice word — into effectiveness, you know, and how you play.

The following season, ironically, was a disappointing one for the Canadiens, and Plante did not get his name on any more trophies that year. Rocket Richard retired. Toe Blake was probably muttering "The Mask, The Mask," as Plante's goals-against statistics got worse and worse. The Canadiens made it into the playoffs, in fact were top team for the season, but were quickly eliminated by Chicago who went on to win the cup. When the season was over Plante went in for a surgical repair to a torn ligament in his knee, which might have weakened his goaltending a little during the season, and then into intensive physiotherapy to get the leg back into shape. But the next season, 1961 to 1962, he was superb. Red Fisher was concerned at first because Plante's most reliable defenceman, Doug Harvey, was gone.

When Harvey was traded to the New York Rangers, of course the big question that everybody asked Plante: "How are you going to do without Doug Harvey on defence?" Plante said, "Listen, we all know what a great defenceman Doug Harvey has been and is, but I'll tell you what: I'm going to win the Vezina trophy this year without Doug Harvey." And sure enough, he won the Vezina trophy without Doug Harvey. Not only did he win the Vezina trophy; he also won the Hart trophy as the most valuable player in the league.

The Hart was to be his last trophy with Montréal. His asthma was getting worse, and so was his relationship with the coach. Red Fisher was witness to one encounter. Between the two when they were playing against the Maple Leafs.

[Jacques] didn't want to stay at the Royal York Hotel because he said that the bedding in the room brought on asthma attacks. He wanted to stay at another hotel by himself and Toe Blake eventually let him do that. But just for one game. Because, you know Toe and I went to Maple Leaf Gardens one morning to watch the Maple Leafs practice and we were walking up the steps and coming around the bend is Jacques Plante with three young ladies on his arm. Toe Blake said, "Good morning, Jacques!" and Jacques said, "Good morning, Toe!" and Plante kept walking and Toe and I kept walking with Toe swearing under his breath saying: "That so and so, he'll be back at the Royal York before he can blink."

And that night on the train, Plante said: "I want you to know, Toe, that those three girls, they were my cousins." Toe said "Fine! Your cousins can come and visit you at the Royal York Hotel, next time we're in town." And that was the end of that.

It was not long afterwards that Toe Blake had apparently had enough of his war with Plante. The goalie wasn't winning the games the way he used to, Blake thought. The coach was fed up, he said, with what he called Plante's "act." But his behaviour was reprehensible when he made the decision to move. He negotiated a seven-player trade with the New York Rangers. One of the players was Jacques Plante. Blake did not even have the courtesy to tell Plante what he had done; the goalie heard about it for the first time on his car radio. He went off to New York grieving for his real team, the team he belonged to, he always thought, missing Montréal, missing his kids. After a strong first game where he shut out the Detroit Red Wings, the rest of his two seasons with the Rangers was undistinguished. He was thirty-five. He announced that he was retiring.

He had done pretty well for himself financially. Molson's gave him a "representative's" job. He bought a beauty parlour and three small apartment buildings. Radio-Canada brought him in as an analyst for some of the televised games, and he enjoyed that in a wistful kind of way. He spent a lot of time with his sons, coached them at baseball, and stopped talking about the hockey wars.

But hockey had not stopped talking about him. In 1965 when the young coach Scotty Bowman was asked to field a Canadian team against the world and Olympic champion Russians, Bowman talked Plante into the net for that one game, and after only a couple of weeks of practice with those Junior Canadiens, against the genuinely superior opponent, Plante shocked the Russians by letting in only one goal. The Junior Canadiens scored twice.

Three years later, professional hockey expanded suddenly when six new teams were added to the NHL. Scotty Bowman was hired to build a team for St. Louis, and brought in not one but two retired goalies, Glenn Hall and Jacques Plante. The two somehow worked it out and were able to play together. Given the mythology that sportswriters nurture, in this case a legendary enmity between two high-level stars, their playing together on the same team was puzzling to some of the fans. But Jean Beliveau said that anyone who had played in that collegial atmosphere of the old Canadiens would understand.

I suppose that after his first retirement he found that he was still enjoying the game. You miss the action on the ice but you miss . . . I know in my case — and I can speak for many of my former teammates — we missed that great atmosphere we had in the room, the great atmosphere we had together travelling on the train. So, I'm not surprised.

What was a surprise was the grace demonstrated by the two old rivals, Hall and Plante, who played such a great season that they were jointly awarded the Vezina trophy, making it number seven for Jacques Plante. Then came a bigger surprise, when he went up to Toronto to play for his old arch enemies, the Maple Leafs. At about that time he started a new business, Fibrosport, making goaltenders' masks. He brought his son Michel in as a partner. It looked as though he had found something to do that was as rewarding as being on the ice. A soon as the season was over he would give all his time to Fibrosport. Soon he was making enough money manufacturing masks that he could take his Maple Leafs salary and put it in the bank. He was also playing very, very well. His 1971 goals-against average was 1.88, the lowest since his record 1.86 in 1956. The next year he was invited to Sweden to teach his goaltending methods there. He brought out a book, *Devant le Filet* (Before the Net), and in the Series of the Century between Canada and the USSR, he was Radio-Canada's principal analyst.

For a while it seemed as though his temporary retirement had been some kind of aberration. He was forty-four years old when he went to the Boston Bruins for the 1973 playoffs, and then negotiated a ten-year, one-million-dollar contract as coach and general manager of the Quebec Nordiques in the newly formed World Hockey Association.

But his personal life was in some disarray. His marriage with Jacqueline was over, after twenty-three years. His son Richard committed suicide. There were bad times at the fibreglass plant. Perhaps all that anguish rendered him especially vulnerable to a proposal to return to the ice. In any case, he made headlines on the sports pages when Bill Hunter brought him to the Edmonton Oilers. One day, in a practice session in Edmonton, he took a slapshot in the side of his head and severely damaged his right ear. A serious loss of balance followed, as well as sudden deafness with all the disorientation and grief that that can cause. And so now he really did retire, finally and irrevocably. He married again and went to live in Sierre, in Switzerland. He came back briefly for his induction into the Hockey Hall of Fame (in 1978). But although he would die of cancer regrettably young — he was only fifty-seven — Jacques Plante seemed to have come to terms gracefully and cheerfully with the fact that the rich and productive life he had led on the ice was done now, and he could play a new role: the Swiss Retiree.

He went to the same coffee shop every morning and did the grocery shopping. He coached hockey a few hours a week with local kids. He would come back to Canada for the playoffs, and sometimes would be seen at a training camp in September, chatting with the old pals.

And then he was gone, leaving behind a game to which he had given his life, and given an entirely different face.

◆　◆　◆

The original documentary was written and directed by Andy Thompson. It was photographed by Denis Debuc, Dwayne Dorland, Frank Vailaca, and Yves Matthey, with sound by Phillippe Jordan, Larry MacDonald, and Frank Vailaca, and edited by Doug Forbes.

◆ Part Four ◆

RATTENBURY

A TALE OF MURDER AND GENIUS

When the television series upon which these books are based was first proposed, Executive Producers Patricia Phillips and Andy Thompson, of Great North Productions in Edmonton, commissioned a brilliant, crusty, inventive filmmaker from Vancouver, Bob Duncan, to make the pilot. When the CRB Foundation, Historica's predecessor, was invited to consider helping to fund *The Canadians* — this was two years before I became commissioning editor — I was asked to keep an eye on the development of this pilot, and advise as to whether or not it was an appropriate venue for the Foundation's Heritage Project.

I was fascinated from the beginning. Here was a sprawling creative life story revolving around a vicious and almost bungled murder. In the late evening of a spring day in 1935, an eighteen-year-old chauffeur and general servant, a semiliterate boy named George Stoner, stood nervously behind the drunken, slumbering form of the sixty-seven-year-old retired architect Frances Rattenbury. Stoner was drunk and high on cocaine. He was also enraged because he thought that he had heard his lover, the young and voluptuous Mrs. Alma Rattenbury, having sex with her husband, the boy's employer, the semiconscious old architect in the big armchair. Stoner carried a big wooden mallet he had taken that morning from his grandmother's house. He struck the dozing old man three times over the head, and then broke down and raced upstairs to his mistress's bedroom, undressed, climbed into bed with her, and said, "I've hurt Ratz."

The trial, at London's Old Bailey, was a sensation. People slept in lineups in the street to get a place. The papers were full of the salacious and bloody details of the bizarre household and the murder that had taken place there. But curiously they said nothing about the rich, productive, memorable career of the architectural genius who had just been bludgeoned to death.

Of all the provincial capitals in Canada it is Victoria that most vividly strikes the visitor with the harmony of the architecture of its great traditional public buildings: the legislature, the ferry terminal, the Bank of Montreal, and perhaps more than anything else, because for those who arrive at the harbour by ferry or by air it is the first they see, the Empress Hotel. She presides over that landfall like a true empress, and declares unequivocally that one has arrived in a city to be taken seriously, at a palace of elegance that Will Not Let You Down. Some will say that, in fact, the hotel does let you down, it is really all show, "like a cardboard cutout against the sky," but Victorians and visitors alike generally find the building awesome, at least from the outside. And there are few city arrivals in the world quite like stepping off the commuter seaplane from Vancouver onto the stone wharf at sea level, and then climbing those stairs at either end while the Old Empress reveals herself to you, step by step, in all her splendour.

It is a bit jarring to discover that the soaring imagination that gave Victoria these buildings and set the style for this most distinctive of provincial capitals belonged to a man who was not only a genius, but also an embezzler, a fraud, a liar on a huge professional scale, an unconcealed adulterer in a time when such things Were Not Done and Were Not Spoken Of, ending as a battered and bloody corpse in his own living room in London.

Frances Mawson Rattenbury emigrated from Yorkshire to Vancouver in the booming summer of 1892, looking for work and waving an impressive resumé. It declared that he had worked on some of the most eminent public buildings of both Bradford and Leeds. "Ratz," as his friends called him, apparently submitted his spectacular *curriculum vitae* in a way that did not require him to be in the same room with it when it was being read. Had he been present during its reading even the more credulous public officials might have noticed that among the specific projects therein noted was one (on which Rattenbury was listed as senior architect no less) that was finished when he was only six years old, and another built before he was born.

As far as we know, Frances Rattenbury had not in fact built anything before he came to Canada, although he had worked on the design of the ugly Town Hall of Cleckheaton, Yorkshire. This is not to take away from his genius, which was remarkable, nor from his ability to turn out, at lightning speed, the most compelling drawings. Both his preliminaries and his developed work were not only overwhelmingly beautiful and seductive, but also thoroughly practical and professional. But he had not, in fact, supervised the actual *building* of anything in Britain. His first commission in Canada, for a printer named Gustav

Roedde, was a house intended to remind the nostalgic Roedde of his native Germany. When finished, however, it looked rather more like an English Queen Anne cottage, with a crenelated tower added on for a touch of grandeur.

Rattenbury demonstrated a flair for publicity from the beginning. When he first came to Vancouver in those balmy days of July 1892 he managed to get a spectacular report of his arrival published in the *Vancouver Daily World*, which apparently did not check out any of the above fraudulent information. (He did not mention the Roedde house caper.) His sense of timing was that of a showman, for in the same edition of the *Daily World* that introduced that amazing twenty-five year old to the Vancouver public, there was announced an anonymous competition organized by the provincial government, to replace the old colonial legislative buildings (known as the "Birdcages") with new parliament buildings. British Columbia wanted something appropriate to the grandeur of the great mountainous Pacific Coast territory that had been a part of Confederation for twenty-one years, but only five years earlier had at last been connected to the rest of the country by the completion of the transcontinental railway. The citizens felt it was time to show off, and so they put out a call for architects to submit proposals in an anonymous competition. The entries had to be signed pseudonymously, so that established reputations would not count, at least on the first round.

Some of the entries were signed with cute names. One hopeful called himself "Patience," while another signed his drawings "Tah-Ra-Ra-Boom-De-Yay." But one set of drawings bore the simple designation, "B.C. Architect."

Rattenbury, a bit presumptuously since he had been there only a few months, correctly supposed that a British Columbian would be preferred over an outsider, all other things being equal. Things were not, as turned out, all that equal. Rattenbury's drawings were brilliant, exceptionally well executed. They proposed a dazzling building complex that strongly impressed the commissioners, and it is likely that the B.C. Architect pseudonym also helped. In any case, he made it into the finals, which were also pseudonymous. This time he signed his submission "FOR OUR QUEEN AND PROVINCE," the spirit of the time being both royalist and locally patriotic.

A few months later it was publicly announced that "Vancouver Architect" Frances Rattenbury had won the competition and would direct the building of the largest government project in the history of British Columbia. He took the steamer to Victoria to present himself to the authorities. They found themselves congratulating a confident, good-looking, red-headed man with a neatly trimmed full moustache, who appeared to be and actually was all of twenty-five years old. If they had cross-examined him on his actual building experience to date, they might have discovered that it consisted in the building of Herr Roedde's Queen Anne cottage.

The builder assigned to the project was, however, a very experienced local man named Frederick Adams. Adams had stationery printed — CONTRACTOR TO THE PARLIAMENT BUILDINGS — and proudly set out to make his reputation and his fortune. But things did not go well between Adams and his young architect.

Rattenbury wanted thousands of square feet of the marble, sheet after sheet of the very best. As supervising architect he had the right and responsibility to approve the quarry and sign off on the choice before the stone was mined, and with Adams' he looked at samples from all the best sources, and agreed on one. But when the marble arrived, a huge order, paid for by Adams, Rattenbury realized he'd made a mistake; it was not the right colour. To save face he declared that the stone as delivered was inferior to what he had approved, not acceptable. He tried to dump the problem on Adams' shoulders.

The terms of the contract were such that Adams the contractor was responsible for delivering materials that would satisfy the architect's demands and standards. If Rattenbury won this one, Adams would go bankrupt. It dragged on for months, through a series of meetings with lawyers and officials. Rattenbury and the builder yelled at each other during some of these meetings, in a manner that was most unseemly for the project heads of an assignment for queen and province. Rattenbury billed his client, the provincial government, $3,000 for attending at those meetings. This would be the equivalent of close to a quarter of a million in today's money. Historian Tony Barrett at the University of British Columbia said that this was typical of the architect throughout his career, and that Rattenbury had

an idea of how you should handle all the contracts, and he didn't really feel himself bound by the rules, when it came to that, that [he thought that those who did respect the rules] were . . . petty minded, and lacked vision.

Trying to figure a way to avoid ruin, Fred Adams

decided to visit another island quarry where there was marble he knew would do the job. He went over in a small steamer one afternoon, on a day when prudent mariners would have stayed home. A storm destroyed the boat, and the unfortunate builder was drowned. Ironically, a later steamship disaster would almost ruin Rattenbury, but this time his luck was holding.

When some bureaucrats in Victoria began to complain of cost overruns, Rattenbury made mincemeat of them. Magnificence was the watchword of the day, and his appeals to the senior officials' sense of the moment, of the significance of this work in the eyes of destiny and the world, seems to have carried the day. When a bureaucrat suggested that perhaps a lesser stone would be quite satisfactory for the interior of the legislative hall (and would substantially reduce the overruns), Rattenbury sent an indignant letter, which prevailed. He wrote:

The grandeur if the whole scheme would be absolutely ruined should the legislative hall be poor and commonplace, and it would be if the marble is omitted. The whole character depends entirely on the rich and massive marble columns, and we cannot in any adequate way replace these with cheaper imitation.

For a while the bureaucrats and perhaps even some of the politicians worried and fumed about delays and costs. It began to look as though the $600,000 cost that the architect had agreed to might easily double (it nearly did). But as the great structure began to rise, to gleam in its cladding and rejoice in its columns, it soon was seen to be so splendid, so fine, so far beyond the glory anyone had dreamed of, that there was no going back and no way to even seem publicly regretful. It was, quite simply, magnificent. At least, on the outside. Once it was in use the MPPs discovered that the acoustics in the legislative assembly were so hopeless that they had to hang fishing nets from the ceiling to cut down the reverberation. The lieutenant governor, given a splendid third-floor suite of rooms for entertaining, was embarrassed the first time he tried them to discover that there were no washroom facilities and he had to send out for buckets.

Furthermore, there was nothing really original about the buildings. They were probably a direct copy of a "Chateau Style" failed proposal that his employers back in Britain had earlier developed for Bradford City Hall. Indeed that firm, Mawson and Mawson, tried to make Rattenbury turn over part of his Victoria fees to them as the traditional architect's due, on a first assignment, to the firm that had trained him. He ignored them, even though he would continue to claim, dishonestly, that he had been a major architect on some of their most famous projects.

Professor Barrett says that Rattenbury himself was convinced that the splendour of his work excused him from paying attention to normal professional obligations, to interior details, or to the other ordinary concerns of ordinary, responsible architects, and that he had absolutely no qualms or conscience about such trivial things as doubling the costs over what he had "committed" to, especially when the client was the government. He was also somewhat less than correct about his business practices. At about the time he started work on the main drawings for the parliament buildings, he saw a competition advertised for a state capitol in Olympia, Washington, and entered it. Apparently he was concerned neither with the impossibility of guiding two such gigantic tasks at the same time if he won, nor with the damage to his reputation if he lost. When he did not get the Washington State contract, a story began to go around that he had in fact won the competition but refused the commission out of moral indignation when the Washington State commissioners asked for a bribe. The commissioners of course declared this to be an outright lie, and Rattenbury himself said that somebody must have made it all up, he had not submitted a proposal at all, what were they talking about? Then he added privately that the reason he had refused to enter the competition in the first place was that the corruption of the Washington commissioners was of course well known.

His own fee for the parliament buildings was $40,000, quite enough for a man of even substantial appetites to retire on, or at least to rest on his laurels for a while, reflect, and consider what next. His reputation was made. He could have sat back and chosen the best commissions. When the buildings opened officially the press called them a marble palace, and the people came in droves to admire the detail and gape at the grandeur of their new parliament.

But Frances Mawson Rattenbury was not at that opening. He was back in England trying to raise money for a greed-driven boat-building scheme connected to the Yukon gold rush. It was 1898. He had already invested in cattle for the Klondike, at great risk, buying a thousand head and shipping them off to Dawson where a steak could cost you your life savings and cattle with any flesh on them, which you might have bought out of Seattle for sixty dollars, were selling for a thousand dollars a head. Ratz had heard about the huge crowds of prospector hopefuls willing to pay absurd prices for the trip across Bennett Lake on their way to the goldfields. Combined with the continuing appetite for high-priced beef in the north, it seemed to call for steamer service across Bennett Lake, cattleboats with plenty of accommodation for passengers as well. With his spellbinding rhetoric he tried to raise a substantial amount from gold-bedazzled Londoners for this not entirely crazy scheme.

His prudence was less than his rhetoric, however. He did not do well before the investors in The City. Ambition overcame judgment, and he made the classical promoter's mistake, investing his own capital in the project. But it was too late. By the time the company was up and running, the gold rush had exhausted itself and he lost his entire investment.

By this time he had married. Florence Lenora Nunn was a not very attractive girl who was pregnant when they tied the knot. She had gone up to the Yukon with him to christen and launch two of the steamers that had actually been built. The three boats, the *Flora*, the *Ora*, and the *Nora* had all been named for this rather lumpy, unattractive woman. They took the time while there to climb the Chilkoot Pass — which they claimed was easy, just a charming scenic walk, all the hysteria was invented. Rattenbury built them a house in elegant Oak Bay, and went back to work in Victoria, picking up on his still solid reputation as an architect in the Grand Manner. They had two children,

Frank, who had badly deformed feet, and Mary, a nervous, erratic girl who would nonetheless become one of the great beauties of the city. Much later Rattenbury would disown both these unfortunate offspring, but for the time being he puttered about the garden in the early and apparently fairly sunny days of the marriage, and went on with his work. He sketched plans for more monumental projects and set about trying to sell them.

When one project looked as though it might go to competition, Rattenbury wrote an eloquent letter to the appropriate official pointing out that a competition was unlikely to produce the kind of elegant results the project merited (despite his success in the parliament buildings competition). He did the same thing a second time, arguing eloquently that the public interest would be best served by engaging an architect of proven record in the field of magnificent public structures. Somehow, he managed to pull this stuff off, but his rival architects did not forgive and forget, and bit by bit stored up resentment and, as they thought, evidence that might one day be used to bring him to grief.

Rattenbury's offices in the Five Sisters block burned down in 1910, and records of some of those key periods of his life are incomplete. But from the early days of his marriage a letter to his mother survives, in which he wrote:

Somehow the mornings creep on, dodging about the garden, in the woods, and along the beach. Then I get away downtown for a little tiffin. Florrie has a marvellously good temper — a jolly good thing for me because mine is rather short, especially when rushed for work. So we pull along well together.

On the evidence of people who actually knew the Rattenburys this letter seems to be more in aid of keeping his mother from worrying than an authentic description of what was going on. In fact, Rattenbury soon came to despise Florrie, although he doted on and was very good to Mary and seems to have been admired by the crippled Frank long after the boy would have been pardoned for giving up on his father.

He did not have to wait long for new commissions. Tourists and corporate chiefs were coming from far and wide to admire the parliament buildings, and before long the Bank of Montreal took him on as its principal western architect. His reputation flourished. The bank let it be known that they had secured the services of The Best. The rich of Victoria and Vancouver commissioned elaborate private homes. When the architect designing a new official residence for the lieutenant governor began to go way over budget, the government, showing not a great deal of diligent memory either for overruns or bathrooms, engaged Ratz as consultant.

Ratz looked at the residence proposal and told the premier it was almost certainly going to go 50 percent over budget; they should hire a new architect. But who? Seemliness and perhaps protocol prevented Frances Rattenbury from recommending Frances Rattenbury; he suggested one Samuel Maclure. Perhaps he did not mention that he shared offices with Maclure and had partnered with him on a number of projects. The government admired Maclure's work and made him an offer. Maclure said he was not well, and could not take on a project of such importance just now, not all by himself, he would bring in a partner. The partner was Rattenbury. Who went over budget by 50 percent.

In addition to the overruns, there was a buzz of rumour about some materials that had gone missing. Rattenbury's biographer, Terry Reksten, said:

> *In particular . . . a rather large quantity of marble, sheets of marble. And, certainly, there was marble in Government House, but not to the degree that had been paid for. And anybody who had visited Rattenbury's home and seen his recent renovations realized that his kitchen was lined with marble from floor to ceiling, and also that a very special fireplace, that was similar to one missing from Government House, now graced his dining room.*

Rattenbury's many rivals and enemies in the architectural community, incensed that he seemed to be getting all the good commissions despite breaking all the rules and sullying the profession with his constant overspending and his open contempt for his fellow professionals, now knew they had him on the ropes. They wrote an indictment to the provincial government calling for a public inquiry. Rattenbury responded in character.

> *I emphatically deny the charges. They are slanders, maliciously and knowingly made for the purpose of discrediting me in the eyes of the Government and the people of British Columbia.*

He accompanied his letter with a formal notice of intent to file charges of libel and slander. The government did not want a fuss. One of the two firms who had called for the inquiry decided, upon reflection, that their participation in such a public event would reflect badly on them. The whole profession was, in fact, stained by kickbacks from suppliers, inappropriate gifts to officials and other practices that at the very least verged on corruption. Rattenbury was known to be a gifted, relentless opponent. The firm withdrew. The remaining individual architect, who actually took the stand to testify against Rattenbury, could not have been a better witness from his opponent's point of view. He vigorously objected to being sworn, as if it were an attack on his integrity and credibility. He was pompous, evasive, abusive, and forgetful. Rattenbury was cleared. It was December 29th, 1923. His club threw a great party for him. As they lustily sang "For He's a Jolly Good Fellow," a twenty-seven-year-old widow, passing through the lobby of the hotel after playing piano at a reception that night, heard that song sung with what struck her as unusual fervour, and lingered to see for whom all this affection was being expressed. Alma Pakenham, who had lost one husband to the Great War and divorced a second, was a lusty, rich-voiced, pouty musical prodigy very much in demand as a pianist at classy social functions. The man who had aroused her interest was Rattenbury. He was polite at first, then curious, then more than friendly. By then his marriage with Florrie had degenerated into mutual contempt. They lived in separate parts of the house. Rattenbury had begun to drink heavily, but recent splendid commissions had sobered him up, brought a glint back to his still lush red hair, and trimmed off some of the pudginess that he had accumulated during some of the bad days.

He and Alma started a fairly open affair.

The single most important commission in that period was the CPR's Empress Hotel. Sir Thomas Shaughnessy, the railway's president, had done a brilliant job of seducing the city into giving the CPR free land and water and no municipal taxation for fifteen years, in order to overcome the railway's official posture of indifference to a tourist hotel in the capital. It was decided that the stinking old mudflats behind the causeway across the foot of the harbour would be reclaimed. On the evidence of drawings that emerged later, proving that Rattenbury had designed a hotel for the mudflats at a time when a different vacant lot near the parliament buildings was commonly understood to be the site that would be chosen, it is clear that here, as in many other cases, Rattenbury had some inside knowledge which he used to invest in ways that would today land him in court with a criminal charge. The Empress Hotel sealed his grip on the harbour and his stamp on the city. He would design and supervise the building of many important public and private structures in British Columbia — the renovations of the Hotel Vancouver, the Vancouver and Nelson courthouses, a vast amusement centre with three ocean-water heated swimming pools — sixty years ahead of the West Edmonton Mall — (Rattenbury's amusement centre did not get built as such but metamorphosed into his version of the Crystal Palace, known as the Crystal Gardens).

The parliament buildings, predicted by the naysayers to be so big it would take five hundred years to fill them, were by now too small for the burgeoning government and an addition would be needed. Rattenbury was clearly the only man to do the work, despite the whiffs of scandal and the overruns. The results (about 35 percent over budget) were — once again — magnificent (the single word most often applied to this man's work). Queen Victoria's son the Duke of Connaught, by then governor general of Canada, presided over a grand official opening.

Along with these successes Rattenbury did make some bad financial decisions, again based on what would now be deemed the criminal use of insider information. Before the war he had been wooed and won by the new Grand Trunk Pacific railway, whose chief Charles Melville Hays had conceived the idea of making Prince Rupert a kind of San Francisco of the North West. Rattenbury drew preliminary sketches for Grand Trunk Pacific hotels from Alberta to the coast. Grand Trunk Pacific bought a clutch of coastal steamers, and commissioned the architect to redecorate their interiors. By the end of the decade it looked as though travellers from Calgary to Vancouver Island would sleep in Rattenbury-designed hotels throughout their journey, and cross to Victoria in a Rattenbury-decorated ship. He actually completed the work on one of those vessels. Hays went to Britain, successfully raised the capital he needed to push the GTP line through to the coast, convincing investors that it would displace the CPR as the principal east-west carrier in Canada if not the continent as a whole, and boarded his ship for home in triumph.

That ship was RMS *Titanic*. Charles Hays did not survive her sinking. His successor, E.J. Chambers, was a cautious man, not at all convinced of the viability of Prince Rupert as a great commercial and tourist centre. He dithered and delayed. Rattenbury waited patiently. The GTP would, in the end, have to make good on its commitments to its shareholders. Rattenbury had bought up relatively worthless land that would, as the project got underway, make him a millionaire. But 1912 turned into 1913, and then 1914, and January turned into August, and the guns broke out in Europe. No settlers were coming west any more; the GTP plans were put on hold. The hold became permanent. Prince Rupert was finished. Rattenbury lost all that investment, took what he had left from the hotels and the courthouses and the mansions, and began to look for another way to live.

If Rattenbury's marriage to Florence Nunn had been forced by the accidental pregnancy of a woman with whom he was only dallying, it had by now deteriorated into something worse than a sham. He bought a silk-lined cape and wore it with a flourish as he took his mistress Alma to the opera. Before long everyone knew that while he nominally still lived in the Oak Bay home he had designed and built and enlarged into a mansion, he was really living with Alma. He asked for a divorce. The undenied adultery would have made it easy for Florrie, and divorce would have brought her a comfortable settlement, but she refused.

Rattenbury, now openly moved in with Alma, cut off power and water to the Oak Bay house to try forcing Florrie to leave. When that didn't work he brought Alma there and had her play the piano in the parlour while poor Florrie hid her head under the pillows upstairs. When Mary came down to complain that this was all making her mother ill, Alma loudly played the "Funeral March."

In 1929 Alma gave birth to a son, John, and when Rattenbury rewrote his will John and Christopher, Alma's son by an earlier marriage, were the beneficiaries: Frank and Mary were cut off. It is strange that when Rattenbury and Alma, who legally married on Florrie's death, turned their backs on Canada forever and sailed for England, the only person who came to see them off was poor, crippled Frank. They settled in Bournemouth, perhaps the closest they could come to a town that felt a bit like Victoria, and rented the *Villa Madeira*, at 5 Manor Road. This second marriage had disintegrated too, at least sexually. Rattenbury, who had started drinking fairly heavily to help himself over some of the rough spots in Canada, was back at it again, almost a bottle of whisky a day. Alma tried to get him interested in developing new projects, and for a while he brightened up and met with one or two fellow architects whom Alma had gotten to know in London, but these discussions never led to anything.

Rattenbury had been a major figure in Victoria for almost forty years. In Bournemouth he was just another overweight, boozy, retired bloke in his sixties who had once been in some profession or other. He was probably sexually incapacitated. But Alma, at thirty-five, was passionate and lonely. She went up to London often, much in demand as a pianist, and soon began to write songs for a popular tenor named Frank Titterton, whom she accompanied for his Sunday night concerts on BBC radio. Ratz was now sleeping downstairs next to his study, and Alma upstairs. In 1934, they hired a slow, bow-legged, strong seventeen year old named George Stoner as a driver and general helper. Alma gave the good-looking fair-haired boy the small bedroom just down the hall from her own. It was not long before she had overcome any reticence Stoner might have felt, and he was spending most nights in her room. She was disarmingly open about it all at the trial. The judge and the lawyers found it intriguing but puzzling. Here was a sophisticated, worldly woman, thrice married, with two children, who had taken up with someone young enough to be her son, a quiet, withdrawn, late-adolescent person: it had to be purely animal. In that court, at that time, this was not a recommendation.

Rattenbury had become very close with his money. Alma took to lying to him about household and personal finances. He let her pay all the bills and manage the servants, and seems not to have found her occasional demands for large sums unreasonable, although his monthly allowance to her was only a few pounds. Stoner was uneasy about his double life as lover at night and common servant in the daytime, and complained to Alma. In fact, while he was nominally a common servant with a salary of 4 pounds a month, he was given very few tasks apart from driving. He often played cards all afternoon with Rattenbury, and took to swaggering, lording it over the other servants, and wearing a small dagger as an ostentatious mark of distinction.

Alma, however, was worried that her young bed partner might do something erratic, perhaps reveal to her husband what was really going on, or even act violently, as he sometimes seemed to be about to do. She told Rattenbury that she needed 250 pounds "for a woman's operation" in London, and had Stoner drive her to Kensington. They went shopping at Harrod's and checked into the Kensington Palace Hotel as "Mrs. Rattenbury and brother." She bought him fine suits and silk pyjamas, and gave him money so that he could buy her a diamond ring. They spent the week there, dining, drinking, shopping, and going to bed. When they returned Rattenbury was "jolly," as Alma described his inebriated state, and amiable. He did not even ask about the alleged operation. Alma, guiltily relieved, feeling some trace of her old affection for her husband, and mellow herself after an uninterrupted week of satisfying all of her appetites, helped the old drunk out of his chair and into his bedroom. She made the mistake of closing the door.

George Stoner's barrister claimed at the trial that his client, allegedly addicted to cocaine, was hallucinating on the drug that night and had imagined that the sounds he heard coming through the closed bedroom door meant that Alma and her husband had gone to bed together. His slow brain found only one way to deal with this. He resolved to kill the old man. The next day, on a routine home visit, he found a heavy wooden carpenter's mallet in his grandmother's house, and brought it back to 5 Manor Road when he returned that evening. He found the architect dozing, drunk, in the usual armchair, went up behind him, and brought down the mallet, three times, on Frances' Rattenbury's now balding head.

Alma had been out for the evening. When she came home, late, she chatted briefly with her personal servant Irene, assumed that her husband was safely asleep in his own room, and went upstairs to hers. After a while Stoner came up and climbed into bed beside her. She testified afterwards that he seemed very agitated, but that she thought it had something to do with the drugs he was taking. Suddenly she heard a loud groan from below, the voice unmistakeably her husband's.

"What's that!" she asked Stoner. "I've hurt Ratz," he said, blubbering. She ran downstairs.

By the time the police got there she was very drunk. At first she insisted that some intruder had come in through the French doors, but when it was shown that those doors were locked from the inside, she tried to bribe and then to seduce the investigating constable. He remained very correct and quietly kept questioning her. She was, in her confused state, trying to protect George Stoner. She declared that she had finally lost all hope for the marriage, had decided to kill Rattenbury, had bludgeoned him with a mallet, which she had hidden outdoors and would try to find in the morning. When she was sober the next day she stuck to this latter story, admitting that there had been no intruder. The police were confused, and when Rattenbury died in hospital a few days later they ended up charging both of them with murder — to which Stoner also confessed.

At the trial, which started on May 27th, 1935, Alma decided to tell the truth and seems to have convinced the jury that she was doing so. Stoner did not withdraw his confession, but tried to plead insanity due to his addiction to cocaine. He described the drug as being a flaky brown colour with dark flecks. Medical experts disagreed as to whether his known symptoms might reflect a cocaine addiction, but not on the actual colour of cocaine of any quality. The trial lasted five days, and the jury were out for only forty-seven minutes before acquitting Alma and convicting George Stoner.

Stoner was sentenced to hang, but Alma would die before him. She had gone to a nursing home, guilty, despondent, badly needing rest and perhaps to dry out, as she had been a heavy drinker since before they came to England. One afternoon, after a Dr. Bathurst had seen her and agreed that she was now much better, she told the matron that she was feeling well enough to go walking. In fact, she took the train to Bournemouth and there was a witness to what happened after that. A farmer driving his cows back to the barn saw a handsome young woman standing by the riverbank, smoking a cigarette, and scribbling in a notebook. Suddenly, as he strode along after the cattle staring at the well-dressed stranger, she threw the coat back off her shoulders, brought out a small dagger, and plunged it into her chest. As the farmer rushed towards her, not having seen the dagger but aware that she had done something sudden and perhaps violent, Alma pitched headlong into the water, which reddened around her. The man could not swim. He ran for help. It was too late.

The police found a tin of cigarettes, a fountain pen, an empty dagger sheath, and some scribbled notes.

If only I thought it would help Stoner, I would stay on, but it has been pointed out to me all too vividly that I cannot help him. That is my death sentence. . . . It is beautiful here. What a lovely world we are in. It must be easier to be hanged than to have to do the job oneself, especially in these circumstances, being watched all the while. Pray God nothing stops me. . . . I tried to throw myself under a train at Oxford Circus. Too many people about. Then a bus. Still too many people. One must be bold to do a thing like this. It is beautiful here. . . . Thank God for peace at last.

Alma and Frances Rattenbury's son John was five years old when his parents died. When Robert Duncan and his production team found him, he had become one of the United States' more senior and respected architects. He was quietly philosophical about the jungle from which he had emerged, scarred but not impaired.

I was playing once with some children my age, and you know how children are . . . incredibly cruel without really meaning to . . . and one of them just suddenly turned to me and told me, "Your father was murdered and your mother took her own life." . . . It was a terrible shock to me. I would be sitting in class years later, you know? Suddenly I would start to cry and the teacher would look over: "What's the matter with this person?" [But] I've never held it against anybody, not even the chauffeur who fell in love with my mother. Those sorts of things happen. And the fact that it developed into a tragedy . . .

Here Mr. Rattenbury's voice trailed off.

As did the life of his father's killer, in the end. There was a huge public protest against the proposed hanging of George Stoner, part of it driven by a growing anti-capital punishment movement in Britain, part by a widespread conviction that he was, as he had said in court, not entirely compos mentis at the time of the killing, whether deranged by jealousy, or by drugs, or by both. Although the mallet seemed evidence of pre-meditation, in the end the home secretary acknowledged the half million signatures on petitions to save him and commuted the sentence to life in prison. He was released on parole, to join the army when World War II began in 1939. He returned to Bournemouth in 1945, then still only twenty-eight years old. He married, and apparently lived a very ordinary life. He was in the public eye briefly in 1990 when, an old page pensioner, he was arrested wearing only socks and a beret, for sexually assaulting a young boy in a public toilet. He would never discuss the Rattenbury case. He died in a Bournemouth nursing home.

Vancouver writer-director Robert Duncan wrote at the end of his documentary on the life of Frances Rattenbury:

In Victoria, Rattenbury's Empress Hotel still dominates centre stage. His legislature building, a hundred years later, still houses the provincial government. But the stately ferry terminal has been converted to a wax museum. Government House, which almost caused his downfall, was destroyed again by fire in 1957. His house in Oak Bay is a private school, the Crystal Gardens an aviary and botanical garden. In Vancouver his majestic law courts are now home to the city's art gallery.

The man who built monuments has no monument of his own. He's buried here in an unmarked plot in the Bournemouth cemetery. Alma's grave, just a few feet away, is identified only with a cemetery spike, to remind the attendants that the space below is occupied.

◆ ◆ ◆

The original documentary was written, directed and narrated by Robert Duncan. It was photographed by Bob Gibson, with sound by David Heckenberger and Lisa Kolisnyk, and edited by Janice Brown.

ADDITIONAL READING:

A. Barnett and R. Windsor Luscombe: *Frances Rattenbury in British Columbia: Architecture and Challenge in the Imperial Age* (1983)

Terry Reksten: *Rattenbury* (Victoria: Sono Nis Press, 1978)

Part Five

NELL SHIPMAN
"AW GEE. FORGETTING ME."

The credit for performing the first nude scene in a movie is traditionally accorded to the Czech star Hedy Lamarr, in a 1933 film entitled *Ecstasy*. The twenty year old was photographed totally immersed, decorously breast-stroking through a brief scene that became some kind of international scandal in the days when sexual behaviour was a Hollywood obsession. For hundreds of thousands of film enthusiasts the only way to see those delectable few seconds of naughtiness in an otherwise profoundly dull and forgettable film was to belong to a university film society where the usual censorship strictures did not apply.

But there is an earlier and more daring nude scene in a movie, performed by the Canadian producer-director-screenwriter-star Nell Shipman of Victoria, BC, who had herself provocatively filmed disrobing by the edge of a mountain pool, plunging in, and partially emerging as she sensually exposed herself to the spray of a cascade falling into the pool. The film was called *Back to God's Country*. It was produced in Alberta in 1919. Shipman had based her script on a novel by the then popular James Oliver Curwood. The picture was produced by Shipman's husband Ernie Shipman, and starred the writer herself. The distributors tried to turn the nude scene into a market-boosting scandal by means of a mildly salacious advertising campaign ("Please do not ban this film!"). The movie was a great success but the nude scene generated almost no comment, and Shipman went on to build a movie career that peaked when she was in her late thirties, and then slowly declined into a final couple of decades of poverty and obloquy.

The Shipman films did not find their way into the university film societies. Perhaps the reason her pictures disappeared after flashing briefly and successfully onto North American screens was largely Shipman's own impulsive and erratic business methods and romantic idealism. But it was at least partly — some say mostly — because this pioneer filmmaker's stubborn independence was a way of declaring war on the big studio movement as it blossomed in the 1930s, a movement that ruthlessly set out to grind down and destroy the Independents, of which proud company Nell Shipman was an exemplary member.

Whatever the reason, disappear they did, until the archivist D.J. Turner began the long process of tracking down and acquiring the lost footage, and Bill O'Farrell, a former production executive for another Canadian film pioneer named Budge Crawley, began the process of physically restoring the few badly decayed prints of Shipman's work that Turner had been able to find. Their most important acquisition and most challenging restoration was Shipman's great 1919 success *Back to God's Country*. These films had been shot on a film stock known as acetate, a transparent forerunner of celluloid. Acetate film was unstable, decaying with a distinctly vinegary odour. Its cousin nitrate film was explosive and caused a number of serious fires before they both were superseded by celluloid, which became and still is the preferred material for both still and motion pictures.[5]

The very word *archives* suggests the smell of dust in narrow corridors, old stone and sunlight slanting through narrow windows. But the National Archives of Canada are housed in an almost futuristic glass-and-steel building in the nation's capital, and in the basement of that building is a cold storage room where film is kept at zero degrees Fahrenheit (minus 18 degrees Celsius). Archivists dress in parkas and gloves to visit it.

Dozens of reels of Shipman originals are in those vaults. When the film restorers began to work through them, the task was daunting. The film had turned a dark orange-brown colour and was giving off the characteristic vinegar odour of decaying acetate. Whole sections were physically falling apart, frame after frame looking as though moths or mice had been at them. D.J. Turner kept scouring the world's repositories of old films, however, and over time acquired a sufficient number of copies, some of them in versions quite different from the one the restorers had begun with, to assemble a *Back to God's Country* painstakingly transferred frame by frame onto modern celluloid (and archived in electronic digital format as well), until they had a projectable finished copy. This movie is really the centrepiece of our story of Nell Shipman, as it was in so many ways the centrepiece of her life; so it is worthwhile hearing a few more words about the task of

5. This will probably change before long. Digital imaging with its ability to be stored in tiny solid-state chips is coming up fast, although even digital's staunchest enthusiasts agree that celluloid film will, for some time, remain the preferred medium for projection in theatres.

rescuing it from its very close brush with annihilation. Bill O'Farrell says,

> Back to God's Country . . . *remains one of the most complex restorations we have ever undertaken. One of the issues we had to deal with . . . was . . . restoration ethics. By that I mean you're faced with some interesting subjective choices, because of the fact that we had literally two versions of the film to work with, from two different camera angles. There was one shot where Nell is walking along the ravine. And in one version she is walking . . . [only] up to a certain point. And in the other version she walks the rest of the way. . . . There were probably two cameras rolling but only one camera got that entire shot.*

The restorers were faced with the question of trying to determine which shot, or combination of shots, would be most faithful to the intentions of the original producers. In the end they had to guess — or often to just go with the only version that was sufficiently intact to be copied onto a fresh roll of celluloid.

One of the things that writer-director Patricia Phillips discovered as she began to assemble this television biography of Nell Shipman is that in *Back to God's Country*, and in other Shipman films, there are striking parallels to Shipman's own life, enough of them to make director Phillips' documentary a running set of images drawn from these old movies, and interwoven with the story of a real life.

That life began in Victoria, about as dramatically as anything the child once grown would ever conceive for her dozens of novels and films: she died almost immediately after she was born. At least that was what seemed to happen, so unequivocally that the baby's despairing mother ran out into the night, to the edge of the forest, with the inert little body in her arms, holding it up to the sky, when suddenly the tiny limbs began to twitch and grope, and the baby came back to life. They named her Helen, Helen Barham.

It was at about the time that the little survivor was taking her first faltering steps in British Columbia, that in Paris the brothers Lumière helped a new industry and a new art form take their first faltering steps. For the first time in the world, in December of 1895, they projected onto a screen in front of a paying audience the image of a passenger train puffing its way grandly into a suburban Paris station. The power of that moving image was so great that as the locomotive grew unstoppably larger and closer on the screen some members of the audience ran screaming from the theatre, convinced that they were about to be crushed under the wheels.

As we begin to look at the new industrial and artistic world upon which Nell Shipman had such an impact, it would richly repay the film enthusiast to rent a video entitled simply *Lumière*, a brilliantly conceived centennial project (1995). For it, an original wooden-box Lumière brothers camera called the *Cinématographe* was put back into working order, reels of the special film were manufactured, and a couple dozen famous contemporary directors were invited to make a movie each, within the space of the available single reel running time — which was only fifty seconds! They had to stick to the techniques of the day, which meant little editing and no synchronous sound. Spike Lee, Agnes Varda, John Boorman, Liv Ullman, and some twenty other

well-known directors had a go at it. The first of the productions in this eccentric and sometimes brilliant collection
took the camera back to that same suburban station for the
arrival of an express, with predictable and hilarious
results. An hour and a half with this inspired work will
give any viewer a whole film course's worth of insight into
the demands and strictures of early filmmaking.

Helen Barham had not yet acquired the nickname Nell;
that would come with her first marriage, more than a dozen
years later. But she had acquired a taste for public enter-
tainments. It is likely that she saw her first motion picture
in a vaudeville house when she was still pretty young. She
was precocious, and her father gave her more freedom than
most girls would have had growing up on the West Coast
at the end of the nineteenth century. It seems likely that he
took her to the popular vaudeville theatres to see this new
phenomenon, the motion picture. Movies in those days
were often travelling shows. An enterprising fellow with a
projector and a bag or box full of short films, completely
silent of course, would go from town to town and make a
deal to split the receipts with the management of a local
hall. He might hire a local pianist to provide an accompaniment. Because of the entertainment level of many of the
early films — five or six-minute simple scenarios of a bank
robbery and chase and apprehension, for example, there
was a natural affinity for the vaudeville theatres with their
tradition of short snappy acts. Bit by bit the vaudeville companies began to install their own projectors, order their
films directly from the distributors, and even use the movie
shows to promote upcoming live events. The bank robber

would be shot to death in the street, and then up would come some rudimentarily animated graphics of stars and moons, and words would spread across the screen:

SEE THE GREAT MANDRAKE THE MAGICIAN
LIVE ON THIS STAGE
NEXT THURSDAY AND FRIDAY ONLY AT 7 PM
LIVING MYSTERY TO THRILL AND *AMAZE!*[6]

Barham *père* was a remittance man, one of those younger sons of traditional British families who was not going to inherit, was a bit of an embarrassment to the family, and was shipped off to the colonies with a small allowance just to get him out of the way. Nell's father drank to comfort himself with his misfortune, which probably included a substantial dose of contempt from his neighbours — the remittance men were looked down upon as ne'er-do-well snobs. And it may be that the adolescent girl's acting ambitions seemed to her father to be some kind of opportunity. He had moved the family to Seattle, and in Seattle there was an acting teacher of reputation, Frank Egan. Nell gave up on school, enrolled with Egan, and by the age of thirteen was on the road with a repertory theatre, travelling up and down the West Coast. This was a trial by fire. You were not paid very much, and you had to cover your own hotel and meals and even make your own costumes. Nell's mother went on the road with the adventurous adolescent, primarily to protect her virtue, as they used to say, but also to comfort her, advise her on wardrobe, and give her moral support. The life was

6. See Part Twelve for the role of film announcements like this in the life of the real Mandrake the Magician, another notable British Columbian.

hard on both of them, but Nell refused to quit until she too got tired of eating inadequate meals in dirty rooms in horrid little fleabag hotels, and came home exhausted but experienced. She was sixteen years old.

She tried a stint in Alaska with another Seattle repertory company, managed by a man named Charles Taylor, who had hoped to make his fortune with a vaudeville company playing to the gold rush guys. But it was too late; the gold rush was over. Taylor's company went broke, and Nell came home.

Something about the North had grasped her imagination, and would not lie dormant for long. Back from Alaska, broke, but still confident that the theatre was her proper place in the world, she walked into Seattle's Pantages Theatre and met a man who was to radically change her life. His name was Ernie Shipman — "Ten Percent Ernie" — because as an agent, manager, and promoter he lived on that percentage of the earnings of all the talents he took under his wing. He was thirty-eight, pot-bellied, a rake with a reputation and an improbable and unattractive red hunting cap. She was eighteen, big-bosomed, voluptuous, with seductive eyes and the confidence of a road warrior. Improbably, they clicked.

They talked together about this new moving picture thing. The new moving picture thing was in California. So they got married and went to California. She began to think about writing; a book was taking shape in her mind. A collection of short stories called *Under the Crescent*, it would be tales of love and intrigue in an exotic Turkish environment. Ernie Shipman, for all his harebrained schemes and unsavoury ways, must have been an effective promoter, because before long he sold the film rights to *Under the Crescent*, landed Nell a contract to write a two-reeler based on it (some sources say a series), and launched the career of a screenwriter who would soon become a star.

Her ability to turn out screenplays quickly made them if not rich at least sufficiently well-off to take a gracious Victorian house in Glendale, which is still there and still lovely. Stories of this svelte and seductive young woman sliding into a production executive's office with one new screenplay and out with a contract for another began to attract a lot of attention in Los Angeles. A company called Vitagraph decided to contract her as an actress in one of the then famous James Oliver Curwood's outdoor adventure stories. She was by now a recognized writer, at the age of twenty-three. Nell got the screenwriting contract for the Curwood project, as well as the principal role, and then talked her way into both producing and directing her own script.

The picture was a full-length feature, *God's Country and the Woman*. It put Nell Shipman back into the northern wilderness she had come to love in Alaska. And it gave her a name. For the rest of her career, the girl from Victoria would be known as the Girl from God's Country.

Sam Goldwyn, then still working under his original name of Samuel Goldfish, tried to secure the glamorous newcomer with a seven-year contract, the maximum allowed by law in those days. Nell came in for a test and a costume fitting. When she found that they were trying to force her big-breasted, wide-hipped long-limbed outdoors

woman body into the then fashionable mould of a tiny del-
icate starlet, she went back to Vitagraph and another
Curwood story, *Baree, Son of Kazan* (1917). Now she was getting cockily independent. She insisted on doing her own
stunts in *Baree*. She was good at them, and perhaps it would
save the cost of a salary to a stunt artist. But it was insubor-
dinate, and Vitagraph decided they had to show who was
boss. Her next few acting assignments were secondary
roles. Nell went to Ten Percent Ernie and complained.

In the overall profile of the life of Nell Shipman *née*
Helen Barham, the role of her first husband is mixed and
not always savoury. But he did know how to make a deal.
He went around by the side door, straight to Curwood
who was a great deal more valuable to those Vitagraph pictures than Vitagraph was to Curwood. Curwood liked
what Nell had done to God's *Country and the Woman*. He
presciently saw the value of the same approach that years
later would give us Rocky from I to V, and he proposed to
go *Back to God's Country*. Nell Shipman would be star and
co-writer with Curwood. Ernie was not only a full partner
in the new production company, Shipman-Curwood productions, but also the producer of the seventy-three-
minute feature.

As they began work on B*ack to God's Country*, the
Great War was just winding down in Europe. Much of the
Western world had been hit by a severe epidemic of
influenza. Nell and her mother Rose were both stricken. As
Nell lay in a coma in an upstairs room, Rose died in the
room below her. Before she was fully recovered from her
illness, and in the midst of her grief at the loss of her mother,

Nell had to start shooting some incidental scenes in California, while Ernie headed north to Alberta, where most of the film was to be produced, to line up financing.

It was probably one of the earliest instances of what has become a mainstay of feature-film production funding in this country: persuading governments, citizens, and businesses in the region where you are going to produce that they should put up the money for the production. Ernie Shipman met with the Edmonton board of trade. They all knew *God's Country and the Woman*. They didn't all know that Nell was a Victoria girl and were probably charmed to learn that little detail. They were told that it was going to be a great movie, much greater than its predecessor, so of course it was a huge investment opportunity. And they bought it.

The actual production, on the shores of Lesser Slave Lake, went less smoothly. When Curwood himself turned up on the set he found a script that had inverted the intentions of his original story, in which a hero — according to the convention of the genre — rescues an enchanting but vulnerable heroine. This latter was not a character that appealed to Nell Shipman, who had to play the role. So by the time Curwood arrived in Northern Alberta, with shooting too far advanced to make major changes, Nell's character (Dolores LeBeau) had become the prime focus of the narrative. The film historian Peter Morris told us, "She is the one who defeats the villain in the end. She is the one who protects her husband. She is the one who develops the very sensitive rapport with the dog . . ." And Curwood was distressed by all these changes until Nell got hold of him and buttered him up and told him how wonderful *his* concept was and how little she had had to alter it for film purposes . . . and doubtless other things that contemporary directors and screenwriters find themselves using to soothe the novelist who has arrived on the set. On the *Back to God's Country* set, although Shipman had no official role other than co-screenwriter and star, it is clear from the many accounts of that production that it was she who chose the key scenes and gave the film its natural look. It was she who discarded the flesh-coloured leotards to play the swimming scene described earlier. The leotards looked like leotards, she said, not like skin. So she would play it naturally.

It was a shoot with a lot of drama that was not all caught on camera. Another interesting man on set who turns up in the official cast list of some later films though not, it seems, in *Back to God's Country* — so it is not clear exactly what he was doing on that set — is Bert Van Tuyle, with whom Nell began to have an affair when Ernie went back to California in search of more financing.

Then the weather turned ferociously cold. The carpenters quit. Bert got severe frostbite, which turned to gangrene. The romantic lead, Ronald Byron, a handsome young Australian, developed pneumonia after a few days of shooting and soon died. When you examine the film closely, you find that the leading man in some scenes looks oddly different from the supposedly same man in other scenes.

This was the beginning of a whole series of films in which Nell Shipman would develop important relationships with animals. She was fiercely loyal to her animals. She would not permit cruel restraints like nose rings and genital rings, nor would she allow stun guns on the set. "They can sense it, you know," she insisted. No whips, no lassoes, no drugs.

In *Back to God's Country* they used two different Great Danes to play "Wapi the Walrus," a key role (and the title of the Curwood story on which the screenplay was based). One of them, Rex, was a soft and easygoing sweetheart dog. The other, Trésor, was a trained killer who could be counted on to be fierce when required, but you wouldn't want to get too close to him when he wasn't muzzled or when his trainer was not at hand.

The dogs got mixed up once, when Nell was supposed to play a close and affectionate scene with Rex. Shortly after they started to roll camera on the scene someone realized that a switch had taken place and whispered to director David Hartford that this was really the killer dog. Hartford said quietly, Keep 'em rolling. Nobody told Nell. Nell caressed and hugged the killer dog, which appeared to return her affection, and the scene went off perfectly. They cut. Someone told Nell, who did not seem very surprised. The director David Hartford came over to them laughing and said sarcastically something like "Some killer dog!" Trésor then leapt for Hartford's throat and they had to rush in and pull the dog off the terrified director.

Back to God's Country was possibly the most successful film in Canadian cinema history. It earned some 300 percent profit for its investors. Nell does not seem to have shared that profit. It seems likely that she was cheated out of her share as a participant in several of the companies involved. The fading marriage may have played a part.

Ernie was having his own affair in California while Nell and Bert Van Tuyle were keeping each other warm at Lesser Slave Lake. Nell was paid as star and screenwriter, but when it was all over she broke away from Shipman-Curwood productions, divorced Ernie, and set out on a road of stubborn independence that would be, for a while, exhilarating.

She founded Nell Shipman Productions, of Los Angeles. Bert Van Tuyle was her front man and business partner. Joseph Walker, a cinematographer who had worked on *Back to God's Country* and would go on to a brilliant career shooting for Frank Capra, helped her with an insignificant little two-reeler, *Trail of the Arrow*, and with *Something New*. She wrote, directed, and starred in *Something New*, a Maxwell Automobile promotional film that was supposed to be a two-reeler but grew into a hilarious feature-length film, set this time not in ice and snow but in the Mojave Desert. She found an "angel," a man named William Clune. Even though there were signs that the future of film was in the hands of the growing big studios like Universal, he took a chance on this brave new independent woman and financed what was going to be her really great film. This one was "take three" so to speak of the God's Country theme. They called it *The Girl from God's Country*.

The maximum length of a feature until then was nine reels, about an hour and a half. *The Girl from God's Country* finished up at thirteen reels. Nell's contract gave her editing control, but Clune believed that exhibitors wouldn't touch a two-hour film. He seized it, recut it, and put out a standard length version. That was the end of Clune. Historian Tom Trusky at Idaho's Boise University (where a centre of Shipman archives and studies has been created) told us that Nell took out trade paper ads saying, "That's what they do to women in China. They bind their feet and produce malformed beings. And that's what happened to my film. Do not book the 9 reel version of *The Girl from God's Country*."

"You can imagine how popular that makes her in the industry," Professor Trusky said. "The word is out that she is . . . blackballed in Hollywood. . . .The decision to start her own company was wonderful, but . . . wrong-headed. The industry is starting to centralize. [That's] going to be the pattern for the next forty years or so. [But now] Nell's going to try to do what Ernie did in Canada . . . go out and get local investors, the sort of people who had invested in *Back to God's Country*, and repeat that success."

Her former director, David Hartford, joined the blackball bandwagon and wrote to the newspapers warning potential investors, but the investors chose to stick with Nell.

Nell had not only started a new company, she had begun to assemble what soon became the largest private zoo in North America, a substantial menagerie that she intended to ship to Priest Lake, Idaho, for the location shoot on her next big project, *The Grubstake*. The studio scenes were shot in Spokane, Washington, at the Minnehaha studios, with a roof that rolled back to let in sunlight and equipment that was as up-to-date as anything in Hollywood.

Then, when it was time to move the cast and crew —

and the menagerie — to Idaho for the location shooting, dozens of animals, including a cougar and several bears, had to be crated and barged up Priest Lake to Forest Lodge, a resort they rented from a man called Sam Byars. The shoot went overschedule and overbudget. Labs were pursuing Nell for the costs of processing the film. She was afraid they might impound the footage, and set up secret editing rooms, sometimes in the homes of friends. Actors who hadn't been paid for their work at Minnehaha Studios were making trouble, and actors at Forest Lodge were getting pretty touchy. Whether or not the picture would ever get finished was a cliff-hanger, and, like many of the events in Nell's life, had its parallel in the film itself, with a genuine cliff-hanger ending. Tom Trusky said,

Nell takes that word literally. We have one of the most dramatic finales . . . ever. . . in The Grubstake. *We see Nell hanging by one hand to . . . a twisted, gnarled tree root on a huge cliff. And she spliced together a scene of Lookout Mountain, over at Priest Lake, with some [fake] cliffs at Minnehaha which are only maybe ten or twenty feet high but spliced together so this woman [appears to be] hanging on for dear life, about . . . to fall from the cliff, thousands of feet to a dreadful death below.*

Somehow, holding the creditors at bay and keeping the actors and crew from mutiny, she finished the film, took a train to New York and started screening for releasing companies. The first one seemed indifferent. The next day American Releasing offered her about $75,000. She accepted, only to have the first company call her later that day with a much better offer. It was too late.

Perhaps Nell Shipman was trying to do too much: conceive and write the story, raise the money, direct and act, and then try to market it herself. Perhaps a more realistic businesswoman would have recognized the changing world, and changed with it. But a more realistic businesswoman might not have made the breakthroughs and created the work that Nell achieved. Who knows? In any case it was not just the producers and distributors who were growing into huge corporations: the small independent exhibitors were leaving the scene as well. Film historian Kay Armatage at the University of Toronto told us:

The studios started buying up . . . the . . . independently owned vaudeville houses and making their own circuit. And of course there are all kinds of rumours about organized crime. If an independent vaudeville owner, for example, didn't want to sell, he might find his equipment smashed, his theatre burned down, his being knee-capped, whatever. Gradually they all fell.

With the money she got from American Releasing, Nell went back to Idaho only to find that Sam Byars had tripled the rent on Forest Lodge. She brought in the barges again, cut leads through the thin ice, and moved the zoo and the gear down the lake to Lionhead Lodge where she built a studio and started producing a series of outdoor shorts for the Selznick organization. To make ends meet she did a vaudeville show, and to avoid the difficulties with the Hollywood actors who were, by now, doubtful about getting paid, she hired locals and tried to train them. She even put her twelve-year-old son Barry to work as an actor on the project.

In one scene Barry was to drive his mother across the lake on a sled. A patch of ice had been cracked open with axes so that it would break under the weight of the sled and Barry would fall in, only to be saved by the dauntless woman who jumps in after him. This was no studio tank with Styrofoam ice; it was Priest Lake, Idaho, in January. The moment Barry felt the freezing water penetrate to his skin he grabbed at the solid part of the surrounding ice and began to pull himself out. But that would have weakened the suspense, and close scrutiny of the restored footage reveals that Barry's later account, of how Nell grabbed his belt under water and held him back as he thrashed against the cold, while doing her best to appear as though she were trying to rescue him, is accurate. "Her priorities were . . . for the movie," said Barry's surviving daughter Nina.

The Selznick projects moved ahead quite well, as it turned out. Nell decided to celebrate with a Fourth of July Party. The former landlord Sam Byars, apparently seeking revenge for his having lost a lucrative contract, slipped ashore by canoe that night while the cast and crew were partying, and tossed a cyanide-laced piece of meat on the ground in front of the Great Dane Trésor, who by now was Nell's favourite and had been posted as a guard. Trésor knew Byars from Forest Lodge, accepted the delicacy, and died. Nell was trying to deal with that grief when she learned that American Releasing, who was also distributing the Selznick shorts, had gone bankrupt.

Now winter was coming on again, 1923 to 1924. Nell's relationship with Bert Van Tuyle was not surviving the financial strain. Bert's gangrene returned. Nell wrote in her autobiography that you could see a toe bone emerging through his diseased flesh. The lake was frozen again. Van Tuyle became emotionally unstable. Without telling Nell, he staggered out, hitched up the dogs, and tried to drive himself across the lake to get medical help. Nell saw him go and, with more cinematic sense than prudence, decided to follow at a distance so that he would not be humiliated. Once again her life imitates her art because it is almost exactly a scene from *Back to God's Country* (with the two different actors after one died), and filmmaker Phillips was able to illustrate this episode in the actress's real life with footage from that earlier film that parallels the actual lives of the actors and crew. An account of that whole winter — although it is about a group of real people struggling with real life-and-death issues — reads like melodrama. Nell began to spend time with a good-looking young local actor. Bert, now at least partly recovered from the gangrene, found out about his rival. One night, drunk and raging, he started threatening to kill somebody. Young Barry, having lived most of his life around cinematic melodrama, picked up a gun and stood at the window with his sights on Van Tuyle, thinking he would heroically save his mother if things got violent. Nell appears to have lost all sense of perspective at that point. She broke from the party, ran out across the lake, and seemed suddenly, madly, bent on suicide, heading for the open water at the edge of the ice. Barry dropped the rifle, tore after his mother, and forcibly brought the broken, deranged woman back to camp.

As historian Tom Trusky talks about the Priest Lake

winter of 1923 to 1924 it sounds as though almost all the people in that settlement were constantly confusing their fictional stories with real life. But the reality was closing in on the play-acting. Soon the money was gone, there was not enough food for the animals, people were leaving, and Nell, finally, had had enough.

She never went back to Priest Lake. Trying to pull herself together she went to New York where she met a gentle, aspiring painter, Charles Ayers, who fell in love with her and took her off to Europe. It seems as though she was, by then, quite content to say good-bye to the world of film. In Spain she had two children, Daphne and Charles Junior. She rested and got herself back into shape, and when Charles Ayers decided to go home to America, Nell began to think about performing again.

Florida, 1928. America is riding an illusory economic boom. Nell gets a job. It is not the movies, but it is show business. Ringling Brothers cast her as queen of the circus, with silver dress and silver shoes — well, painted cardboard — and the glamour of her career takes on a different tone. She starts to write again.

She was a prolific writer, banging away at her old typewriter turning out articles for women's magazines, novels, trying more film scripts. She sold a serialized novel to *McCall's* magazine, then turned it into a screenplay (to star Nell Shipman), and tried it out on the studios. But whether her bad name was lingering on, or the studios had decided they now preferred male screenwriters, or both — nobody bought. The marriage with Charles ended. Charles Jr. seems to have become estranged from his mother, and Daphne's mental health was precarious. Once more Nell was alone.

In New York she met a fraudulent sometime director who was on contract to the British company, Fox, in England. He was passing himself off as an Italian count, "Amerigo Serrao." They started to live together. Nell worked on a screenplay for Paramount, which was produced with Myrna Loy and Cary Grant. For a while this looked as though it might be the launching pad for a renewed career: the fame of a script for those two great stars was bound to open doors. But somehow, when the movie was released, there was no screen credit for Nell. She and Amerigo tried scheme after scheme.

"There are a series of letters," historian Kay Armatage says, "where Nell writes to Barry and says, 'They're going to rent a studio for us; the money will be in the bank by Friday.'"

But it was probably all fiction. In fact they were sometimes sneaking out of hotels to avoid paying. Her typewriter, bought on time, was repossessed. They were constantly dodging bill collectors. In Virginia they managed once more to intrigue local investors. Nell wrote and directed *Mr. Hobbs*, a twangy Virginian country love story. It was never released. She wrote an autobiography. She left Amerigo in New York and, now sixty and not well, tried her luck in California once again. She never saw Amerigo again. He died in a New York flophouse. Hollywood acted as if she were an unknown old bag lady. She was not far from it. She was destitute.

There is a comfortable seniors' Hollywood home for aging and indigent members of the profession, funded by the Motion Picture Relief Fund. Nell swallowed her pride and applied for a room. She was told that there was no record of her ever having been a member of the profession. The ranks that had closed against her in her proud and independent days stayed closed. She was saved from the streets by an old friend name Dick Diaz who had a dude ranch for dogs in the small town of Cabazon, and there she lived out the last few years of her life. You can hear her voice, in the documentary, sending a grandmotherly Christmas message to Barry's children.

Film historian Peter Morris said, "You know, when I think the last words of her autobiography . . . if I'm remembering correctly she ended up saying, 'Aw Gee. There they go. Forgetting me. So what?' Like . . . I had my moment in the sun and it was great, you know, when I was sort of a star. And then it didn't work."

"Pan. Well, Okay."

When she died in 1970, thieves broke into the little house in Cabazon during the funeral; her four big theatre trunks of costumes, scripts, and other memorabilia were stolen and never recovered. As these prodigiously original early films begin to surface and are restored and screened, they show the pioneering work of a Canadian who made blockbusters in Alberta half a century before Telefilm Canada was even thought of and who then vanished. It has been a difficult time for the historians and archivists — and documentary biographers — to piece together the Nell Shipman story. But it has clearly been a labour of love, and that love shows through on the screen.

Note: This writer was able to locate one copy of her novel *Under the Crescent*. It is offered for sale via the Internet for $225 (US). It does seem as though there are some people who remember.

◆　◆　◆

The original documentary was written, produced, and directed by Patricia Phillips. It was photographed by Douglas Munro, CSC, and edited by Doug Forbes.

ADDITIONAL READING:

Ally Acker: *Reel Women: Pioneers of the Cinema, 1896 to the Present* (New York: Continuum,1993)

Kay Armatage: *Animals in the Films of Nell Shipman; Nell Shipman: A Case of Heroic Femininity; The Silent Scream and My Talking Heart*

William M. Drew: *Something New: The Speeding Sweethearts of the Silent Screen, 1908–1921*

William K. Everson: "Rediscovery: The Films of Nell Shipman," *Films in Review* 40 (4) (April 1989): 228–30

Gwendolyn Foster: *Women Film Directors: An International Bio-Critical Dictionary* (Connecticut: Greenwood Press, 1995)

Tom Fulbright: "Queen of the Dog Sleds," *Classic Film Collector* (Fall 1969): 31

Peter Morris: "The Taming of the Few: Nell Shipman in the Context of Her Times," in *The Silent Screen and My Talking Heart* (Boise, ID: Boise State University Press, 1987), 195–205

Nell Shipman: *The Silent Screen and My Talking Heart: An Autobiography* (Boise, ID: Hemingway Western Studies Series, Boise State University Press, 1987)

Anthony Slide: *Early Women Directors* (New York: Da Capo, 1984)

Joseph Walker and Juanita Walker: "Danger in God's Country," *American Cinematographer* 66 (5) (May 1985): 34–43; The Light on her Face (ASC Press, 1984)

On the web: www.utoronto.ca/shipman and another at http:\\english.boisestate.edu.ttrusky are interesting sites. Simply entering the name of Professor Tom Trusky in a good search engine will bring up a number of Shipman-related sites.

Part Six

BILL MINER
The Truth about the Grey Fox

It has to be confessed from the start that including the life of Bill Miner in a book of Canadian biography is, as Huckleberry Finn might have said, a bit of a stretch. Miner was born in Michigan and died in jail in Georgia, and the only place he could ever have called home for any length of time was the famous San Quentin prison in California. But the man they called the Grey Fox, Last of the Old Time Bandits, did become a hero in western Canada. He did humiliate one of the more detested of the great Canadian institutions of the time, the Canadian Pacific Railroad. And he seems to have negotiated with that same powerful Canadian corporation, a deal involving the equivalent of hundreds of millions of dollars in today's money. The deal appears nowhere in the record books, but it is historic in every sense of the word. And — we argued at History Television — that part of the story more than justifies giving Old Bill Miner a place in our gallery of Canadian rogues and heroes.

San Quentin is the oldest (1852) maximum-security prison in California. You can get there easily by bus from San Francisco, look at the virtual reality display by the gate, visit the museum for $2 or half that if you are a child or a senior. If you are a journalist or sociologist or have other credentials, and call well in advance, you might even get to interview the warden, Jeanne Woodford. Her annual budget of $120 million pays a staff of more than 1,500 people to look after more than six thousand inmates in an institution designed to house about three thousand. About six hundred of those men (women were moved to another prison in 1933) are on death row, and the prison houses California's only gas chamber.

Billy Miner spent thirty-three of his sixty-seven years in San Quentin. He went there as a teenager, convicted of his first robbery, when the United States was riven by the consequences of a bloody civil war and the murder of a great president. None of these events seems to have left any mark on the kid. He had chosen the way of the outlaw, and it seems that from then on the outlaw life is all he really thought about. California was, in any case, a long way from the war and relatively untouched by it. If Lincoln's death had seared the consciousness of the East and the South, California then as now had its own agenda and its own preoccupations, one of which was the out-of-control crime that had spiralled up out of the gold rush after 1849. That was why they had made San Quentin.

The prison still had the system of boss cons in those days. This let the toughest convicts actually control the discipline in the prison yard. If other prisoners didn't say good morning to a boss con, they could be beaten for disrespect, and if they did say good morning, they could be beaten for insolence. There was an average of ten whippings a day. Prisoners were routinely and savagely beaten and tortured. Sexual assault was routine.

The new boy was slight of figure, rather girlish in appearance, not effeminate but somebody who would be quickly seized on by the aggressive "wolves" among the inmates. Miner was probably sodomized on his first day. Later he became a wolf himself, was well known to inmates and staff, and, ironic though it sounds, was well liked by most of them.

This legendary bandit began his career of crime as a stagecoach robber in the great old tradition of the Western movies, pulled off the first train robbery ever committed in Canada, and was sentenced to life in prison as a result. Two years later he slipped away from the prison brickyard with two other cons one afternoon, under circumstances that only recently have focused on the strange role of the bandit's greatest victim, the CPR.

That set of events, around the CPR heist, was the most spectacular and the most successful of his many capers, many of which were hilariously bungled. But Bill Miner is remembered not so much for what he did, or even for his dramatic and comical ineptitude ("a very *bad* bandit," says historian Mark Dugan, meaning incompetent, not nasty). It was his character that struck people, perhaps his skill as a storyteller, weaving his own tales of derring-do and failures into a lasting legend. To the San Francisco historian John Boessenakker, the durability of that legend has little to do with Miner's one big multimillion-dollar success:

He's remembered today for a number of reasons. One is the longevity of his career, almost fifty years as an outlaw. He had the personality of a man who just refused to give up. He was able to adapt very quickly to new environments, new geographical areas, new societies, new technology. And he was a charming man, he was funny, he was bright, he was educated, and he was somebody who revelled in his reputation. At the time of his death, he had a national reputation as a criminal. We don't know much about his mother, Harriet Miner. She was definitely an educated woman. Bill in later years always said that she'd been a schoolteacher. We couldn't find any proof that in fact she was a schoolteacher. However, the evidence of his handwriting makes it appear that he was well educated. He certainly was literate; he could read and write. He was very well spoken and very gentlemanly and obviously had a very good upbringing.

The one photograph we have of Harriet Miner shows a serene and lovely woman of thirty or less, in an elegant heavy silk dress, looking dreamily off into infinity with a book in her hand. She had brought her two boys out to California from their hometown of Onondaga, Michigan, six years before Billy's first failed robbery and subsequent imprisonment. They had settled in a gold rush town called Yankee Jim where the reigning values were get-rich-quick and violence. John Boessenakker said,

What you had in California, was something historians call the bachelor cult of masculinity. This was a real culture that existed among young men in the nineteenth century whether it was on the east coast or in the frontier regions, where young men congregated in political clubs, volunteer fire companies, saloons, and they engaged in the favourite pastime, which was bare-knuckle fighting, and this is the kind of community that existed on the east coast and in the California gold rush. That's the kind of community that Bill Miner grew up in.

The prison records showed him convicted of robbery, and he served six years in San Quentin for that one, where he made friends with a professional stagecoach robber named Alkali Jim Harrington. They got out together in 1871, and before long had held up a stagecoach near San Andreas. Billy was apprenticed to Alkali Jim, but according to historian Boessenakker he was also already asserting himself as a kind of leader.

They robbed this stagecoach, and the driver, Cutler, was ordered to take his boots off and he complained about that and he said, "This is pretty rough on a guy to make me drive back in my stocking feet." And then they took his watch, and he said, "you can't take . . ." — the driver, Cutler, said, "Listen, you can't take my watch. It's a gift from my dead mother," and Miner said, "We respect men's mothers," and gave him the watch back.

Cutler was also able to identify the men when they were arrested not long after the robbery. Before their cell bunks had cooled off, so to speak, they were both back in San Quentin sentenced to fourteen years with hard labour.

Billy Miner was twenty-five years old. In his prison photo that year he looks forty and he looks sad and bitter. The babyfaced kid look of the teenage years has been replaced by the trademark long inverted V of a moustache. The eyes are crinkled and sad, the expression distant. His sidekick Alkali Jim would die in San Quentin, but Billy was beginning to think about escaping. The rock quarry seemed an opportune take-off point, but it is probable that he did not seek as much advice as he should have when he made his break about three years into the term. Escapes from the quarry were enough of a natural temptation that the custodial staff was used to them. Tracking down the escapees was almost routine. They got him within hours, gave him twenty lashes, and threw him into the Dungeon.

If you get to San Quentin and visit the museum, the museum director Dick Nelson can tell you, as he told us, about the conditions Miner lived in there in the 1870s. How long and how badly you were punished would depend not only on your behaviour, but also on how you got along with the Captain:

> And then [he] probably would have, for a period of time, been sentenced to the ball and chain, to preclude any further escapes — in the immediate future, anyway. It doesn't take very long to assimilate into the prison society, because there's nothing else to do. The morning would start at about 6:00, and they'd be served a breakfast, probably in those days just a mush. Then they'd have to report to work. They'd come back in about 4:00, and they'd be counted, locked up, and then go to their evening meal. There's no record . . . of any nighttime activities. They were locked up from dusk to dawn.

Photographs of the prison yard show those afternoon lineups for the count, several hundred gaunt men, drooping with fatigue, many of them chained to a heavy cast-iron ball, all dressed in the long coarse cotton prison jacket and pants, with broad black stripes running horizontally across the chest and back and around the legs and arms. There was no concept of prisoners' rights. But as any inmate will tell you, there was a moral code and a highly structured society. Study after study of long-term inmates show that while they learned to live and conform effectively inside, life on the outside is often so baffling to them that after ten or fifteen years of prison it is almost a relief to be caught and to come back "home."

Was that part of the Miner story? With almost forty of his sixty-seven years of life passed behind bars, and so casual and unplanned an approach to each of the jobs he pulled that it almost seems as though he wanted to be caught, there is a temptation to think so. And yet it doesn't seem to fit the character. Miner had a self-confidence and a social ability that would not have left him ill at ease in the outside world. A later episode back in Onondaga, Michigan, attests to that. He was not unintelligent, but there may have been an almost pathological inability to distinguish myth from reality, a need to map his life out according to a romantic notion, a need so compelling that it overcame any training he might have received from mother about planning ahead and considering the consequences of your actions. Part of the romance was the partnership model — the James Brothers, Butch Cassidy and the Sundance Kid. Billy Miner ultimately paired up with a succession of very unpleasant people whose one attractive feature was their dedication to the criminal life.

The next one of these guys was Billy Leroy. Miner had earned four years off his sentence for good behaviour and an apparently convincing promise to leave California. He said he would go to live with his sister in the state of Washington and turn his prison training in shoemaking into an honest living. He had no intention of doing this, although it does appear that his sister held out hopes for a while, and that he did in fact spend some time with her. But he kept looking out for the next accomplice, and he met Billy Leroy on a train.

The American historian Mark Dugan specializes in the study of rogues and rascals of this period, and has become an expert on Billy Leroy. It does seem an unusual subject for a historian to specialize in: Dugan himself finds little to admire in the little crook.

Well, he's just kind of a brash, cocky kid from Iowa who got tired of working, and he gets on a train and Miner's sitting next to him, and Miner's — what? — thirty-something at that point? And they start talking on the train.

We can be pretty sure that the talk — from Miner's end — was well-embroidered storytelling, an account of a daring and successful life of crime that would easily turn a boy's head. Dugan went on:

And the kid jumped at the chance to work with him. But in this case, I do not think there was any sexual relationship between the two. Billy Leroy, he turned out to be kind of a tough kid. In fact, in the end, he takes over control of the robberies. He takes Miner's place and puts Miner in a secondary role . . . in their last robbery. . . . I don't think Miner cared much for that at all. I think that really irritated him.

Irritated or not, Miner found Leroy an effective fellow bandit. For the first time in a long and undistinguished career he was actually a success. He was robbing stagecoaches and getting away with it. But in the end he couldn't stand not being in control, not being number one, unable to control Billy Leroy. They soon split up. Leroy formed a new gang and kept on robbing stages in Colorado until he and his partners were caught and put in jail in the town of Del Norte. While they were there, the good citizens of the small town paid them a visit, and there is a photograph of the two of them, in suits and ties, with bowler hats — they hadn't even gone to trial yet — hanging from a couple of trees on the Del Norte main street. So Miner's decision to break off that relationship was fortunate in a way, although without LeRoy to keep things disciplined he went back to his bungling ways when he next turned to crime.

But that was not for a while. He took the considerable haul that was his share from the Leroy partnership, and inexplicably headed back to Onondaga, the Michigan town he had not seen since he was twelve years old. Nobody there remembered him as the adolescent kid who left with his serene-faced mother almost twenty years before. He told the townspeople his name was William Morgan and that he owned gold mines in California. He flashed a lot of money around, and for the first time in his life he fell in with local society. A portrait taken in Onandaga shows an elegantly trimmed moustache and goatee, a serious cigar (not lit, in the photograph), and a kind of soft bowler hat with a very tall round crown. His look at the camera still has that careful, appraising look, but there is a bit of a twinkle this time. Let John Boessenakker and Mark Dugan pick up the tale here.

John Boessenakker:

He met the mayor of Onandaga, and, more importantly, he met the mayor's daughter, young Jenny Willis, who was a very attractive young woman about twenty years old, and he was extremely well dressed, handsome, debonair, and Jenny Willis fell madly in love with him.

Mark Dugan:

Well, Bill got there and he played like a hotshot, mining man from California, and he's got all these mines in South America and California and all over the place, and he's got all this money and whatever, and he starts squiring one of the local belles.

John Boessenakker:

They were engaged to be married. Bill Miner was the toast of the town. There was an engagement dinner in which Jenny's father toasted Bill . . . and this romance went on for a number of months.

But it is now that the power of that confusion between myth and reality kicks in again and sabotages Bill Miner's capacity to make a workable plan and carry it out. He has been spending unrestrainedly, and he is almost broke. It is time to pull another caper. Were he a man who can learn from experience he would have sought out a successful partner again, someone with "management skills." But no. He invented a story for Jenny. His mother was ill in California and he must take her on a cruise for his health.

John Boessenakker:

[His] elderly mother was back in California. She was living in poverty in Sacramento, and he needed to go back to California to do another robbery . . . to be able to continue this romance in Michigan.

So he hit another stagecoach in November of 1881, just outside Sonora, and got away with $3,700. That is the equivalent of about a quarter of a million dollars in today's money. There was no reason not to speed back to Michigan and get on with life. Bill Miner stayed in California. A few days before Christmas of that year they got him, in Sacramento. He was sentenced to twenty-five years.

John Boessenakker:

Jenny Willis was certainly heartbroken, but she eventually recovered and she had a long, happy, and productive life. She died in 1945 at the age of eighty-five, and she told her children of her romance with Bill Miner. She wasn't ashamed of it in the least. She was proud . . . of this romantic adventure she'd had as a young woman.

We do not know much detail of the next few prison years, which would bring his San Quentin total to just over thirty-three. The Spanish-American War had come and gone. The Boer War was winding down. Queen Victoria had celebrated her diamond Jubilee. McKinley had been shot to death in Buffalo, and Theodore Roosevelt was about to enter the White House. Just as he seems not to have noticed the Civil War forty years earlier, there is no reason to think that Bill Miner took any interest in these matters.

He was almost fifty-five when he got out of jail. There weren't any stagecoaches any more. In the new-fangled moviehouses of California they were showing *The Great Train Robbery* in 1903. Billy Miner probably saw it. Perhaps he took notes. He did have the good sense to get out of California, and head up towards Canada. He stopped off in Oregon on the way north, and had a go at this new drama, the train robbery, although he found it a whole lot harder in real life than it had looked in the movie. He had enlisted two accomplices this time, one of them only seventeen years old. They put up a set of red signals to stop the oncoming train, but they put them on the wrong side of the tracks, for trains coming in the opposite direction, so the engineer of the train they wanted to rob didn't even see them and the train didn't even slow down. Four days later they decided to simply board the Oregon Express as passengers when it stopped at a station. Then they put on their masks and clambered over the coal tender to the engine where, with guns drawn, they told the engineer to stop, which he did. They knew the money was kept in the express car, but they didn't know that it was guarded by an armed agent. The guard shot at them and hit one of the bandits in the head. Miner and the boy, Charles Hoehn, ran away empty-handed. Police picked up the injured man, who squealed, and soon they had Hoehn, but this time Billy managed to stay out of sight.

By now the famous Pinkerton Detective Agency was half a century old. Its first major assignments had been with the railroads, and they were building a file on Bill Miner. Our crew visited the Pinkerton archivist Jane Adler, who showed us stacks of photographs of the man who would soon earn the soubriquet, the Grey Fox. She told us about the founder, Alan Pinkerton, and those early railroad contracts.

Five railroads building northwest out of Chicago hired him for $10,000 a year — which was a very sizeable sum in those days — to protect their lines, because they were building out into construction camps, and there were Indians and there were robbers on the trains, and their own employees were cheating them and taking the money. So there was a lot of embezzlement going on. . . . The

Central Illinois Railroad was the principal line that Pinkerton first worked for. Later, his commissions or his engagements were with the major trunk lines in America, and occasionally, he did have to go out west to deal with somebody like Bill Miner.

Jane Adler showed us the reward poster Pinkerton put out on Billy Miner, which not only reviewed his career, showed his photograph, and listed all his prison sentences, it also added that Miner was "said to be a sodomist." They were very frustrated by his unusual invisibility this time, according to Mark Dugan:

They were so mad at him, they were hot. I mean, they were going to put everything they could get in there. Look, he robbed . . . he tried to rob that train in Oregon. They knew he did that. Then he went up to Canada. They knew he did that. And then in 1905 he hits the one in Washington . . . above Seattle. They knew he did that. And they're hot, you know, they can't catch him, they can't find him. . . . Here he has spent twenty years in prison, they let him out and boom, he starts this!

He began to look for another partner, and this time he came up with a very experienced thug he had met during those last twenty years in San Quentin. Jake Terry was as naturally violent as Miner was courteous. His prison picture resembles a lean, bald Robert Duvall in a sinister role. Terry was a gunfight man. Why Miner picked him is not entirely clear from the record: Terry on his own had been as inept at keeping clear of the police as Miner himself was, and that should have been a warning. But in fact they worked well together, better than they ever had on their own. Jake Terry would eventually die in a gunfight, but not before he helped Bill Miner turn himself into the Grey Fox, become a hero to British Columbians, and take the Canadian Pacific Railway Company for a staggering sum in bearer bonds.

They picked up a third small-time crook named Shorty Dunn, and set out for Mission, BC, in the fall of 1907. There was no fumbling with badly placed signals this time. The hard-faced Jake Terry may have been a killer but he had also been a railroad man and he knew something about the technology. He figured out that if you had a telegraph key (which he knew how to operate) you could climb a pole and wire your key into the line and send a message that would look official because it came in on the company line. The message he sent was simple: COMBINATION LOST. LEAVE SAFE OPEN ON TRAIN.

Unbelievably, it worked. When the CPR express stopped for water near Mission, the three men went aboard and in five minutes were off again with $1,000 in cash, about $6,000 worth of gold dust, and a package of Australian Bearer Bonds worth some 50,000 pounds sterling. Added up in today's money we are talking about half a million dollars or so in cash and gold, and more than a hundred million in those redeemable bonds. Miner and his pals apparently did not understand exactly what the bonds were; nonetheless Billy buried them in a safe and secret place.

The railroad was not insured; it was responsible to their owners for the value of the bonds and would have to make good. The gang divided the money and went their separate ways, and this time Billy Miner acted more or less rationally for a while, perhaps thinking that in time he would find someone through whom he could make something out of those buried bonds. He went to Princeton, in the BC interior, and by John Boessenakker's account seems to have had a reasonably normal kind of life for a while.

He was able to ingratiate himself with people. The evidence is pretty clear that he loved children. He certainly loved women. Women were one of the driving influences of his life. . . . There are numerous stories of Miner's kindness and the things that he did while he was hiding out from the authorities. He would generally go by an alias, William Morgan being the most common one [and the one he used here].

So "William Morgan" got a job with a rancher, and simply smiled when he heard local people chortling over the train robbery. The CPR was not exactly the most loved of Canadian corporations. The Montreal historian Bob Stewart said:

Miner was perceived as a hero by many, many people in the area because, simply because he robbed the CPR, because of his victim, really, being so unpopular. I recall reading a quote from an old resident of BC who said, you know, "Hell, Bill Miner ain't so bad. He only robs the CPR once every two years, and the CPR robs us every day."

Ironically, Miner and his gang were never charged with the first train robbery in the history of Canada, the one that involved the CPR in what turns out to have been a bizarre manipulation of the justice system. After a decent interval, and feeling pretty cocky about the big one, Miner and Shorty Dunn and a twenty-eight-year-old drifter named Louis Colquhoun (whose prison ID photograph has a Russell Crowe look to it) decided to rob yet another CPR train just east of Kamloops. Without Jake Terry in the gang, Miner lapsed back to his sloppy old techniques, and made about all the mistakes it was possible to make. The biggest being that while they had intended to hit an express car full of registered mail and gold, they got the wrong train. This one didn't even have an express car. Miner ran off with a paltry $15.50 and a bottle of pills.

At about this time his admirers began to refer to the elusive hold-up artist as the Grey Fox. When the North West Mounted Police joined forces with the BC provincial force and brought in a group of native trackers, they were soon posing for their photographs as the men who had captured the Grey Fox. This time Miner gave his name as George Edwards, but before long he was identified and went to trial in Kamloops. John Boessenakker said that even though the robbery for which he was charged was trivial, the law acted almost as if they were nailing Miner for the Big One.

They saw this man as a very dangerous threat to transportation, to commerce. Here's a single outlaw who managed to steal the equivalent of millions of dollars in bonds and securities. This is something that the Canadian Pacific Railroad is very angry about. They were a common carrier, and under Canadian and American law, they're responsible for making good a loss like that, and that has a lot to do with the stiff sentence.

Well, it was armed robbery after all, whatever the size of the haul. But it does add to the comic dimension of the Miner saga that, for stealing $15.50 and a bottle of catarrh pills, Louis Colquhoun got twenty-five years, while Shorty Dunn and Billy Miner were sentenced to life in the BC penitentiary. As the sentence was pronounced, and Miner was asked if he had anything to say, he smiled at the judge and replied, "No walls can hold *me*, sir." It was sheer showmanship. But in this case it proved to be true.

The boss con system that characterized Billy Miner's early years in San Quentin did not operate in British Columbia, and here the concept of the inmates' rights — while limited — somewhat eased the pain of confinement. The inmate had five declared rights: a cell of his own, adequate food, adequate clothing, adequate health care, and an hour's exercise each day. The definition of adequate was determined by the "joint," and the food was pretty bad, pea soup and burnt pea coffee and seldom enough of anything. The work was hard and the cells were cold in the winter. But Bill Miner's time there was made a little easier by a series of visits from a detective who worked for the CPR.

His name was Bullock. He had been charged with recovering those securities, and he was bound and determined to do that. The talks went on for more than a year. Bullock said that he was authorized to offer the Grey Fox a pardon in return for his showing them where the bonds were. Miner — more prudent than usual — demanded to see it in writing, which the detective could not of course provide. But in the meantime life in prison began to seem a little easier. Every other prisoner was shaved, face and head. The Grey Fox was allowed to keep his hair long and his long inverted V of a moustache just the way we know it from the movies. He asked to be assigned to the brick-yard, which was not only thought to be an easy assign-ment, but was also easy of access from the outside, or, more importantly from the inside to the outside. One day in August the newspapers reported that the Grey Fox and three other inmates had tunnelled a hole under the wall, from a corner of the brickyard where they could not be seen from the gun towers, and had walked away.

There were, however, a number of contradictions. Reporters invited to examine the getaway site were shown a hole, all right, but it looked far too small for a man to have wriggled through. They concluded that it was simply not possible for four men or even one to spend an after-noon digging the said hole, in full view of the rest of the yard, without their being seen. Tony Martin spent most of his working life on the custodial staff of that penitentiary. He has made a study of the institution's history, and has a theory about the Miner escape:

My guess is somebody was bribed, and not necessarily the warden. After this whole thing was over, the warden was allowed to retire and get his superannuation, and prior to that, the guy could be fired for inattention on duty. Even in my time, I saw . . . I used to collect fines. An officer was fined if he fell asleep or missed something he should have done. So a warden losing a guy like Miner [and then] being allowed to retire and get his pension, it had to be organized by somebody with great political power. And there's absolutely no doubt that the CPR had tremendous political power.

There is indeed no question that the CPR did have

substantial political power, and that influential politicians, at every level, owed their electoral success to the support of that company. Does this mean what it seems to mean? For historian Mark Dugan there is simply no doubt that the escape was engineered by the CPR. Jane Adler, at Pinkerton's, agrees.

It would not have been at all difficult. It's not difficult to imagine. Certainly it would have happened in America, easy as pie. In Canada, it's probably a bit of a shock to people, and certainly . . . and they didn't do a very good job of it. I mean, the men were supposed to have escaped. Somebody went and examined the hole where they were supposed to have burrowed out of the brickyard where they were working. Apparently, it wasn't big enough for, you know, a small boy to get out of, let alone three adult men. So the effort was made to cover up what was happening, which I'm sure everybody was well aware. And the people made a fuss about it in the House in Ottawa. . . . It had been arranged. That was it.

The fuss in Parliament died down after a few days. There were bigger things to worry about than an escaped train robber, particularly when — by coincidence it was said — the railway detectives stopped looking for the bonds once Miner was gone.

And gone he was. The Grey Fox had slipped over the border and back into the States. He lived quietly for a couple of years and it seemed that he'd finally retired. But in 1911 the sixty-four-year-old incorrigible was in the state of Georgia preparing to rob another train. There were, once more, two younger accomplices. On February 11th, 1911, at

Sulphur Springs, they had the distinction of committing that state's first train robbery. The take was $2,200, which was a very good year's salary for a professional man at the time. The public were enchanted with the image of this "Old Man," a former friend of Jesse James it was said again and again, hitting the trail again — in "the best traditions of the Wild West" said the press. When they put him away — for twenty-five years once more (remember he was nearly sixty-five), reporters came long distances to interview him. The warden let him sit on the porch and tell his story.

Although the nearest he ever came to doing anything remotely Robin Hood-like had been to return the stage-coach driver's watch four decades earlier, the public imagination turned him into a good guy. Milledgeville Pen was new, state-of-the-art, when they put the Grey Fox there. It was a tough joint. Cons were chained to their beds at night and chained to a ball by day when they went out to work. But the warden took it easy on Old Bill, and let him sit there and tell the reporters about his diamond mines in the Transvaal and his days with Jesse James, and they wrote it down, and the people of Georgia lapped it up. Mark Dugan says that by now he was lying most of the time.

I think he lied; he had lied so much, even at the end, I don't think he knew truth from a lie. He didn't know one thing from another. He couldn't have told the truth in the end, I don't think, if he'd wanted to, because he had lied so much through his lifetime.

That does seem a bit harsh. And yet when, on October 17th, 1911, the chairman of the prison board, one Robert E. Davidson, visited the prison and asked Bill Miner to keep his promise not to escape, the Grey Fox is reported to have replied, "Old Bill keeps his word. I am going to stay right here as promised."

He escaped at 2 a.m. the next morning. Tony Wilson tells it like this:

A guard had fallen asleep, and there was a large peephole where the guards could watch the prisoners. Apparently, one of the prisoners got out of his bunk and looked through the peephole, the other direction, could see the guard was asleep. The fellow in question was small. He squeezed through the peephole, took the keys off the sleeping guard and got back in, and he and two other fellows — Bill Miner . . . I can't remember the second guy . . . Tom Moore was the third fellow — opened the door, up over the walls, and they escaped, much to everybody's embarrassment, as you might imagine. I think part of the appeal, in that sense, of Bill Miner, was that sort of appeal of the rebel against the establishment, because the South was suffering in those years. The cotton economy was on the decline [and] the sense that large corporations were [the cause of it], particularly the railroad companies, the freight rates they charged for shipping cotton were so outrageous that you could barely make a profit. Well, here's somebody that's robbing the trains, that's standing up to the Georgia Railway. . . . He played on this, you know. "I never robbed poor people or innocent people," which wasn't true, but he said that. "I just robbed trains."

They got him a couple of weeks later, and put him back in Milledgeville. Somehow — he was after all about to turn sixty-six — the custodial staff let their guard down, and this time two of them sawed through the bars in the window — in Approved Wild West style — made ropes out of their blankets, lowered themselves to the ground and got over the wall and away. They waded downriver — to throw the dogs off the scent — and then got lost in the swamps for four days, and were so wrecked with dysentery from drinking swamp water that they gave themselves up. When the car brought them back to the prison there was a crowd outside; the cops feared that a lynching was about to take place; but in fact the Georgians were there to cheer the Grey Fox. They gave him cigars and let him know he was an OK Guy.

But Billy never recovered from his time in the swamps. He was taken to the prison hospital suffering from acute gastroenteritis, and on September 2nd, 1913, in his sixty-seventh year, the last of the old-style Western bandits died. The citizens of Milledgeville had a collection to pay for his funeral, and he was laid out in what was then the local funeral parlour for four days while people paid their last respects. "And he gets headlines," Mark Dugan told us: "'HE WILL GO HURTLING THROUGH GEORGIA HISTORY!' . . . His picture when he died was . . . the President's picture was in the same edition, and his was bigger than the President's."

They buried him there, with mistaken dates on the stone. Writer-director Robert Duncan wrote, at the end of his biographical documentary of the old escape artist, a kind of filmmaker's epitaph:

BILLY MINER, THE GREY FOX,
THE LAST OF THE OLD WESTERN BANDITS,
REMAINS IN MILLEDGEVILLE, GEORGIA
—AS FAR AS WE KNOW

◆　◆　◆

The original documentary was written and directed by Robert Duncan. It was photographed by Al Lopez, Ngaio Killingsworth, John Collins, Doug Sjoquist, Dieter Melhorn, and Tony Zappata, with sound by Hing Lo, Ademah Hackshaw, Buddy Schwandt, Chris Horton, and Bill Bass, and edited by Tim Reed.

Part Seven

KATHERINE RYAN
THE SAGA OF KLONDIKE KATE

From the archival records of the Klondike gold rush of '98 it is easy to get the impression that there were more photographers per square mile in the Yukon Territory than in any other part of the world. Photographs come tumbling out of the files (and nowadays the hard drives and the CDs) by the thousands. The shots of departure points, where romantic hopefuls tried to board the steamers out of Seattle or Vancouver for Wrangell and Skagway, and the trains out of Skagway for Whitehorse, are reminiscent of railway history pictures from India at the turn of the century. People hang from ledges and railings, scrambling to board a boat or train that is already bursting with humanity, crowded onto docks and station platforms as if they were escaping from the latest maraudings of Godzilla.

You also have the impression that *style* was a prime consideration for entry into the ranks of the hopeful. They almost *had to* be wearing a tall hat with a round crown, a walrus moustache, yellow-tanned calf-high boots with pointed toes or else foot soldier–style laced boots with double thick soles. The famous panoramic photographs of the Chilkoot Pass with spider-sized men bent over under their murderously heavy packs ("like hairpins" Pierre Berton famously said) has become an icon of the period. Less familiar are these grainy, water-stained images packed with hundreds more people than could ever board the packets or the stern-wheelers or the trains that already look as though they will sink or collapse from their human burden. But after only a few minutes with those archival files, the researcher realizes that the Chilkoot Pass picture, while it eloquently speaks the challenge and the difficulties, is nowhere near as powerful as these mob scenes. They are the depiction of a tragic madness that seized what looks like a whole generation of adventurers, few of whom would find any gold, many of whom would starve or freeze to death, and most of whom were miserable most of the time that they spent in the territory.

Whole sequences of these photographs compose a fascinating majority of the historic images in this documentary, the motion picture having been invented only three years earlier, and not having much penetrated into the frozen Canadian north. One of the reasons for the misery is that there are virtually no female faces in these acres of packed humanity. No mothers, no girlfriends, no wives, sisters, nurses, cooks. The men range in age from adolescence upwards. Some of the early arrivals will head into the wilderness woefully underequipped and undersupplied, and when the North West Mounted Police get on the case after the initial confusion and disasters, one of the first things they will establish is a Proving-Up procedure whereby you don't even get into the territory unless you can demonstrate that you have brought enough grub to keep yourself alive for months and enough warm clothing to get you through the winter without freezing to death. The few women who did make the trek to the Yukon would have to Prove Up — if they trekked in — just as the men did. Among the requirements for one leg of the journey were 400 pounds of flour, 150 pounds of bacon and the same of split peas, tinned milk, beans, a sleeping bag, a rifle, and a Bible.

This is the story of an adventuress from New Brunswick who did all that, proved up, trekked, mushed her Huskies, and drove her pack horses, went into business, acted as vicarious mom, real nurse and real cook, girlfriend perhaps, never a wife, came away with a modest fortune and a great reputation, lost her fortune in the crash of twenty-nine, died poor, but left a name and a mark on the Yukon that have not been forgotten.

Along the way she would build, run, and sell at a profit some half a dozen restaurants. A trained nurse, she would be the first and only woman engaged by the Royal North West Mounted Police as a special constable and a "gold inspector." She would become a pal of Robert W. Service, and used to say that she gave him some of the stories that turn up later in the famous *Songs of Sourdough* and *Ballads of the Yukon*. She was also a close friend of a dynamic entrepreneurial north country butcher named Dominic Burns who was one of the few who would stick with her right to the end. She was, in her late teens, plump, comely as a girl, and then towering, solid and daunting as a mature woman. She was smart, determined, tough. Her name was Katherine Ryan, and they called her Klondike Kate.

She was not the only woman on the gold rush, of course. There were the dance hall girls, famously so up in Dawson, which at the height of the madness was said to be the biggest North American city north of San Francisco and west of Winnipeg. The Dawson dance hall girls worked long nights, sometimes as many as 150 dances a night. Part of the deal with the proprietors was that, on commission at so much a shot, you drank watered whisky with the men in order to encourage them to buy as much as possible. There was an active white slave traffic, the young prostitutes largely recruited — or kidnapped — in Seattle, Washington. It was a trip to that city to heal a broken heart and work as a housekeeper that would launch Kate Ryan on the road to Whitehorse.

A few years ago the historian T. Ann Brennan, who lives in the Johnville region of New Brunswick where Kate Ryan was born, realized that the round pile of field stones wrested from the stony soil by a pioneer ploughman and still there near her own family homestead, had to be the Ryan place. It is just down the road from the Brennan place near the top of Campbell hill, surrounded by a coppice of lilacs and weeds, a familiar sight on old farm properties throughout the eastern woodlands. Anne Brennan was able to find the well and the site of the original orchard on the farm settled by Pat Ryan and his wife Anne Holden early in the 1860s, before Canada was a country, and when you could get a hundred acres for next to nothing if you undertook to clear it and farm it.

Katherine was born there two years after Confederation, one of five children, two girls and three boys. The boys were favoured. Katherine's sister Nora eloped with an actor, to Bangor, Maine, when Katherine was fourteen. The parents were disgusted and disowned the impudent thing. Katherine missed her sister, but seems to have accepted her duties as labour hand on the family farm, and got on with life. She was already over six feet tall and embarrassed at her size. She may have felt more at ease out in the field or the barns than she would have in town, and for the next several years, long after most girls in her circumstances would have married, she stayed on at home lending a hand with the farm and helping her brothers with their children.

Ann Brennan discovered that there were people still living in the region, seventy years after Katherine Ryan's death, for whom the saga of Klondike Kate was still so much part of the gossip and texture of their young lives that they talked as if they could remember the woman herself. Ann Brennan decided there was a biography to be written here, and set to work on it. One of her early contacts was a neighbour, Frances Cullen, herself well into her fourth quarter-century, who talked, as if it was just a few years ago that Katherine — disappointed in love — left home

broken-hearted. And I would suspect in her young days, her dream would have been to marry that man, settle here like people were doing, the pioneers at that time, but I think she was destined for something else. And I think there are people that no matter what their plans are, I think that their plans are, you know, I think a greater power changed their plans.

The man in question was Simon Gallagher, whose family owned the big general store and whose mother wore expensive furs and looked down on farm people. Simon and Katherine stepped out together for several years, and it is said that he was the only real love of her life. It may be that Simon's mother was the cause of it, but whatever the real nature of the break-up, Simon did briefly enter a seminary. Brennan speculates that it was a device — invented by the mother, by which she could engineer his split with Katherine. He then later came back to the family business and married someone else. By then Katherine was long gone from the Johnville homestead.

Mary Healey, a friend (and a cousin of Simon Gallagher), had married and gone to live in Seattle. She invited Katherine to visit. Katherine turned the visit into a job when she found Mary Healey overwhelmed by a fragile constitution and too many children, and took over as housekeeper and nanny.

It seems that she supplemented her income here by making the first move towards what would become a calling: the restaurant business. She helped run the dining room in the Crifton Hotel in Seattle, at least for a few months. She also enrolled in a nursing school run by nuns at nearby Nahomish. In two years she had earned her nurse's certificate.

One of the difficulties in producing a biography of a person who leaves as few written records as Kate did is that the recollections of those who knew her (or knew someone who knew her and had told stories about her) often contradict the recollections of the next witness. In Katherine Ryan's case there is a curiously validating second stream of evidence: the photograph. There are photographs from Johnville when she was just a girl and photographs taken there at the Ryan farm when she came home for a visit, famous and prosperous a quarter of a century later, photographs in Vancouver, in Alaska, on shipboard, in front of her makeshift wilderness restaurants, in the little tent she lived in on the trail, in Whitehorse, in Stewart, BC.

So as our television team assembles the story from oral accounts on the one hand (with their evident fragility) and the solid reassurance of the photographs on the other, they are often in the position of having to conjecture, in building the links between fragmentary bits of evidence. "Well, it must have been *something* like this." A great deal of history is written that way, of course, and the amount of judgment and speculation that goes into any account of the past will vary both with the inclinations and experience of the historian, and the amount of incontrovertible documentation there is to work with.

Katherine's grandniece Kit McKernan is one of those witnesses who was not really *there*, but so vivid is the Kate Ryan legend that she seems to feel almost as though she had witnessed it.

The difficulty in getting there was the fact that it was very very hard to get passage on the boats, they were all booked very very quickly. And there were no women that really wanted to go. It was all the men going. So she had to find men and the only ones she knew and happened to find out were going were Danny Gillis and Peter Stokes. She always called Danny, Sandy. Sandy Gillis was his name. And they had an in. They were importers/exporters. They were going to Wrangell, and, ah . . .

Here Kit McKernan's voice drops to a conspiratorial whisper, as she confides that "they were taking liquor into Alaska, *which was dry*!"

Wrangell is a port on the Alaska Panhandle, named for Ferdinand Petrovich Wrangel, who was the first governor of Russian America. It was founded in 1835 by Russian fur traders, as a fortification against the Hudson's Bay Company. That didn't work; The Bay just moved in and occupied the place in 1840. It seems odd today to think that Russia had a substantial piece of North America a century and a half ago, with settlements as far south as Northern California. The United States bought Alaska from the Russians (for $7.2 million) in the same year that Canada became a country, 1867. The Russians had introduced agriculture and logging into the territory, and left behind some churches and place-names, including this ragged little town.

There is a clipping from a Seattle newspaper in August 1897, announcing the impending arrival of the steamer Portland bringing men back from those first gold-hungry forays into the Klondike, before it had become a rush. The paper says the ship's arrival is anticipated with increasing interest each day because there are rumours of "GOLD PILED ON THE DECKS LIKE CORDWOOD." That was a headline writer's invention, we can suppose. In one version of the Klondike Kate story it was those men gobbling up the steaming dinners at Katherine's Crifton House tables whose exciting stories about nuggets like slabs of cheese and fortunes being made overnight that got Katherine thinking about opportunities in the Yukon. However, Ann Brennan's book finds that when the spectacular reports of the Yukon gold strikes began to make their way south, Katherine was already in Vancouver, visiting more New Brunswick friends, and once again running a small restaurant.

In any case, it was reports of this kind that drew her towards the north, and on February 28th, 1898, with her two bootlegger friends, Katherine was one of the very few women to board a Canadian steamer, the *Tees*, out of Vancouver for Wrangell. The preparation that she undertook, with no experience of this kind of thing, is staggering. She went to the Hudson Bay Company's special top-floor wilderness supply section, found a sympathetic salesman, and spent almost everything she had on the best clothes and equipment. In addition to the necessary gear and supplies she had acquired a dogsled and a team of five good huskies, in Vancouver, and loaded them onto the *Tees*. The dogs travelled on a lower deck with an odorous company of cattle and mules, in the care of a group of not very happy deckhands who had to spend a good part of the day shovelling cowpats, horse manure, and dog droppings overboard, and hosing down the filthy decks.

The records show that she had also acquired a Canadian "free miner's pass." That would allow her to travel into the Klondike, and to prospect and stake claims. We have to assume that the actual mining or panning for gold was something she at least considered as an option, although there is no evidence that she ever actually did either of these things. She certainly could have. Being out on the creeks with all those men was not likely to distress a farm girl from New Brunswick, used to working alongside boys and men, with little of the privacy and gender distinction that a town girl of the period would have expected. So to be at sea or on the trail or in a mining camp where she was the only woman or one of few seems never to have struck her as daunting.

She was twenty-nine years old now, but photographs of that year show a woman who seems much older, seeming close to early middle age. She is big, wide-jawed, solid, with a huge bosom and a daunting expression. If she was worried about being the only woman in that crowd, she left no record of it. Throughout the many and often dramatic tales that make up the legend, there is no suggestion that she was ever sexually harassed. It is likely that the prospector hopefuls assumed at first that her turning up there at all meant that she was a prostitute, but even more likely that it did not take long to disillusion them. As a serious Catholic with what appears to have been a Protestant touch of the puritan, it may be that she simply never recounted any of the encounters she had. But looking at the photographs of this square-jawed, broad-shouldered, over-six-foot, two-hundred-pound woman suggests that her sheer *presence* may have kept predators at bay. It is history's loss that she did not keep a journal, nor, in her letters, say very much about the day-to-day challenges she met as she made her way into the wilderness.

She begins to be called Kate at about this time. It was four days from Vancouver to Wrangell. There Kate learned that up the frozen Stikine River there was a staging point called Glenora, nominally a village but in reality not much more than a collection of tents and huts. It was said that the Canadian government intended to build a rail line from Glenora to the goldfields, trains to take the prospectors and miners in, and bring the gold out. The British

Columbia government was also promising a wagon road. If governments were taking the gold rush that seriously, it must be a reality.

Whether or not she was ever serious about getting her hands on a miner's pick and shovel, Katherine Ryan was one of those fortunate people who assume that anything they set out to do they will succeed in. Whatever she had in mind when she applied for the free miner's pass, everything points to her having two primary objectives: to be a part of a great adventure, and, more importantly, to make money out of it by running a restaurant. She was now experienced and adept at the trade, and she enjoyed the social buzz and the whirr of gossip that swirled around her tables.

She knew that with all that money flowing into the Yukon in the form of the miners' stakes, and about to flow out in the form of gold dust and bullion, there would be no time for people to settle down and make homes for themselves with kitchens in them. There would be hungry men with money to spend. She could deal with that. Kate knew a business opportunity when she saw one: Glenora was going to need restaurants, a trade she knew a lot better than mining. But it was not going to be easy to get there. There were no roads, Wrangell was on an island and there was at least one more boat trip to the mainland. The rivers were frozen.

Kate made friends with a contingent of Royal North West Mounted Policemen who were staging through Wrangell to Glenora. When she visited their encampment, the first young constable she met complained to her that their cook had not turned up and he, who knew nothing about a kitchen, had been saddled with the job. Kate made the obvious bargain, provided the young cops with the first decent food they had had for a while, and when they set off for Glenora, along the Stikine River she went with them as company cook. If there was some risk of exploitation (from steamboat operators and packers) that she would have encountered as a woman on her own, her temporary job with the police force would serve her well.

The NWMP contingent was under the command of Inspector Phillip Primrose, who would be a good friend to Kate for the rest of her years in the north. Primrose's surveyor, Jim Callbreath, told his commander that he believed that the rumoured Ottawa government-sponsored railroad was a fantasy, impossible to build in that territory, and that they should be pressing the BC government to make good on its more practicable wagon road.

Kate appears to have left the slower-moving police contingent at some point on this journey up the frozen river, and headed off on her own with the dogs. On the first or second night on her own, she was just setting up camp when another traveller turned up, a Presbyterian clergyman named Pringle, on his way to set up a mission. Pringle travelled with her the rest of the way to Glenora and they would be friends for the rest of her life.

In Glenora Kate found that the surveyor Callbreath had transformed his surveyor's warehouse, a sixteen-by-twenty-four-foot frame shack, into a rough little two-storey hotel. Kate tacked a tent onto the side of the building and opened a canvas-covered restaurant. Soon she would not be the only woman in Glenora. Helen Dobrowolsky, a historian specializing in the story of the North West Mounted Police, set the scene for us.

There were thousands and thousands of people pouring into the territory. There was a very small force of mount-ed police that were expected to collect customs, to ensure that all these greenhorns who knew nothing about living on the country had enough supplies that they wouldn't starve to death. They were trying to patrol the entire waterway, between the mountain passes and Dawson, and just generally keep law and order. So to deal with this, the government of the day decided to put together a special force of 200 soldiers of what became known as the Yukon Field Force.

When the Yukon Field Force arrived in their totally inappropriate tall white pith helmets and a great deal of brass to polish, they were escorting a group of very digni-fied ladies. The government at Ottawa had recognized that in addition to maintaining law and order — and dealing with what would become a serious disagreement between the United States and Canada — there would be humani-tarian needs to be met. Ottawa had financed a contingent of women from the Victorian Order of Nurses, under the sponsorship of Lady Aberdeen, the wife of the governor general and founder of the order. A Toronto newspaper-woman named Faith Fenton was also travelling with the nurses, and her accounts of Glenora for the Toronto *Globe* give us some of the little narrative documentation we have of that hastily built town.

Their presence was at least in part an international political move on the part of Prime Minister Wilfrid

Laurier. With the US–Canada borderline in dispute, a military unit in the Yukon, Laurier hoped, would help him demonstrate Canadian sovereignty in the territory. If there was going to be a boom in gold there would be revenues for the national coffers, and Ottawa was going to establish a presence.

More stories were coming in about new discoveries of gold, and Jim Callbreath decided that he had better ride north towards Teslin to check out the route and see what the conditions would be like for men who wanted to head up towards the goldfields before any road or rail line was a reality. He was away two weeks. The river had thawed and there was steamer service now, all the way from Wrangell. In the two weeks Callbreath was away on his survey, the miners pouring into Glenora in response to the flood of gold rumours had swelled the little settlement from a village of about a hundred people when Callbreath left, to a town of more than three thousand. By the time he got back people were setting up three more hotels, a smithy, several outfitters, a barbershop, a newspaper, and even a brewery.

In the end the BC government's promised wagon road north out of Glenora never materialized. In Ottawa Sir Clifford Sifton, Laurier's minister of the interior, was spectacularly successful in getting Parliament to agree to finance a rail line, but in the Senate the Tories — who had a majority in the upper house — shot it down. A lot of hopes were dashed with it. The terrain between that staging village, Glenora, and the actual goldfields was desperately difficult. Some gave up and went home. One young man shot himself when the news came about the government's abandoning the rail line. The toughest and most determined swallowed their frustration, bought packhorses, learned how to tie the diamond hitch (without which you could not, it was said, really claim to be able to run a pack train) and headed north across the muskeg and the hills. The people — and the money — were moving out of Glenora, towards Teslin. If the money was migrating that way, the need for restaurants was too. Kate decided to sell the dogs, buy some horses, and pack herself north, alone.

Tom Radford, our documentary's director sought out a modern-day pack train outfitter, Rob Touhey, to demonstrate on camera the famous diamond hitch and to comment on just what Kate would have been up against, as she followed each stream, the Thaltan, the Nahlin, the Twoya, and the Teslin Rivers, up to their headwaters, over the passes, down into another mosquito-infested valley and up another river. Touhey said that for an experienced team of packhorse men in prime condition it would have been a daunting trip; for a lone, inexperienced woman of thirty it was quite simply an astounding achievement.

First of all five horses is a handful in any kind of situation. I mean you can certainly take more, if you're experienced, but five horses is a handful for anybody. Now if you're on a trail with a lot of bogs and windfall and you know wasps and all those lovely things that wreck horses, and you're by yourself and you've never been over the trail, that's a hell of an accomplishment!

By the time Kate arrived in Teslin, still a long way from the goldfields, it was late fall. Freeze-up came early in 1898. She set aside her plan to reach the goldfields by

Christmas. She heard that a settlement at Aitlin, back south in British Columbia, needed a nurse. The cook/restaurant-manager/packhorse woman was a trained nurse. She traded her horses for another dog team and joined a party of prospectors from Quebec. The Klondike historian Mack Swackhammer describes the conditions of a trip like that in winter.

> *Just imagine yourself walking, you're a woman that has maybe thirty-five pounds of clothes on — it's all wool and leather — and you're carrying perhaps forty-five to sixty-five pounds of gear and you're going to do that thirty times in six weeks, and its bloody cold and you can't have trousers on.*

Ladies don't wear trousers, and Katherine Ryan would not relinquish her status as a lady. The whole of that winter, the lady worked as a nurse, travelling out to tiny settlements by dogsled. In the spring she went over to Bennett City, on Bennett Lake at the headwaters of the Yukon River, with still about three hundred miles to go to Dawson, the centre of the goldfield action. In Bennett she began to hear vivid and discouraging tales of the squalor and viciousness of life in Dawson. At the same time they were talking about what a great place Whitehorse was turning out to be. She was tired of living in a tent. As she thought it over, the lure of the goldfields began to fade. With a new restaurant in a stable, civil town, she would have steady business and lots of company; she could keep warm. When a boating company started rafting people across Bennett Lake, she went with a party who were willing to let her off at Whitehorse.

If this were a movie, it is here that the subplot would be introduced by a couple of puzzling scenes, their central figure a much younger woman. It is not clear whether or not Kate ever met a dance hall girl in Bennett, an eighteen-year-old opportunist from Seattle named Kitty Rockwell. But Kitty Rockwell heard a great deal about Kate over the years, and will come back into the story a little later on. Kate got off the barge at Whitehorse, and Whitehorse, as Helen Dobrowolsky told us, was booming.

The railway from Skagway [on the Pacific coast, in the Alaska panhandle] had been recently completed. Just over here by the train station, this was the head of navigation for the Yukon River, so tons of goods and hundreds and thousands of people were coming over that train, offloading on to all these ships. All along here was all shipyards and docks, and stern wheelers tied up as well as all kinds of various more eccentric craft. It was a bustling little community.

A butcher named Dominic Burns helped her get a restaurant started and gave it its famous name, *KLONDIKE KATE'S*. Kate Ryan had decided she was finished with dog teams and pack trains; it was time to settle down. "I built my first home, a twelve-by-sixteen-foot log cabin, and finally put my first log on the fire," she wrote to her sister in Bangor.

(In the meantime, our subplot heroine, Kitty Rockwell, had gone the other direction, north to Dawson, and was building herself a hell of a reputation with something called the flame dance. "I'm here to make as much money as I can," she said.)

Down in Whitehorse, Katherine Ryan, restaurateur, added yet another set of skills to her already considerable repertory: police work. She had been helping the Whitehorse NWMP detachment in an informal way, coming around to some of the rowdier drinking spots on a Saturday night with a cartload of pies, which distracted the guys from their obsessive pursuit of oblivion. Soon she would have them all gathered around her table wolfing down pie dished out by a now rather stout, motherly-looking big person, the kind of person many of them missed or thought they missed and certainly sentimentalized about a lot when they were in their cups.

So she was well liked by the constabulary, and when they suddenly were directed to enlist a Special Woman Constable it is not surprising that they turned to Kate. The Woman's Christian Temperance Movement, as well as campaigning for the prohibition of alcohol, was also working on women's rights, including the vote and the rights of women in prison. Those dance hall girls and the prostitutes were getting jailed pretty frequently, and while their employers usually paid their fines and got them out again in short order, to get back to work, they were entirely in the custody of men while in jail, and the WCTU convinced Ottawa that this would not do. Kate was sworn in. Now she put in a few hours a week as a warder, and that inevitably meant counsellor and advocate. Later, when the NWMP had to start searching people for contraband gold, she was sworn in to a second police function, the first (and only) female gold inspector in the history of the force.

As the gold was shipped out of the Yukon there was

sometimes as much as $400,000 a day moving through Whitehorse. This was a Canadian resource. Canadian taxpayers had footed the bill for policing and other services. The feds were determined to have a share of the proceeds, in the form of an export tax on gold leaving the country. Not surprisingly the smuggler's art was being practised with considerable ingenuity. NWMP historian Helen Dobrowolsky explained what that meant to Kate.

There were two routes out of the territory. Downriver by ship from Dawson, or you could come up the river, take the train from Whitehorse to Skagway and go out in relative comfort. And of course you couldn't expect a male police constable to be frisking these dignified female passengers. You needed a woman of tact and force of character to handle this. And this became Kate's job. There's one story of a woman who she asked if she had any gold. And the woman wouldn't say anything and the woman was wearing a particularly elaborate upswept hairdo. And amazingly enough she had this little cache of gold nuggets right in the middle of it.

That particular smuggler was the wife of a general in the United States Army.

Still a practising Catholic, Kate Ryan had something less than a deferential attitude towards the clergy. Her grandniece Kit McKernan likes to tell of a priest, new to the territory, who got into Kate's bad books.

They had great missions up there, that the young priests used to come in for, the mission. And all of the Native people would come, all dressed up in their great costumes with buckskin and their moccasins on. And this young priest got up and said that the Natives' ways were so pagan, and that if you come into the house of God you don't come dressed in skins and moccasins. . . . Kate Ryan got up and walked out on him. Took the train over to Skagway, took the boat down to Rupert and talked to the Bishop because it was such an insult to the Native people.

Katherine Ryan had never completely lost interest in mining. It was, after all, the motive power of her restaurant business and the economic engine of her territorial world. She invested a substantial part of her profits from the restaurant business in the claims of a number of prospectors and start-up mining companies. In a few years, as the gold rush began to wind down and Whitehorse to settle down, she had some money put away.

By 1904 she was a pillar of the community, a member of the Catholic Women's League, the Hospital Committee, the North Star Athletic Club, the Yukon Liberal Association and the Yukon Women's Protective League. She became friends with a literary-minded young Scottish bank clerk who had come to work for the Whitehorse branch of the Bank of Commerce. Kate would later laugh and tell people that when she first peeked through the bank window to get a glimpse of the new clerk people were talking about, she thought, Well, *he* doesn't look as though he knew enough about the North to write anything about it! And it is said that she would later complain that the tales she told Robert W. Service about life among the sourdoughs got very badly distorted when he retold them in verse. This, like a lot of the Klondike Kate folklore, is pretty doubtful since he did not begin to publish until 1907, long after Service and Kate are supposed to have met. And if Kate did so complain, she was almost certainly only one of many who would, as Service's reputation blew into flame, declare that they were the ones who had told him the story of The Lady That's Known as Lou, or The Cremation of Sam McGee.

Now here comes the subplot again. There is an archive newspaper photo of Service and Klondike Kate together. It has been considerably retouched, apparently with the picture of a different woman pasted in where Kate was in the original, posing in front of *KLONDIKE KATE'S* restaurant. The woman pasted in is Kitty Rockwell.

Now a touch of the subplot again, still not clearly attached to the main story. As the high life in Dawson City wound down, Kitty Rockwell had gone back to Seattle to seek out Alexander Pantages, whom she had known in the North. The story of Kitty and Pantages is clouded by the myths that both of them created about themselves, but it is likely that they were lovers in the Yukon, where Pantages worked as a bartender, learning how to pick up tiny bits of gold dust that collected on the bar, and slowly accumulating the capital that would buy him his first theatre, the Orpheum, in Nome, Alaska. It seems probable that Kitty Rockwell, who was already prosperous when the young Pantages arrived in the north after losing his shirt to gamblers on the boat from San Francisco to Skagway, had lent him money and never got it back.

Pantages had worked as a waiter for a while in Skagway, then persuaded a party of innocents that he was an experienced guide, and somehow managed to get them all the way to Dawson, where he met Kitty and then abandoned her. When he became the successful proprietor of a movie house in Seattle, and married a Seattle girl, Kitty sued him for breach of promise. She had a publicity sense, and perhaps thinking it might help her suit, she passed herself off as "the Real Klondike Kate." Now the Kitty Rockwell story comes into contact with the Kate Ryan story. The lawsuit with its deliciously scandalous echoes of Dawson dance halls, gold, and immoral behaviour, became a national news story. *KLONDIKE KATE SUES PAN-TAGES*. So the real "Real Klondike Kate" had some explaining to do to family and friends. The embarrassment of it bothered her for the rest of her life.

The last years of Kate Ryan's life take her far from those adventurous beginnings in the late 1890s. During a home visit to New Brunswick in 1903, her brother John asked him to take one of his sons back to Whitehorse; his wife was frail, and pregnant again. Later she would die in childbirth with their fifth son. While it is not clear whether their father just dumped the four boys on his sister Katherine, or perhaps brought them out to her in Whitehorse, we soon find her back in Whitehorse raising the boys as her foster children. The photographs of them as slight, winsome boys give way to a quartet of heavy-set, serious-looking men, and then that quartet is reduced to a trio in the later photos, by the death of Kate's favourite, Leo, who wanted to lie about his age and join the army during the last days of the Great War. Kate would have nothing of it, and sent him back to New Brunswick, the trip starting by train down to Skagway and then by steamer, the *Princess Sophia*, down to Vancouver and the train back east. The

Princess Sophia never made it to Vancouver; she ran aground on the Vanderbilt reef during a storm, and broke up. More than three hundred passengers and crew died, among them Leo Ryan.

Kate associated Leo's death with Whitehorse; that was where she had become deeply fond of him, where she had found real family at last, with her four handsome nephews. Now that she had lost Leo, she wanted no more of Whitehorse. She could afford to pick up and go; she had put away enough of her profits from KLONDIKE KATE'S that she did not have to run restaurants any more, or nurse the sick. She tried Stewart, BC, for a while, and even dabbled briefly in politics. They wanted her to run for office now that women had the vote, but she was afraid that the Kitty Rockwell/Pantages scandal would be raised all over again by her opponents, and declined. Kate, in her fifties now, poses in formal, bustled gowns and heavy hats, broad-beamed and broad-chinned and broad-smiled, grandmotherly, settled. The girl who packed five horses up the frozen Stikine is nowhere to be seen, except perhaps in the dreaming eyes. She tells people who ask, that she just wants to be left alone, once the boys are grown and gone. A reporter from *Maclean's* magazine says, "Why did you never marry?" "No man ever proposed to me," is her published answer, "And I don't really understand why!"

But it doesn't seem to matter any more. She goes back to Johnville for another visit, in 1923, and there is a photograph of her with her now very elderly parents in front of what has become a huge, sprawling frame farmhouse of several buildings growing out of each other. She makes friends with a Great War hero, Colonel George Pearkes, VC. This gives this writer "three degrees of separation" from Kate Ryan, as George Pearkes was my father's commanding officer in the 116th Battalion in that war.

Kate leaves Stewart and moves in to Vancouver. She is comfortably off and buys a house on Robson Street. Vancouver is growing at an exponential rate. She hears a lot of talk about what a wonderful thing the stock market is. Friends are making fortunes. This looks pretty interesting to a woman who, after a life of risk and adventure, is quietly clipping coupons and living on her investments. She puts virtually everything she has into the market. It is the autumn of 1929.

It is all gone now, the stories, the dreams, the gold, the restaurants, even the legend. The title *Klondyke Kate* has appeared on movie screens and the covers of hit songs that you buy at the sheet music stores, and serialized tales in the short story magazines, but they are all falsified — thefts from her own once very authentic adventures. They have brought some momentary glory and wealth to Kitty Rockwell, formerly of Seattle. But Katherine Ryan doesn't care about any of that now. Weakened by cancer and by the despair that hit her when the market crashed and all that KLONDIKE KATE'S had earned for her is gone, Katherine Ryan is close to the end. It is 1932. She is sixty-three.

Dominic Burns, the butcher from Whitehorse who had told her to call the place KLONDIKE KATE'S in the first place, shows up, right at the end, and so does the youngest of her four foster-sons, Charlie. She was in Saint Paul's hospital, Kit McKernan told us.

But no one I think expected her to die. She died on a men's ward. It was the only private room that was available at St. Paul's at that time. And she said, "I lived my whole life with men so I just as well die among the men, too." It didn't bother her one bit.

It was a grand funeral procession, they say. She had made many friends in Vancouver, and despite her reclusive last years she was, after all, a celebrity. The cortege wound its way out to Ocean View Burial Park, where her body was interred.

There is no marker.

◆　◆　◆

The original documentary was written and directed by Tom Radford, in collaboration with Dave Cunningham, who also edited the program. Camera was by Jim Jeffery and sound by Jim Jeffery and Randy McKenzie.

• Part Eight •

SIMON GUNANOOT
CHASING SHADOWS

This is the story of a man whose life was suddenly put in jeopardy by a double murder, and then saved by the power of the land he lived on — the land that he was *of* — and by the ancient culture in which his view of life was nurtured.

The Cassiar country north of Hazelton in northwest British Columbia was some of the last wilderness to be explored in North America. It is a vast, sprawling land of picture-book mountains reflected in mirror lakes, rich vegetation in summer and cutting snows that slant down the precipitous slopes in winter. A bald eagle perches motionless in a tree far below you, and below the eagle, down in the marshy flatland, a many-pointed elk picks his aristocratic way through the deep grasses, across a wide, shallow river, and up the far shore.

British Columbia patriots may tell you that this country is so huge that you could plop the whole of England down in the middle of it and come back next week and not be able to find it. Clouds come down to the ground and hang on the shoulders of the mountains and foothills so that a photograph can look like an ancient Chinese painting, with only a line or two emerging from the soft white envelope to suggest the outlines of a landscape. Early European adventurers getting lost in that territory would often stay lost. As distinctive as some of those mountain silhouettes can be to the knowing eye, after a few days trekking up the vertical canyons floored by shouting rapids, and passing through one meadow after another only to find yourself back in canyons again and confronting another breathtaking panorama, can lead to a deep disorientation in the brains of all but the most sanguine or experienced.

The Gitskan[7] of the Cassiar region say that their people came into being at Temlehan, in the shadow of Mount Roche Deboule. Their proud, brooding totem poles and gate poles were, according to one modern European cultural anthropologist,[8] part of the greatest art the world has ever seen, more powerful than Ancient Egypt or Ancient Greece or the European Renaissance. Ironically, the apex of that art was achieved after the arrival of the Europeans, who brought the steel-cutting tools that made it possible to easily and elegantly work the great cedars. Museum visitors at Toronto's ROM, Vancouver's Museum of Civilization, or the national Museum of Civilization at Ottawa or the Museum of Natural History in New York cannot escape a skin-tingling sense of ages immemorial, as they stand in the shadow of those immense North West Coast poles, but the truth is that their growth to meet the sun was brief. It crested in the 1880s, began to fade under the oppressive cultural genocide of the ruling population early in the twentieth century, and then flowered again in a renaissance in the hands of young artists from the many nations of that region. To some extent inspired by the sculptural adventures of the great Bill Reid, their work *feels*

7. Say "GISS-kan."
8. Claude Levi-Strauss, in an interview with the author, Ottawa, 1971.

like ancient work.[9] It reaches back into the deepest cultural consciousness of peoples who felt such an affinity with the animal kingdom that in their art is often difficult to know where the animal stops and the human begins. You can see the artists who made them in the turn-of-the century photographs and motion pictures of Edward Curtis, assembled in both a book and a film entitled *The Shadow Catcher* by Terri McLuhan. Curtis found them still going to sea in their whaling canoes carved out of a single immense log, the paddlers dressed ceremonially to go and greet the killer whales. And they are there among the stupendous poles, unlike any other national culture in the world.

Some of those weathered old giants of the early period still stand in the Cassiar country, cracked, tilted, fading into the undergrowth, but most are gone. The photographs of Kispiox village that were unearthed for our documentary show forests of them, taller than the tallest tree in a mixed eastern forest, gracefully watching over the spiritual life of their villages, watching for enemies, watching for danger, watching for the touch of life.

In the 1960s the renaissance of the old arts and the old values led to the building of 'Ksan, a replica Gitskan village on the Skeena near Hazelton. 'Ksan became a major training centre for Northwest coast native peoples who wanted to learn the styles and skills of their ancestors. Cultural anthropologists use the term *Tsimshian* as a collective name for the Tsimshian, Nishga, and Gitskan peoples. But the 'Ksan style is distinctive, clear of line and sharply detailed, positive, using the traditional U-forms and split

9. Bill Reid is a Haida sculptor: b.1920; d. 1998.

U-forms in elongated or truncated versions, often outside the figure depicted. 'Ksan has brought thousands of summer visitors to the region to feel the power, through dance and mask and silkscreen works growing out of these rich ancient cultures.

And it was in that rich mix of nature, art, and a turbulent encounter of conflicting cultures, that a baby was born to two Gitskan chiefs, in 1874. His mother was a hereditary chief of the Fireweed clan, and his father a hereditary chief of the Frog clan. His childhood at his father's side prepared him for the great drama of his life. His father was a trapper and hunter who knew the land and its creatures and its ways, and how to survive in it, as deeply as millennia of tradition could provide. And Simon Peter Gunanoot, the child, would need all of that when he was thirty-five. He would be suspected of a double murder, made the object of one of the longest and most famous manhunts in Canadian history, and survive on the run with his family, in that fearsome landscape, for nearly a decade and a half.

The then active British Columbia Provincial Police, the RCMP, and even the legendary American Pinkerton Agency would pursue him, fruitlessly and at enormous cost. Rewards offered for his capture were the equivalent, in today's money, of hundreds of thousands of dollars. Yet nobody turned him in. He was seen in a number of the towns and villages of the region, whither he would glide like a shadow out of the mountainscape, to pick up a little salt, a bottle of whisky perhaps, leave word for his friends that he and his family — for his father, wife, and children were with him and two children would be born during his exile — that they were all right, and that the friends were doing a good job of throwing the pursuers off the scent and warning the Gunanoot family of who was hunting them and where. For thirteen years nobody turned him in.

Violent death was not a stranger to that family. Some years earlier Simon's older brother Din had accidentally shot and killed a companion when the boys were playing with guns not far from Hazelton. Din disappeared into the bush. His parents hunted for him for days, but before they found him he had hanged himself.

Simon took up ranching. There was a place on the Skeena River where the packhorse trains taking prospectors and explorers into the Big Country could cross over in the shallows. Simon married Sarah, a woman from the village of Kitsegas, and together they developed a horse-breeding ranch on prime bottomland near that ford on the Skeena, calling the farm *Anlaw*, which meant River Crossing in their tongue. Simon Gunanoot appears to have been able to live comfortably in both the Gitskan and the white cultures. He was educated in a church school, spoke an accented English fluently, and wrote in a clear, cursive hand, samples of which appear in the documentary, legible and elegant. Competent and at ease living off the land, both in the bush and on the ranch, he was also a successful businessman, running a general store in Kispiox village and travelling into town to buy supplies for his business. He bought and sold furs.

In the spring of 1906 Sarah heard that there was a good catch of fish for sale at a village a few miles away. Photographs of the river fishermen of the period show magnificently precarious log platforms slung out on beams over the gorges, and men standing on them casting nets down into the teeming rush of water a dizzying distance below. Salmon were so plentiful that workers on the CPR as it pushed through into British Columbia in the 1880s complained of having to eat it every day. Simon set off on foot, over the infamous wooden suspension called the Terror Bridge and down through the semi-outlaw community of 2-Mile, where he stopped in for a drink. The town council in Hazelton, then just a few muddy streets and wooden buildings clad in unpainted cedar bevel siding, were determined that their little frontier community be a "respectable" place; so they outlawed such popular but unseemly institutions as brothels and taverns anywhere closer than two miles from the town centre. 2-Mile had its supply of both services and did a regular and successful business although nobody lived there except the practitioners themselves. The big saloon was well furnished with brass spittoons and hand towels hanging under the lip of the bar every two feet along the polished mahogany panels. We have to guess what the towels were for. But that was where Simon stopped in for a shot of something, and then, apparently, another, in the company of numerous other well-lubricated packers, trappers, and prospectors.

The bartender's name was Cameron. From the evidence given at the inquest it seems that Cameron was already too drunk to work by the time Simon Gunanoot came in, and a dock labourer named Macintosh had taken over behind the bar. Macintosh was a big, powerful brawler fresh out of jail, probably for assault, under orders to leave the region within twenty-four hours, and making the best of a last night in 2-Mile. Witnesses said he baited Gunanoot with racist remarks and hints that he, Macintosh, had been "close to" Gunanoot's wife Sarah. When the inevitable fight broke out Simon was no match for Macintosh, who threw him out in the street badly beaten and bloodied with a ragged wound on his face that left him with a long scar for the rest of his life.

Somebody told the police they had heard Simon say that he would be back with a gun and Macintosh had better watch out.

But Macintosh was in bad shape too. There must have been broken bottles involved, for the pinch-hitting bartender's hand was bleeding so badly that the trail boss of his pack train sent him over to the hospital in Hazelton to get it treated. He never arrived. In the morning he was found dead on the trail with a single bullet neatly centred in his back. People still point out the place. The soaring mountains loom in the distance, and there on the trail wild lilies are growing.

It was Constable James Kirby of the BC provincial police who opened the investigation, with his rangy handlebar moustache and heavily lashed walrus eyes. "After investigating the grounds all around," his report reads, "I went back to the 2-Mile Tavern and discovered the circumstances of the night before," much of which has been related above. There was no morgue. The body was laid out at the police station. Kirby was sitting down to lunch when word came that a second body had been found on the trail, that of a farmer named Max LeClair, a newcomer to the valley with no connection to Macintosh. He too had been shot neatly in the middle of the back with a single bullet.

It must have seemed pretty clear to Constable Kirby that Gunanoot was his man. As soon as Doctor Wrinch completed the obligatory autopsy, they got out a warrant for the Gitskan rancher, and the long search was under way.

Kirby swore-in a posse. They lined up on the porch of the courthouse and had their photo taken. The photo still exists, and in it the posse look as though, well, this will all be over pretty soon. They saddled up and rode out to *Anlaw*. Sarah and the children stared at them mutely, and just shook their heads when Kirby tried to question them.

"Searching around the house," he wrote, "we discovered three horses had been shot, a fourth killed by a pick, which we found with bloodstains on it. We searched the grounds thoroughly, but no sign of the accused."

And indeed it would be thirteen years before he saw his prey, thirteen years of confusion, not without its humour, but based upon the desperate run for his life of an Indian in the days when Indians were still considered less than human by many whites, certainly less than civilized by most, and no more likely to be acquitted by an all-white jury — as it would inevitably be — than a black man in Mississippi in the 1930s. Gunanoot knew perfectly well, and so did his friends, that the likeliest outcome were he ever found would be a round of gunfire on the pretext of self-defence, and a clutch of Gitskan corpses left for the relatives to claim. He had no choice. The many photographs of this man show a watchful, appraising gaze, strong eyes that turn up sharply at the outer corners and always seem to have an exceptional glint. Sometimes he is in the ceremonial robes and bear-claw headdress of his national culture, and sometimes in the suit, vest, and tie of the white world. However he is dressed we do not see him smiling much. Perhaps it is just because we already know a great deal of his story, but this looks like man who will not readily be surprised.

Indeed, Constable Kirby never got close enough to pull a gun. He found tracks on the trail heading north towards Sarah's home village, Kitsegas. That seemed a likely lead, so Kirby and the posse rode north. Somehow, as they were interrogating the Kitsegas villagers, the posse's horses got loose and disappeared. Kirby and his men had to walk the forty kilometres back to Hazelton. There they learned that while they had been looking for him in Kitsegas, Simon had come back to the ranch, collected supplies and his family, including a brother-in-law named Peter Himadam, and once more vanished. Simon's father Nah Gun was rounded up. Perhaps Kirby hoped that when Gunanoot learned his father was in jail he would come out of hiding. Instead the old man escaped on his own, and before long word was going around the valley that he was with Gunanoot and the rest of the family-in-exile. A local historian, Bob Henderson, wryly narrates the next phase, which is not distinguished by a high degree of admiration for Constable Kirby.

He wrote to superintendent Hussey, who was chief Counsel of Victoria, and said that it was very difficult to chase Simon and Peter because they had access to horses and he didn't. And he really needed a horse. So it was allowed that *he could go out and buy a horse. And eventually he writes back to Hussey and says, "I have found a very gentle mare, and she's going to cost $100, and then I'll need the upkeep." So it was decided that he would get $100 and $15 a month as the upkeep. [But] these horses were mythical. The province [sent] them $15 a month to feed these mythical horses, and . . . he . . . actually asked for a barn to be built for the mythical horse.*

Hussey, in his bowler hat and greatcoat, superbly sculpted great bush of a moustache and eyes that glowered with deep civic menace (reminding the reader of Sherlock Holmes's pompous rival at Scotland Yard, Inspector Lestrade), was not long taken in by the bumbling Constable Kirby. He pulled Kirby off the case and sent in another moustache, Constable Berryman. Berryman got as far as Kitsegas and reported back that he needed more supplies. When Hussey learned that Berryman had been seen actually talking to Gunanoot, interrogating him without knowing who he was, he pulled Berryman off the case and sent a couple of real professionals out from the capital, Constables Munro and Wilkie. *The Victoria Daily Colonist* reported:

By canoe and trail the constables are vigorously pushing their quarry into a corner of the country where they will certainly in time round him up. Both Munro and Wilkie are hard, sinewy, tough men, and the task is to their liking. That they will be able to stand the tire of the trail, with its packing of grub, carrying of canoe, lining through rapids and resting at nights with the round boulders of the gravel bar under their heads for pillows, is no less certain than they will bring the bad Indian to civilization and justice.

But this was just a lot of romantic gush. The man they were up against was far less likely to tire on the trail than were his pursuers. They went all the way up to Dawson City chasing rumours of Gunanoot along the Yukon Telegraph line. Native workers on that line kept Gunanoot well informed. That winter of 1906 to 1907 was a killer. The mercury dropped to minus 45 degrees Celsius. Wilkie and his partner reported confidently that nobody could have survived that kind of a winter, and that the Gunanoot family had certainly frozen to death. They went back to Victoria. Spring came, and with it unequivocal reports that the Gunanoots were alive and well, and on the way to becoming heroes among the tribal peoples. The natives might, Hussey feared, use the symbolic figure of the fugitive as the rallying-point for an uprising or some other form of resistance to provincial authority. When a prospector named McPhail gave a statement to the police, in the fall of 1907, that he had met and talked with Gunanoot, Hussey sent Wilkie back on the trail. Wilkie's telegram to Hussey is still in the archives

We constructed a raft to go down the lake and put our effects on board and started, but had an accident, the raft running onto a sunken snag and throwing everything into the water.

Another man, Haggard, went out with three juniors. They fell out over cooking duty and the juniors quit. Haggard hid his food and other supplies in a cache and went back in for orders. Gunanoot and his family rifled the cache and disappeared again. By now Premier McBride had given up on his own police and sent for the Mounties.

The Mounties insisted on travelling in uniform, so everyone, including Gunanoot, always knew about their movements. By 1909 Hussey and McBride decided they needed something special, and went for the Pinkerton Agency.

The Pinkerton posters of the time show a great engraved single eye, with the motto *We Never Sleep*. The agency had become world famous; it even figures in a Sherlock Holmes story. Pinkerton men had hunted down Jesse James and Butch Cassidy and the famous but incompetent Canadian bank robber Billy Miner, the Grey Fox (see Part Six of this book). They specialized in undercover work. Their two agents took on the role of coal prospectors in the Groundhog Mountains, where Gunanoot was last seen. They were told to sign their telegraphed reports to Hussey with numbers (#8 and #26) instead of names. Sometime that fall they met a packing contractor up the telegraph line, and sent in the first report to suggest that maybe they were getting somewhere:

"We spent nearly all day with George Beirnes, [who] told us . . . that Simon had a special hunting ground, and that he had met Gunanoot there."

In the provincial archives there is a dirty watermarked slip of paper with a pencilled map that Beirnes drew for the Pinkerton men, believing them to be legitimate prospectors whom Gunanoot would help, although he warned them that Gunanoot would know they were coming long before they got close, and would decide whether or not to meet with them. Gunanoot decided not to. They came back, in the spring, as empty-handed as their predecessors.

And so Hussey called off the search. It was costing a

fortune, earning the law only ridicule, leading nowhere. He announced a reward for information leading to the arrest of Gunanoot and Peter Himadam. Perhaps he hoped that bounty hunters would achieve what the lawmen could not. The reward was at first $300. This was raised to $1,000 and then to an unprecedented $2,300. Stories began to go around among the Gitskan that people were coming all the way from Europe to go on the hunt. But it was hopeless: not only did Gunanoot and his family know the land and how to live on it, but also they had become heroes to their people. They could slip into a village for supplies, a friendly word, and information about where the police were, or who the newest hopefuls were on the bounty trail, and there was simply no way that they would ever be caught. Gunanoot's son David, who was born on the trail, gave an interview much later in which he told of being at the head of the Skeena, and hearing of someone coming there to find them. The children were packed on the sled with the best dogs in the country, and, with Simon and Peter both perfectly fit within twenty-four hours they were miles away. That was family life for the Gunanoots, for thirteen years.

It was not without hardship and loss. Whether it was revenge or accident, Gunanoot's store in Kispiox along with all its inventory was destroyed by fire. His father Nah Gun died on the trail; consistent with tradition, Gunanoot carried the body to the old man's chosen resting place at Bowser Lake and buried him there. At least one of Sarah's babies died at birth. Peter Himadam's wife died and was buried in the Spatzi wilderness.

One evening Simon slipped into the town where he was most likely to be recognized, and was. A fur trader named Dick Sergeant had decided to try his luck as a motion picture exhibitor, and had bought a projector and hung up a sheet and put out a poster. Half of Hazelton came along one night to see their very first movie. Dick Sergeant later said that he had recognized a figure standing in the shadows at the back of the hall. And Gunanoot later told how he had gone back to his family in their tent in the bush and made shadows on the tent wall, with his hands and a lamp, to try to tell them about the moving picture marvel he had seen in town.

There is a significant political context within which this adventure unfolded:

Historian Tom Buri:

There was a great deal of . . . unrest with the native people. Alliances were being formed between the tribes. Declarations of rights were being promulgated. A delegation was led to England by Squamish Chief Joe Capilano to see King Edward. All of this while railroads were getting put in, trap lines were being taken away, land was being alienated. It was an extremely volatile political situation, when Gunanoot disappeared.

The weapon of conquest that seemed most visible to the Gitskan was the surveyor's transit. That was the seemingly innocent, but more and more powerful tool that opened the way for those steel invaders, the tracks — the tracks and the grade, connecting Prince Rupert on the Pacific coast with the inland wealth and markets of Eastern Canada. Those lines of steel, with the flat gravelled grades that supported them and changed the land forever: those were seen as scars on the territorial flesh of the Northwest native peoples.

Gunanoot was too busy staying ahead of the law to be actively involved in land claims issues as they began to take shape, but he became a symbol of the new assertiveness of his people. When an uprising was rumoured to be forming in the Hazelton area, even though Gunanoot had no possible way of being involved in it, his name turned the rumour into an event.

There was a big Irish constable at Hazelton, named Deane. Deane was new to the job and to the region, a guy who, by reputation, liked to "fight first and investigate later." Deane heard that the influential Squamish Chief Joe Capilano was visiting the local Gitskan leaders. He became seized with the notion (which he may have invented), that the Gitskan were going to lay siege to the town. The *Omenica Herald* ran a story saying that Gunanoot was ready to lead the Kispiox in battle, if that was what was needed to achieve their land claims. Deane organized a defence and rounded up a task force of bewildered residents. These people had been getting along just fine with the Gitskan; and just that day the Indians had helped with a major packhorse crossing of the Skeena. Nonetheless Deane somehow bulldozed the white residents into starting to dig a defence trench. He even brought out a forced labour gang from the town jail to help with the shovels. It was all a fantasy, but it brought Gunanoot back into the limelight, and at this point Premier McBride told the attorney general he wanted the hunt to be re-activated: "Bring in Gunanoot at all costs."

That packhorse man, George Beirnes, now becomes the crucial figure.

"[He] came here about 1908, and he packed for the Yukon Telegraph Line, and he was also a good friend of Gunanoot," Dorothy Allen told us. She knew him when she was a girl, and lives now on the very ranch that Beirnes had settled when he first came to the valley.

Beirnes knew where [Gunanoot] was most of the time. . . . In the summertime he used to come in and hay for George Beirnes. And George would bring him groceries and all that. And then in wintertime when Gunanoot was trapping, George would take his fur and sell it to the Hudson Bay, and bring groceries for his winter supply. George Beirnes talked Gunanoot into giving himself up.

Gunanoot trusted Beirnes. Beirnes told him that he had become such a hero, not only to the Indians, that he could count on a fair trial. There was enough money from the furs to hire a top lawyer. The lawyer's name was Stuart Henderson, one of the top criminal lawyers in the country. When Gunanoot came out of the bush, he walked between Beirnes and Henderson.

The newspapers of the time used to stack subheads over a story, two or three or even four, above the column where the story began. The *Victoria Colonist* wrote, in its edition of June 25th, 1919:

Indian Whom Authorities Had Sought For Years Gives Himself Up

Is Accused of Killing Two Packers in 1906

Came in under Direction of G. Beirnes and Stuart Henderson

By the time he came in out of the cold on that June day in 1919 the Western world had come through and had been transformed by a cataclysm. When Gunanoot and his family went into the bush they were in hiding all through the war that killed tens of millions and exhausted the treasuries of Europe. The federal government had come up with the idea of special university subsidies for returning veterans. The airplane had come to British Columbia, and so had the now world-famous "Mohawk Princess" the renowned Six Nations poet and stage performer Pauline Johnson.[10] Women had won the right to vote. New notions of equality and social justice seem to have been born out of the horrors of war. Not only had that Gitskan nemesis the Grand Trunk Railroad been completed, but also — in the year that Simon Gunanoot gave himself up — the Grand Trunk declared bankruptcy.

Some dim beginnings of a sense of the greatness of the native culture, and the injustice of their segregated and oppressed life had begun to form in the minds of a few members of the dominant white population, and not so dimly in the minds of people like George Beirnes and Stuart Henderson. "The Bad Indian," as a 1906 newspaper had called him, was now being lionized. Chief Inspector Parsons of the provincial police came over from Victoria to be photographed with the famous fugitive. The *Colonist*, which had once called him "that murdering Indian," wrote,

Many stories are told by his fellow Indians of his prowess,

10. See *The Canadians: Biographies of a Nation*, Volume I, for an account of Pauline Johnson and her relationship with Chief Joe Capilano.

of his ability to fell an ox with a blow of his fist, of his ability as a hunter and trapper and his fidelity to his friends. His escape and successful eluding of capture for so many years has made him a species of hero.

He was a quixotic figure who had defied authorities, overcome immense adversity, saved his family, and found his freedom in the hills. Now he was exposing himself to the ultimate penalty of death by hanging should the jury find against him. This had to be the act of an innocent and much wronged man. It was a profile that must have had many saying, "I wish I had done that."

When he left for Vancouver by train, for the trial, they all came out to see him off. Peter Muldon, a Gitskan man from Hazelton, was nine years old that year, and remembers that Simon Peter Gunanoot had a rose in his lapel when he got on the train.

The prosecutor was also named Henderson, Alexander Henderson. He was up against a man who had become a myth, and he had little to work with. The luckless Constable Kirby was one of the first to testify, and everybody knew his story and knew that it was nothing more than circumstantial evidence and hearsay. There was no weapon, no witness, nothing but a co-incidence in time and the hearsay account of a drunken threat. There was one witness whose appearance made defence counsel Stuart Henderson anxious. That prospector, McPhail, who claimed to have talked with Gunanoot thirteen years earlier just after he disappeared, had given police a signed statement, in which he said:

Simon had acted strangely. He came to our camp. . . . [He] said he had killed a white man at Hazelton a short time before he came to Bear Lake. He thought his name was Macintosh. The white man had treated him badly, he said, and had said something bad about his wife, too.

Strangely, that statement was not offered as evidence in court, and all that the dapper, goateed little prospector would testify to on the stand was that Gunanoot had said, "I killed a white man."

"Could have been the other white man," the judge said sourly, directing the jury. Gunanoot had not been charged with the other murder.

The only possible case that prosecutor Alexander Henderson might make would have to come from his cross-examination of the accused. The one question that troubled even some of Gunanoot's loyal supporters was, If he were innocent, why did he run away? "Even Moses fled," his lawyer said. "There's two different worlds out there." Here is how the *Colonist* reported the testimony of the accused:

After the fight my face swelled up. I was ashamed. I never fight before. I went into the bush. Not wanting to see anybody until all better. I would have come back in three or four days. But I hear shooting and see them kill all my dogs. And my father comes and tells me they are after me. So I go behind Glen Vowell for a few days, and then when my father got away we crossed the Skeena and started up the trail to Kitsegash.

That seemed reasonable to the jury. The judge took pains to warn them that they might convict only if they were certain of Gunanoot's guilt beyond a reasonable doubt, and of course there was all kinds of reasonable doubt available, even to a white jury, in the case of a fugitive whose story had climbed such legendary heights. They took just thirteen minutes to deliberate, one year for each of those years in the wild. Not guilty!

"As far as this court is concerned," the judge said, "you are entirely innocent." The courtroom dissolved into cheering and the shaking of hands. Gunanoot smiled. Friends and strangers pressed in to shake his hand and wish him well.

Perhaps those thirteen years had taken it out of him, or perhaps they had brought him a more tranquil sense of what life was for. In any case he gave up the store in Kispiox, leaving it in Sarah's hands, and went back to the ranch and did a little trapping and prospecting with George Beirnes and Stuart Henderson, who had become a good friend.

Simon Peter Gunanoot lived fourteen more years, and when he died in 1933 his son David carried him to the gravesite at Bowser Lake where Simon had carried his father years before, when they were still on the run.

"Because that was his father's wish," says cousin Gilbert Johnson.

In the old days, the . . . High Chiefs chose where they wanted to be rested. It was an honour for the other person to deliver that person to where he wanted to rest, and bury him there. That's his favourite ground.

The Gitskan say that Gunanoot's courage and example inspired and re-enforced their determination to campaign for their rights in the succeeding years. David would later be a principal witness in a major case about tribal boundaries, the Delganote Land Claim. In 1997, the Supreme Court of Canada ruled in favour of the Gitskan claims and found that West Coast aboriginal rights had never been extinguished, despite what their opponents had claimed.

There is, of course, one question that still troubles students of the story: Was Simon Gunanoot *really* innocent of the murder of Macintosh? In the Cassiar country today, you can hear both yes and no.

◆　◆　◆

The original documentary was written and directed by Monty Bassett.

◆ Part Nine ◆

KIT COLEMAN
KIT OF THE MAIL

Violet: I cannot see why you should feel it necessary to sac-
rifice yourself to "comfort" a man for whom you do not
care. You say, "He kisses me, and I kiss him, and tell him I
love him because he pleads so hard to hear it. But I do not
love him." . . . You need a cold douche; you have no right
to go on like that. The young fellow will have every right
to call you a jilt and a flirt. You think you'll marry him to
"comfort" him. Some comfort you'd be!

    Kit.

In the Hamilton Cemetery in Hamilton, Ontario, there is a
handsome, classical Celtic cross over the grave of a journalist named Kathleen Coleman who died in that city on
May 26th, 1915. Born in Castleblakeney, Ireland, in 1856,
Katherine Ferguson, sometimes Kathleen Willis, Kathleen
Blake, and Kathleen Watkins, was known to tens of thousands of newspaper readers simply as Kit. She was a successful pioneer women's page columnist, a widely travelled special events reporter, and the world's first female
war correspondent.

    If the Fergusons of Castleblakeney were indeed "ten-
ant farmers," as the family history says, they certainly did
not fit the famine-driven image of the shoeless starving
agricultural indentured labourers who fled the stricken
island in those dreadful years between 1848 and 1852.
There appear to have been several layers to the tenant

farmer class, and the Fergusons, with their comfortable house and seventy-five productive acres of land were well up towards the top of those layers. They may even have owned a pub, and there is speculation that, indeed, they may have done well out of the dreadful famine, perhaps acquiring some land that in prosperous times they would never have been able to afford. Dr. Carla King, a historian at St. Patrick's College Dublin, says that they were part of a rising Catholic middle class whose economic and even political influence were on the upswing in those years. They had farm hands working for them on the land, and domestic servants in the house. They were able to give young Katherine and her sister Margaret riding lessons, and send them to a finishing school in Belgium.

The young girl was devouring the books in her father's extensive library from a very early age as well as doing her formal studies at Loretto Abbey, where her uncle, Father Thomas Burke, was the boarding school's popular chaplain as well as spiritual advisor to the nuns who ran the school. Katherine adored the independent-minded cleric, who once took his niece (now calling herself Kathleen), disguised as a boy, to walk the streets of Dickensian London with him, and see whether or not the famous novelist had got it right.

An unfortunate aspect of all this prosperity was that family, property, social position, and public status had a lot to do with whom you married, and whom you married was not a matter upon which the bride was always consulted. This is an unfortunate part of the social picture of aristocratic Europe that invaded the lower classes as they moved upwards. It is said of the brilliant French minister and diplomat Talleyrand that when his daughter came to him on the eve of her wedding to a certain duke and complained that she detested the prospective groom and did not want to marry him, her father replied brusquely and formally, *"Mélez-vous de vos affaires!"* If the twenty-year-old Katherine Ferguson returning from her Belgian school with refined manners and a modest fluency in French ever expressed any demurral when she discovered that she was engaged to a middle-aged merchant named Willis, the best she could have expected was a "There there, dear."

The marriage was a disaster for Kathleen, but probably brought her husband the equivalent in today's money of hundreds of thousands of dollars in dowry money. The husband, Thomas Willis, already wealthy, rode to the hounds, slept around profligately and cursed his bride when their first child turned out not to be a male.

The little girl died at the age of two. Kathleen became deeply depressed, and her philandering husband was not even interested in helping her. Not long after, he fell from his horse during a foxhunt and died from his injuries. Because there was no male heir there was no inheritance for Kathleen, either. Her beloved uncle Father Tom had died a year earlier. Somehow the determined young widow managed to establish her rights to part of the dowry, namely, the furniture she had brought into the marriage. Relieved to no longer be the domestic property of the noxious Mr. Willis, she sold everything and left for London, where she quickly found work as a governess. It was through her London employer that she met a Canadian government official, a

Miss Richardson, who had been assigned to encourage educated women to emigrate to Canada. Kathleen Ferguson Willis began to save her money.

In 1884 she boarded a ship for Quebec City, symbolically erasing at least part of her eight hideous years of marriage by registering as "A Lady: Aged 19." She was really twenty-eight. From Quebec she took the train to Toronto, quickly found work as a governess, and married a flamboyant travelling salesman named Edward Watkins, who took them off to Winnipeg to try their luck there. He appears not to have been very good at his job, and, like her first husband, a drinker and a philanderer. Watkins was a remittance man, a younger son whose British parents had sent him out to the colonies to keep him from agitating for part of the succession, and "remitted" a small allowance to keep him from coming home to England. Remittance men were figures of fun in Canada (see Part Ten on Calgary Bob Edwards) and it is clear that after the excitement of the first months together, the marriage fairly soon began to come apart. Kathleen taught French and music to help pay the rent. They had two children, Edward and Patricia, "Taddy and Patty," but before long, Watkin's irrepressible behaviour in other people's bedrooms gave Kathleen a legal opportunity for divorce, for which she may have applied. There is no record of a divorce having been granted, but the family legend is that Watkins was discovered to already have a wife in England, so that Kathleen would have automatic cause for annulment.

In any case, Kathleen is on her own again, has taken the distinguished County Galway surname of Blake, returned to Toronto with her daughter (Taddy stayed with his father), found a cheap apartment, re-established her teaching career, and enrolled Patricia in a boarding school.

Toronto was beginning to feel like a genuine literary city in the late nineteenth century. Magazines sprang up and flourished and died, and others replaced them. Newspapers were prosperous. On a whim Kathleen wrote a couple of stories, signed them "Kit," and to her delight sold both of them to the *Daily Mail*. A new weekly newspaper called *Saturday Night* had just started up in 1887 under editor E.E. Sheppard. It actually went on sale sharp at 6 p.m. on Saturday night. Kit sold three articles to *Saturday Night*, also signed simply "Kit." Suddenly the *Daily Mail* became interested in her as a regular. Christopher Bunting, the *Mail*'s editor, had decided it was time to launch a woman's weekly page. He liked the energetic, confident, handsome, red-headed Irish woman and asked her if she would take charge of the new page.

The column, entitled "Woman's World," was a hit from the start. Author Ted Ferguson, whose book on Kit contains samples of a good deal of her writing, said,

There were lineups outside the newspaper, to buy the column, every Saturday. . . . I don't think that . . . ever happened in Canadian journalism before or afterwards. People just absolutely loved everything she did.

And Mick Lowe, a Sudbury journalist who has also written a book on Kit, said,

The modern newspaper columnist that most newspaper readers would be familiar with, whose work would fill one

linear column of a newspaper — that's eight hundred words. Standard length. . . . An average "Woman's Kingdom" — I did a count — would run from six to seven thousand words. And it was in three parts. The first part would be an essay that . . . might run, say, two thousand words. The second part was called "Pot-Pourri." And it was kind of a collection, a mish-mash of things. Sometimes reprints, but often just . . . observations [or] news of the day . . . that she would be commenting on. And the third part was correspondence.

She started a lovelorn column, of which the quote at the head of this chapter is a sample. God knows she had had some experience in that department. Biographer Barbara Freeman said,

This became an incredibly popular feature. . . . "Oh Kit, I've met this wonderful man. But you know, he seems to have a drinking problem. What do you say, Kit? Should I marry him? And Kit would write back and say, "No. You can't save a man from drink by marrying him."

Not exactly a head turner in the era of Dear Abbie and her sexually explicit television progeny. But in a time when discussion of such matters was simply not done in public, this appears to have taken off instantly. There was a striking directness about it:

You are jealous of your husband's first love, jealous of his musings, his silence on occasion. [But] every human being . . . has a secret garden . . . each human soul is absolutely alone. . . . Respect the individuality of the man you love. His past does not belong to you. Let him walk in his garden.

She was even-handed in her support and her criticism, to men and women alike:

Harry P: You have made a little tin god of yourself and, mounted on a little tin bicycle, you are careering around, watching the public and thinking it has eyes only for you. Dismount, little god, and be a sensible little human worm, wriggling along like the rest of us.

At first, because of the gender ambivalence of her nom de plume, there was some uncertainty as to whether "Kit's" columns were the work of a woman or a man. There were not many women journalists working then. Photos of the *Mail* newsroom show an all-male collection of suits and ties. There may have been a slight stigma attached to the idea of a woman working in that environment. When she wrote a column once about riding to hounds she admitted to swearing at her horse when it got cranky. A reader wrote to say, "Well you must be a man, because ladies don't swear." For a few years she was able to maintain some uncertainty as to what sex she was. At one point the *Mail* ran a cartoon featuring four possible Kit characters, each one depicted as both a man and a woman.

The correspondence ranged far beyond the usual pangs of unrequited love, and Kit dispensed advice on everything from diet to how to react when a man does not give you his seat on the streetcar.

You were a very foolish woman to have had a fit of crying over so small a thing. I have often been left hanging on my strap in the street-car while gentlemen have got up and made room for nice-looking young girls. One has not forgotten the time when such attentions were paid to oneself.

They will be paid again, you know, when one's hair is white and one's back bent. . . .You and I and the rest of us ought to be glad of the humble crumbs.

People eventually figured out that she must work at the newspaper, and she began to get visitors there. One angry reader came to the office and attacked her verbally over an article he said was outrageous. Kit grabbed a pair of scissors and went for his beard. The man fled, but later wrote a letter demanding she apologize for trying to cut off his beard. She published a reply that said "I did not try to take off your beard, I was trying to take off your nose because you were sticking it in someone else's affairs."

She was working sixteen hours a day now, and when Patricia was away at school she kept a pet white rat for company. She had become sufficiently important to the circulation of the *Mail* that she felt she could ask for some special assignments. Perhaps recalling her visit to London with Father Burke some twenty years earlier, she persuaded Bunting to send her back to Britain to walk those streets again and write about the disappearing London that Dickens had recorded. She visited the Whitechapel district where tourists and would-be sleuths still came to see where the notorious Jack the Ripper had committed his crimes. She interviewed a woman who claimed to have overheard one of the assaults, and saw an apartment where there were still bloodstains on the wall. This visit produced four weeks' material for the *Mail*.

In 1893 she covered the Chicago World's Fair, and wrote, of a technological marvel that was apparently used outdoors there for the first time, "At night, when the vast buildings are flooded with electric light, that is past description."

In February 1895, as she was about to turn forty-one, the *Daily Mail* merged with another Toronto paper, the *Empire*, to become the *Mail and Empire* (still published under that title into the 1930s when it merged with the *Globe* to become the *Globe and Mail*). On assignment for the *Mail and Empire* in Ottawa, having heard gossip that the prime minister was a steady reader, she introduced herself to him in the hallway of the House of Commons and asked him straight out if it were true. Wilfrid Laurier replied courteously that he liked the unpredictability. He seems to have indicated that he would be glad to hear from her, and Kit took advantage of this cordiality to ask Laurier to open a few doors for her at Queen Victoria's Diamond Jubilee later that year, where the PM was going to be knighted. When the *Mail and Empire* assigned her to the Jubilee story, the newly knighted Sir Wilfrid arranged for her to have a front seat for the procession, and even invited her to join him and Lady Laurier for a visit to H. M. the Queen. She wrote about the procession, and the figure of the "benignant" monarch in the carriage, with all the patriotic fervour that people expected of her, but she did not lose her sense of proportion, and sent this back to the *Mail and Empire* as well as the glory pieces:

The Royal Family has dreadful taste in furnishing their palaces. The Queen's drawing room at Balmoral is absolutely frightful. . . . Can you imagine anything more hideous than walls and windows hung with tartan?

While in London she also took time to visit a famous

fortune-teller, the White Mahatma, whom Kit hoped to expose as a fraud.

A door behind me opened and a limp, faded little creature walked slowly in. . . . She brought me a blank card, told me to write on it my name, age, profession and one question. [I wrote] Name: Jinkins. Age: Sweet twenty-two. Profession: Journalism. Question: Does he love me? Madam took the card (written side face down) and sealed it in an envelope. She sat down and laid the envelope, the fastened side up, before her.

"Your name is Jinkins. I cannot tell your first name, it is not given to my mind to see. I see you surrounded by paper and pen — writing, writing — you do a lot of this work." She looked at me shrewdly. "You are younger than you look . . . about twenty — two, but you look many years older."

"Would you mind letting me have that envelope," I said gently. She changed colour. "I cannot do that. I would lose my impressions."

"The back of the envelope is transparent. I know it madam. But don't worry. I'll pay your fee."

Kit's reportage on the Jubilee demonstrated to her host of readers that this was a journalist of consequence, but Kit never gave up her touches of playfulness in her column. She still called her readers "the paper people," and their domestic animals, about which she was consulted along with the love affairs and the wayward children, were "the jungle people." All the same, London had given her an appetite for larger stuff, and she kept her eyes open for the next big foreign assignment.

In the meantime, with a little more security and time for some social life, she had begun to "walk out" with a physician named Theobald Coleman, from Seaforth, Ontario. Kit had been scarred by her earlier marriages, but she was a passionate and social creature; devoting hours of writing time every week to matters of the heart was not merely a professional device. Coleman was a quiet, decent, humorous, and successful doctor, but Kit had been forced into one nightmare of a marriage and had allowed infatuation to rocket her into another. This time she was going to make sure.

In April of 1895 revolution broke out in Cuba, which was then a Spanish colony. Quite unlike their behaviour in a subsequent Cuban revolution sixty years later, this time both American business interests and popular opinion backed the rebels. Spanish rule had been harsh in Cuba. That is really where concentration camps were first used. The Spanish called them "strategic hamlets." Thousands of rebels real and suspected died in them. It was to become a very special war for newspapers, partly because printing techniques had been developed that made it easy to rapidly get photographs onto the printed page. The American president, William McKinley, appeared to be vacillating about Cuba, and the media, which meant primarily the newspaper empires of Joseph Pulitzer and William Randolph Hearst, had a field day stirring up outrage against the atrocities of the colonial government of Spain. Hearst sent the famous illustrator Frederick Remington to do provocative paintings of the turmoil. When Remington cabled that all was quiet in Havana, could he come home, please, Hearst told him to stay, and added a phrase that has become famous in the history of Journalism: "You furnish the pictures and I'll furnish the war."

Kit had no illusions about Hearst. She had written, years earlier, that he was

Neither an honest nor a great journalist. His newspaper methods are Standard Oil methods. Libel suits are settled privately for cash, no public apology is printed. . . . Mr. Hearst maintains that since the magazines use fiction, newspapers have the same right. [He] has bought up the maddest imaginations in the market today.

But those papers were what she had to turn to when she wanted to read about the Cuban rebellion, and she felt she could do better. As the tension built, Kate watched in fascination from Toronto. She became convinced that a real war was going to break out, and that she would go to it. Americans owned some 50 million dollars worth of Cuban property, in sugar, tobacco, and iron. One politician, Senator Thurston of Nebraska, said openly,

War with Spain would increase the business and earnings of every American railroad . . . every American factory . . . every branch of industry. J.C. Breckenridge, the American Major-General of Volunteers, said, "Our policy should be always to support the weaker against the stronger, until we have obtained the extermination of them both, in order to annex [Cuba]."

It didn't require the journalistic sophistication of a Kathleen Willis Blake Watkins to see that it was just a matter of time, and in 1898 when the USS *Maine*, a battleship on a "friendly visit," was sunk by a mine in Havana Harbour; the war was on.

The invading Amerian forces were ill trained and ill equipped. The Spanish were even worse. Spain sent her fleet, the US Navy bottled it up in Santiago Bay, at the east end of the island, and virtually destroyed it. Kit got herself assigned. There was no response to her telegrams to Washington for permission to go to the island. She got on the train. In Washington, if the Secretary of War, General Russell Alger, thought he could politely turn her away, he soon found out he could not, and ended up giving her a pass. In Florida the army's commanders said quite rightly that they, not the secretary of war, were in charge in the field and they had no way to protect a woman in or on the way to Cuba. Kit tried the Navy, out of Key West.

It was a short war, and by the time Kit finally persuaded the Navy to take her across the less than a hundred miles of Gulf Stream that separate Cuba from Florida, hostilities were over. That did not stop Kit from writing affectingly from the hospitals, the battlegrounds, the site of the sunken Spanish fleet.

A ghastly ship with torn sides and battered decks. Half a mile further on, at Juan Gomalez, the Almirante Oquendo *lay half upon the beach like some dying monster that had tried to crawl out of the sea and died in the attempt. We . . . crept as best we could from beam to beam of the torn deck, and peered into what had been the cabin of the Spanish Admiral, Cervera. We saw a charred and battered little room.*

It was stuff that had not been reported on by a woman before. Kit had the clarity and the skills to wring everything she could out of "the human angle." The international press picked up her reports. She had become a world famous journalist.

The awful cruelty of war, the pitilessness of men when set as foe one against the other — crying out there, dumb things as they are, against man's inhumanity to man, against the breaking of the great covenant of the Brotherhood of Man. And yet necessary, say the gentlemen [who] from Senate houses and Parliaments guide the destinies of nations. Perhaps . . .

In the end, what America wanted out of the Cuban conflict America largely got. Spain was out of the way as a military power in the Caribbean; so the area was secured for the next big US project, the building of the Panama Canal. It was a war that brought America out of a century of isolationism; she had become an international player. When it was over, official America downplayed the role of the Cuban rebels, and trumpeted an American military success. Cuban forces were not even allowed to attend the surrender ceremonies, and Cuban representatives were not invited to the signing of the peace treaty in Paris. Even the American soldiers were not very well dealt with. Kit came back to Florida on a troop ship with the returning wounded. She wrote heart-wrenchingly about the appalling conditions, oppressive heat, insufficient water, food, and medicine, terrible crowding. Back in port in Florida neither the troops nor the correspondents were allowed off the ship for days, until they had completed quarantine for yellow fever. By the time Kit got ashore she was exhausted and sick.

She rested for a few days, and took the train to Washington, where Dr. Coleman met her. He proposed marriage. Kit thought about what she had been through, and about Coleman's patience and kindness in the year or so they had known each other. She accepted. They married then and there.

Her son Edward came to live with them now, and Patricia came home from boarding school. They had help in the house. Kit — now very happily Kit Coleman — could take it easy for a while, perhaps start writing that novel she had been daydreaming about. She went to concerts and began to include comment on the arts in "Woman's World."

An artist, giving a concert, should not demand an entrance fee but should ask the public to pay just before leaving, as much as they would like. From the sum he would be able to judge what the world thinks of him — and we would have fewer mediocre concerts.

And, "Literature would pay better if there were not so many dead men still in the business, hogging the customers."

It was also in 1898 that the great Sarah Bernhardt played Montreal. Kit decided it was time to see something better than what Toronto had to offer.

Why can't we have better plays in Toronto? For the past two seasons we have been no better off than the merest village. Burlesques . . . we have had in plenty, but plays — good plays and good actors — have been as rare as oases in the Sahara. . . . Caesar with a Scotch accent — by the Gods!

Her reputation got her backstage in Montreal and right into the Divine Sarah's dressing room. The two women looked at each other in shock. It was like looking in a mirror, so striking was the resemblance. "My God!" the great actor exclaimed, "We are like sisters!" She invited the journalist to stay as she dressed and made up.

Then she drew dark violet lines about her eyes that elongated and narrowed them, touched her ears with rouge, her lips, her cheeks, slightly, very slightly. And then she bolted the door for a moment, and taking a little phial, poured from it a drop in each eye. It was belladonna. Afterwards I noticed the effect of the blinding fluid. The pupils large, black, were dilated to their fullest effect.

Kit watched the play backstage.

I saw this woman who had been so particular as to her appearance a moment before change in an awful way as . . . the role forced itself upon her. . . . The face grew gaunt, haggard, old. Every line showed. She grew pallid, drawn. It was an old woman who faced the people.

But Kit's next move would take her far away from that world. In 1899 her husband got a well-paid commission with a mining company, and they moved to Copper Cliff, a desolate, sulphur-contaminated bleak landscape that destroyed Kit's images of the romantic north and set her down in a smoke-stained frame house where she had to carry water in from a well and make her own fires. From time to time, when there was an accident at the mine, her husband asked her to come and nurse the wounded. She continued to write the "Woman's Kingdom," and she was happy with her husband, but it was a bleak life. She missed the buzz of the city. She got her correspondence as before, and enjoyed writing her goofy or helpful replies; but it all seemed terribly far away.

On Valentine's Day in 1901 Theobald Coleman diagnosed a case of smallpox in Copper Cliff. Only six years earlier Montreal had been closed down by an epidemic of the disease, the port closed, the railways stopped, the last great smallpox epidemic in a Western industrial city. The Copper Cliff city officials were slow to respond, but Kit wrote a series of articles in which she urged a municipal quarantine, and finally the city built a quarantine centre, which probably prevented the outbreak from turning into a real epidemic. Both she and her husband felt that they had had quite enough of Copper Cliff, and so when the mining company cancelled Dr. Coleman's contract they were both relieved, moved back south, and settled in Hamilton, Ontario. It was a short train ride over to The City, to see her old pals and gossip with the guys at the paper, take in some theatre, get back into the swing of things.

There was one field of journalism that Kate had not yet tried: crime. It was becoming big stuff on the front pages, and she was fascinated. She was handed an opportunity when Cassie Chadwick was arrested in Cleveland for defrauding a number of American banks. It was a matter of millions of dollars, Chadwick was a woman, and she was from Ontario. An obvious assignment for this veteran of the Diamond Jubilee, the World's Fair, and the Spanish-American War. Her editors agreed. Ted Ferguson tells how she made out:

> *Kit went down to Cleveland. And when she went to the prison to try and interview Cassie Chadwick, there were so many other journalists that crammed into the cell that she really couldn't talk to her one-on-one. So she left her gloves behind. And then she went to the front desk and*

said oh, I left my gloves behind. And the police woman took her back there. And it was just her and Cassie Chadwick in the cell. And she got a world exclusive.

So now she could add crime reporter to her resumé. The *Mail and Empire* was not displeased. It had a real star on its hands now. She was only a woman, of course, and before long the paper would get a shock when it made the mistake of refusing her a raise in pay. But for now, if she wanted a special assignment, she was likely to get it.

Readers of E.L. Doctorow's novel *Ragtime* may remember a sensational murder story that somehow gets woven into the middle of it. A spoiled young rich kid named Harry K. Thaw had married a showgirl named Evelyn Nesbitt. Nesbitt had been seduced at the age of sixteen by the architect of Madison Square Gardens, a notorious roué named Stanford White. White was part of a kind of club of prominent New Yorkers who got together to see how many beautiful young virgins they could debauch.

Milos Forman made a film of it in 1981 — James Cagney's last appearance ever, with Norman Mailer playing Stanford White. Thaw, a man given to violent rages, apparently found out about his young wife's earlier arrangement with Stanford White some time after they were married. He had already taken to beating her with whips, so it wasn't much of a marriage anyway, but when he learned about Stanford White, he began to carry a gun. One night White had been watching showgirls doing a pistol-duelling number, on the stage of the Roof Garden Theatre at Madison Square Gardens, when Thaw walked up with a pistol, put it between White's eyes, and fired three times.

The sensational details about the seduction club and the strange marriage that came out after Thaw murdered White made for sensational reading, and once more it seemed obvious to the Mail and Empire that Kit Coleman should go to New York.

Kit covered the trial, at which Thaw was declared insane and put into an institution where he spent just over twelve years. His mother paid Evelyn Nesbitt a million dollars to shut up and forget it all, while Thaw gave the press a statement that went:

> *The agony of Evelyn in the years of her girlhood formed the prelude to a long continuous drama of sorrow, the murk and gloom of which was never illuminated by a ray of sunshine until what occurred on the roof of Madison Square Garden and Stanford White fell dead. After ten years during which a crew of moneyed libertines had made life almost as unsafe for virgins as did the Minotaur, a revolver made New York safer for other girls. They are safe.*

This was all very apt grist for the Kit Coleman mill. The *Mail and Empire* presses worked overtime to meet the demand for her reports. She was famous. Her work sold papers. She had become almost an icon among journalists, although the word was not used in that sense in those days. She must have supposed now that whatever she wanted to do next she would get to do.

But that was then, and this is now, and Kit Coleman was a woman. She was never, not once, invited to the *Mail and Empire*'s annual dinners. She could not have covered the proceedings of Parliament even if Sir Wilfrid and her editors had both wanted her to do so, because only members of the Parliamentary Press Gallery could do that, and women were barred from membership in the Press Gallery. The gender equity clause in the Charter of Rights and Freedoms was still seventy years in the future. It is not so long ago that another great Canadian reporter, Judith Jasmin, was kept away from an important number of her contacts when she was CBC correspondent in Washington, and women were not allowed in the Washington Press Club.[11] It is easy for people who did not live through that era to forget that this kind of discrimination still functioned in the years after World War Two, but it most effectively did. Few professional men objected.

Kit started a women's press club. She then asked the *Mail and Empire* for a five-dollar-a-week raise. The newspaper said no. Kit resigned. She was fifty-five years old, at the height of her reputation and her powers. She seems to have taken the end of her relationship with the *Mail and Empire* in her stride. Now she added another first to a long list and became the first syndicated columnist in Canada. For a while she was making more money than she had earned at the Mail. That changed when war broke out in the summer of 1914. Kit thought war futile and foolish. She found it hard to be a rabid anti-German. She said to a colleague, "When the years of your life are slipping fast, it makes you wonderfully kind." Her readers were not so kind. When she began to write pieces that suggested perhaps they should feel compassion for women on both sides of the battlefront, editors began to cancel her column. Ted Ferguson said,

11. See *The Canadians: Biographies of a Nation*, Volume I, for the story of this trailblazing television journalist.

She was very prickly and she was very feisty. And she was a very difficult woman in many ways. But . . . I fell in love with her, reading her columns, because she had courage. She had wit. She had intelligence. She also was supposed to have had the most beautiful sherry brown eyes in the whole of the Dominion of Canada.

Everyone who encounters Kit Coleman's work and her person seems to fall under her spell. Biographer Barbara Freeman said,

There were things that she did that caught the headlines, like going to Cuba. And everybody would say, well that was her great contribution because she did something that a man would do. But I think her greatest contribution was [carrying on] a career for twenty-five years, and by doing that, carving a new niche for women in journalism who were coming after her. Kit, really, I think was depressed [by] the struggle of trying to balance a career and mother-hood. Because there was even less support for that in her time than there would be now. She wasn't a prude . . . she hinted that she knew what sexual passion was, and that was pretty daring [back then] even to hint at that.

Ted Ferguson said,

She was a full-blown flesh and bones human being. But underneath she was a conservative person. She believed that marriage was the most important role that a woman should have. At one point, a Member of Parliament asked her if she'd be interested in running in a Federal election. She said, "The idea interests me, but I'm afraid I'm no good at lying and stealing. So I have to say no."

Mick Lowe is a Sudbury journalist who practises the

trade just a few miles down the road from where Kit helped her husband with a smallpox epidemic. He is writing a Dickens-like serialized novel about Kit's time in Northern Ontario. He said, at the end of our documentary:

I am not sure that her contribution has been fully made yet. She is someone whose writings should be revisited and studied. I really wish that would happen. Boy! It's all there. She really left it on the page.

To help make his point Mick Lowe sent me the following passage, from a New York visit Kit made during the Copper Cliff period. It is partly about journalism: we'll give her the last word.

Woman's Kingdom, May 11th, 1901
— "A Gossip of Gotham"

Away from this unsavoury neighbourhood and out to the middle of the Brooklyn Bridge only to look down on the big city at night. How far down, how pygmy the houses! How narrow and mean those lanes we call streets. Lights everywhere. Burning brightly on the tops of tall buildings, quivering in electric streams over shop and theatre, glimmering faintly in top storey windows, where perhaps one lay a-dying.

To be Asmodeus for one hour! Why should not the Devil Upon Two Sticks alight upon this parapet and bidding us to take hold of one end of his cloak flit with us to yon pinnacle and unroof to our view the houses of this big city! What things one would see. What crimes are being committed this very moment!

Accidents are occurring in the streets. Children are being born, men and women are dying. There is song and laughter and music, beauty and wealth and power, and set over and against all these — what an ocean of misery, what terrible poverty and hunger and naked-ness, what desolation and disappointments and despair of soul! Even now some poor aban-doned wretch is lifting his hand against his life. Even now the forger is signing his own death warrant, as his pen steals over the paper.

At this moment in one of those dark corners down below, black murder is being done, and looking backward to whence the tall newspaper buildings stand, one can well fancy their glitter-ing eyes of light piercing those dark and forlorn places and dancing with delight in the thoughts of the stories they will fling into the greedy maw of the public in the morning.

A chill wind blows from the river. Come away.

◆ ◆ ◆

The original documentary was written and produced by F. Whitman Trecartin, and directed by Chuck Stewart and F. Whitman Trecartin. It was photographed by Patrick Kennedy and edited by Reynold Gregor.

ADDITIONAL READING:

Ted Ferguson: *Kit Coleman: Queen of Hearts*

Barbara Freeman: *Kit's Kingdom: The Journalism of Kathleen Blake Coleman*

Kay Rex: *No Daughter of Mine: The Women and History of the Canadian Women's Press Club*

• Part Ten •

CALGARY BOB EDWARDS
THE EYE OPENER

When he died in Calgary in 1922 the outrageous, challenging, humorous journalism he had given to this country
almost died with him and was not revived for decades. His
pallbearers were police officers in full dress uniform.
Beside him in the coffin were a copy of his first newspaper,
the *Wetaskiwin Free Lance*, the last issue of his great, nationally read paper, the *Calgary Eye Opener*, and a pocket flask
full of good whisky. Calgary Historian Max Foran says that
when the *Eye Opener* was in business, the whole of
Calgary's high society dreaded its every appearance
because they could be in it, and if they were in it they
would be subjected to some kind of ridicule. Catherine
Ford, a columnist now at the *Calgary Herald* said that
Edwards "was a public scold because he could be, he put
his money where his mouth was, he put his money where
his typewriter was, and he had fun doing it."

"Fun," however, while it is a word that many use in
talking about Edwards' work, more accurately describes
their response to that work than the state of mind of the
man they are talking of. He was a serious alcoholic, a lonely bachelor until the last three years of his life, a man who
could dish it out — even against himself in his own
columns — but was terribly wounded when they dished it
out to him. In short, a complex, troubled, brilliant, original
and provocative journalist, both tough-minded and vul-

nerable. He left a legacy of journalistic "attitude" which has never totally vanished. Year after year the legacy of Calgary Bob Edwards is celebrated in that city when his admirers gather to present an annual award in his name.

Robert Charles Edwards was born in Edinburgh on September 24th, 1864, orphaned at the age of five, raised by rigidly moralistic aunts in Glasgow, graduated from the university in that city, and roamed around Europe doing odd jobs for a few years. Before he set out for the New World, his first newspaper experience was in France, as the youthful editor of a short-lived English Language tourist magazine, the *Traveller*. He was self-deprecatory about his university experience, saying sardonically that he emerged a "total ignoramus." However, this may indicate nothing more than the early development of a sardonic voice, a gift for a well-turned sarcastic *bon mot* ("A hypocrite is a man who is not himself on Sundays") — and a reflexive contempt for establishment institutions rather than any genuine diffidence about his own intelligence or knowledge.

This dismissive attitude towards convention — 'tude, it might be called today — appeared early as a kind of editorial currency in his newspaper work. He used it to genuine effect as a device for raising public awareness and discomfiting the comfortable, but it may have been more a rhetorical device than a seriously considered view of either social institutions or powerful people.

He and his brother Jack headed for Idaho in 1892, where they hired on as ranch hands and moved around the American West for a while. Edwards would later say that it was witnessing the lynching of a thief that changed his mind about the Land of Liberty, and started him thinking about Canada. In any case he turned up in Calgary in 1894, virtually broke, and for some reason moved on to Wetaskiwin, a small town south of Edmonton, where he found work as a handyman and part-time bartender in the town's small hotel. Jerry Boyce was the hotelkeeper. Boyce took a liking to Edwards and Edwards took a liking to Boyce's bar. "Some men are hard drinkers," he wrote. "Others find it absurdly easy."

Bob Edwards was one of those others. For the rest of his much too short life (he would die at fifty-eight) booze was a support and a scourge, a subject around which he would build some of his more boisterous humorous writings, and the object of his bitterest scorn and invective. He was seldom able to stay dry for more than a few days, and among his loyal present-day fans there are those who say that self-contempt — linked somehow to the drinking — was an essential part of his makeup.

He would hang around hotel bars a lot for most of his life. When his brother Jack died three years after he arrived in Alberta, he seems to have made a very sudden life decision, left the Wetaskiwin Hotel (at least as an employee), and started a small weekly newspaper, the *Wetaskiwin Free Lance*. In its opening number he declared that its purpose would be "simply and entirely to amuse." But amusement was not, for Bob Edwards, a trivial matter. Alberta historian Hugh Dempsey said that Edwards

> *used humor as a tool. He was a social activist. He was . . .*
> *for the little man, so to speak, and felt that there were*
> *everything from real estate agents to loan sharks to specu-*

*lators who were constantly causing trouble, causing hard-
ship and grief. So . . . his humor would be used as a very,
very sharp sword to whittle that person down to size.*

The thirty-three-year-old editor-publisher and sole
correspondent aimed his blade at personalities and institutions alike. He included his own mistakes and drinking
habits in his catalogue of lampoons, a device often used by
satirists so they don't appear morally superior to their subjects. But if his public self-criticism was ever meant to rec-
oncile the subjects to Edwards' ridiculing them, it certainly did not work in Wetaskiwin, where a committee of
churchwomen let it be known that the town would be better off without him. He picked up and moved on, not set-
tling anywhere at first, and perhaps — as Hugh Dempsey
speculates — influenced more than was good for him by
his friend the hotelkeeper.

*I believe he moved first to Leduc and then later moved to
Strathcona. And I think . . . he was following Jerry Boyce,
the hotelkeeper. He was a very close friend of his, and as
Jerry Boyce left one hotel and bought another or built
another, [Bob Edwards] followed him.*

In 1899 he arrived in High River, southwest of
Calgary, and a couple of years later the enterprise that had
begun in Wetaskiwin as the *Free Lance*, became the *Eye
Opener*. Max Foran speculates that it was during these
years that Edwards first began to look on the newspaper as
something more than an entertaining way to skewer
pompous people.

*I think these stints in these smaller towns honed his jour-
nalistic skills. I think they gave him an eye for story and*

probably forced him to go deeper into finding good stories and pertinent stories, instead of relying on outside information.

He did, however, launch the *Eye Opener* off with characteristic sarcasm, some of it levelled at himself. The paper's reputation — as it grew and grew until it became a national institution — was at least as much built upon the lampooning style as it was upon some of the very solid polemical journalism that he pioneered in the west. This is how the opening communiqué to the *Eye Opener*'s readers went:

> *Clothed in righteousness, a bland smile and a lovely jag, the editor of this publication struck town two weeks ago. The management has decided on the name* Eye Opener *because few people will resist taking it. It will be run on a strictly moral basis at $1.00 a year. If an immoral paper is the local preference we can supply that too, but it will cost $1.50.*

It was here that he began his tirades against the hypocrisy of churchgoers (he was one himself) who characteristically took the opportunity of the Sabbath traditions to clothe themselves in righteousness one day a week. Max Foran said,

> *I don't think he had any trouble with the Sabbath [as such]. It was the way it was compromised in the name of self-righteousness. You go to church and you sing songs and you come home and you might beat your wife or your dog or you might screw someone out of a house you were trying to sell, and then go to church and sing about how good you are. Sunday didn't make you a better man. And he would argue that a lot of these people . . . were much*

different people on Monday than they were on Sunday, and he didn't like it.

Whether it was the hostility towards him of his Methodist targets in High River, or (more likely) a growing confidence that he had something that would sell in a bigger city, he soon moved on again. In 1904 he moved the *Eye Opener* to Calgary. "These small towns are awful," he wrote, as he was leaving High River:

Wetaskiwin threw us down. Leduc threw us down. Strathcona, being dead anyway, shook its shriveled finger at us. High River is passing us up. Ye gods! That we should have lived in such places!

An Alberta social phenomenon that he had found especially entertaining in High River, the remittance man, had led to the development of a fictional component in the *Eye Opener*, and there would be times later on when it became very difficult to distinguish Edwards' fictions from his reporting or his jokes from his diatribes. When he wrote that the three biggest liars in Alberta were "Robert Edwards, Gentleman, Honourable A.L. Sifton, Premier, and Bob Edwards, Editor of the *Eye Opener*," the premier did not get the joke, and launched a libel suit that he later withdrew when Edwards himself filed a similar action on behalf of "Robert Edwards, Gentleman, and Bob Edwards, Editor."

The remittance man theme was a far more elaborate gag. Hugh Dempsey described it in detail:

The remittance man was usually a younger son of a fairly well to do family in England. Very often the eldest son inherited the estate, the second son went into the ministry and the younger son was kind of left footloose and fancy-free. And it was often the younger son that was in the local bars and taverns and getting the local barmaid knocked up and so on. So, as a result they would send the youngest son off to the colonies and every six months they would send him a remittance, enough money to last him for the next six months so that he wouldn't go home.

So he developed this series of letters that this Buzzard Chumley, who was a remittance man, wrote home to his parents, with all these different schemes of getting more money out of [them]. And some of them were absolutely hilarious. One of them was that he had married this Native girl and that he wanted her to share in the family estate, so he wanted to bring her home to meet the family. But on the other hand, he had a chance to buy a ranch. But if he got this ranch he wouldn't be able to come home . . . and kind of left it at that, hoping that the parents would send him the money. And it was very believable because it paralleled the actual kind of situations that were occurring. Buzzard Chumley became a real favorite of the readers of The Eye Opener.

Calgary had gone through a few slow years, but now it was going into a boom. When Edwards arrived there the population was only five or six thousand and descriptions of the city recall Mordecai Richler's later joke that "Calgary will be a very nice city once they get it out of the crate." Jennifer Bobrovitz, the history librarian at the Calgary public library, said that as Edwards settled in,

the economy was rolling along fairly well. There were lots of opportunities and in many ways it was a frontier town in every respect: independence was appreciated. Characters were appreciated. And Bob must have sensed that perhaps he would have an opportunity to succeed in Calgary. Calgary was very much a conservative town. It was centered around the Canadian Pacific railway station on 9th Avenue and generated out a few block radius from there. So the busiest corner in Calgary in 1904 was the corner where the Alberta Hotel stood.

The Alberta hotel building is still at the corner of 8th Avenue SW and 1st Street SW, now overshadowed by the Pan Canadian Office Tower and the needle shape of the Calgary Tower. Bob Edwards got a room there in 1904 for a dollar a week. He made friends with a socially prominent lawyer, Paddy Nolan, who like Edwards was a man who loved a joke and loved a drink. They made a pair of satirically minded raconteurs. Nolan helped Edwards put together the necessaries to start up his newspaper again, and he kept the title he had invented in High River. "It is said the editor has never drawn a sober breath in his life," he wrote when he launched the Calgary version of the *Eye Opener*. "His rag will probably go bust inside six months." They laughed at that and began to buy the paper in gratifying numbers. "Come to Calgary," he wrote, "the Aquarium City. Full of sharks! Boozorium Park!" And that too was taken by the Calgarians as a good joke.

But before long there were people in high places who did not find it funny to open their copy of the *Eye Opener* and find a haranguing banner like this:

If Exhibits bore you to death, and you don't give a damn for horse races, COME TO CALGARY

ANYWAY! And have a look at the Province whose GOVERNMENT GIVES AWAY ITS FATTEST CONTRACTS to New York City.

He engaged a brilliant cartoonist named Forrester, and encouraged the artist to depict politicians as apes and hooligans. When Sir Clifford Sifton, the federal minister of the interior, turned up in Calgary, Edwards ran a front-page drawing announcing the visit, showing a man in a white hood and robe looking almost exactly like a member of the Ku Klux Klan. Sifton was a Liberal; Bob Edwards was a Tory. He was a pretty far-left Tory, who campaigned for free public health care, social justice, the rights of women and of all those who were downtrodden. But he was a Tory all the same, and he made the Liberals mad as hell. He would sit at his table in the Alberta Hotel, where it is said that half the deals and most of the money in Alberta were made, and look around him, and gather energy and material for the paper. The Alberta Establishment at some of the other tables would wonder if he was looking at them, and what outrage he would insult them with next.

That hotel was his domain. Much of the copy for the *Eye Opener* was written at his table. It was thought a grand place, with seventy-five rooms and a great dining room. There were far more men than women in Calgary then, and few of those women would be found at the Alberta. It was not easy to find a good meal anywhere else in the city, and the Alberta's dining room was always full. It was a ritual in the morning to stop in at the basement barbershop for a shave before heading off to work, and, if you liked, a start-up drink as well. Bob Edwards was only one of several prominent citizens who had their own regular tables. R.B. Bennett, the future prime minister of Canada, was another. Bennett was a teetotaller, so it was odd in a way that they should become friends, and it did not start out that way.

Bennett was a lawyer for the CPR. Edwards took the side of those who believed the CPR was a diabolical Enemy of the People. Whenever there was a train wreck he would put big photographs on the front page. The railway retaliated by refusing to carry the *Eye Opener* on the trains. Edwards ran a headline to celebrate a whole week without a wreck at the 9th Street crossing. When another train went off the rails, his caption would say, "Another CPR Wreck," as if they happened all the time. He once said to Paddy Nolan that he hoped he was doing something to give the West a social and political individuality. But to many of his targets he just seemed to be an intolerant bully. Certainly R.B. Bennett must have thought something of the kind when Edwards ran Bennett's photo with the caption, "Another CPR Wreck."

Soon the portly editor with the bushy moustache and eyes that always seemed slightly startled about something became an institution. There were those who adored him and those who hated him, and almost nobody who did not have an opinion about his character. He promoted himself cheerfully, with, among other things, cartoons that showed him as a good-looking, relaxed big guy leaning back in his editor's armchair and thinking up new ways to annoy the pompous. He did not just write about politics and rascals. He did thoughtful pieces on what was then called "The Negro Question," and intelligent pieces about fattening hens and marketing eggs. He championed the Pig Lady, Mother Fullum, a filthy local street person who fed her pigs from garbage collected outside the Alberta Hotel and other restaurants. And then, on the subject of dirt, would write that "The [City] Council should appoint a civic laundryman to handle the dirty linen."

"His job was to irritate people," says Jennifer Bobrovitz, "and he took it very seriously. It was his way of keeping them honest."

In that prosperous, optimistic decade before the Great War there was one political phenomenon that has not changed much since: the Liberals in Ottawa were, then as now, constantly trying to think of ways to gain some ground in traditionally conservative Alberta. They had two mountainous enemies in Calgary: the *Calgary Herald*, which was a Tory paper, and the *Eye Opener*, which was Bob Edwards. So the Liberals funded a new paper, the *Calgary Daily News*, under editor Daniel McGillicuddy. McGillicuddy set out to destroy Bob Edwards.

Edwards went after McGillicuddy through an invented comic character named Peter McGonigle, editor of the *Midnapore Gazette*. He reported that McGonigle, who had been jailed for stealing horses, was given a huge banquet in Edmonton when they let him out. At that banquet a congratulatory telegram was read out, from Lord Strathcona. Strathcona, the former Donald Smith of the Hudson's Bay Company, had helped finance the CPR. He is the bearded figure driving the Last Spike in the famous photograph. Edwards fictitiously reported Strathcona as saying, in the telegram, how glad he was that Peter McGonigle was back, and that if the CPR stocks had gone down instead of up he, Strathcona, might also have gone to jail.

Lord Strathcona was not amused. According to Jennifer Bobrovitz, he

> *was livid and he phoned his good friend in Calgary, Senator James Alexander Lougheed, who was also a lawyer, and said: "I want this guy for breakfast. I want to sue him both in civil and criminal actions." Lougheed said: "You know, ultimately if you take Edwards to court in Calgary, it will turn into a huge farce and you will wish you'd never heard his name." Lougheed finally convinced Strathcona to let it go, but it wasn't without a lot of effort.[12]*

Over at the *Daily News*, McGillicuddy had also been less than amused by the adventures of the satirical Peter McGonigle. He decided that he would serve his Liberal masters well if he could undermine Edwards' credibility in the weeks leading up to the next election. So he wrote and published a vicious personal attack on the satirist, which he signed pseudonymously.

> *I intend to show that he is a libeler, a character thief, a coward, a liar, a drunkard, a dope fiend and a degenerate, A . . . journalistic bully, . . . a "four-flusher," a "tin horn" and a welcher . . . make-believe journalism . . . the contents of which were smut and slander.*
>
> *(Signed) "Nemesis"*

Hugh Dempsey told us that Edwards "went deep into the bottle" when this piece appeared in the *Daily News*. The

12. Sir James Lougheed was Conservative leader in the Senate, and grandfather of Peter Lougheed, the much admired premier of Alberta from 1971 to 1985.

Eye Opener did not reappear for weeks. To his admirers it was troubling that the tough political critic and satirist could be so wounded by an obviously unfair and slanderous attack. Columnist Catherine Ford says, "It's there, take it, it rolls off your back. So what? You know, there is an old saying: Never pick a fight with someone who buys ink by the barrel."

Editors across the country came to his defence. The *Lethbridge News* said,

> *If there were more editors with the independence and fearlessness of Mr. Edwards . . . and fewer prostituted journalists like the editor of the* Calgary Daily News, *the country would be infinitely better off.*

Paddy Nolan took the matter to court, in a libel action against McGillicuddy. The judge found for Edwards, but took the occasion to scold Edwards for the *Eye Opener*'s "debasing and demoralizing content." Edwards came out of the trial thoroughly fed up and decided he'd had enough of Calgary. It was 1909. He tried Toronto for a while. He published the *Eye Opener* in both Port Arthur[13] and later in Winnipeg. By 1911 McGillicuddy and the *Calgary Daily News* were out of business, and when his friends convinced Calgary Bob that he was needed, he realized that Calgary was where he belonged, and back he came.

When Paddy Nolan died two years later, in 1913, it was weeks before Edwards could bring himself to write about the loss of his best friend.

Well might it be said of Paddy that in life he always left

---

13. Now Thunder Bay.

them laughing when he said good-bye. In this last good-
bye of all, tears take the place of laughter.

In 1914 there were dramatic changes on the horizon. Edwards tried to enlist when World War I broke out, but he was too old, and his chronic drinking was well known. The gathering Prohibition movement would have seemed a likely subject for his scorn and ridicule, but it did not turn out to be so. Hugh Dempsey argues that this might have been foreseen.

> *When he missed two or three editions of his paper because he*
> *was on an extended drunk, he knew he was letting his sub-*
> *scribers and his followers down. At a time like that he would*
> *dry out. Actually there were some occasions when his*
> *friends came to him when he was in this drunk state, and*
> *said, "You know, Bob, you need help." And they would*
> *actually take him to his favorite place, the Banff Sanatorium.*
> *And he would come out and seemingly stay sober for a while*
> *and [soon] drift back to his friends at the bar.*

"No man," he wrote, "can appreciate the best of it until he has got the worst of it a few times. And don't we, the writer, know it!" He was talking about the drinking. "When a man is driven to drink," he added, "he usually has to walk back." As the Woman's Christian Temperance Movement gathered on the Prohibition front, he began to support them. He ran a cartoon of a stout man with surprised eyes and a bushy moustache collapsing helplessly into bed clutching a whisky bottle, and captioned it "Why the *Eye Opener* does not come out more often."

When Paddy Nolan reminded him that the teetotal R.B. Bennett was a Tory who hated the Liberals as much as he did, and that he might be an ally in the fight for Prohibition, Edwards agreed to come to a dinner that Nolan would host, and the boozy editor and abstemious future prime minister of Canada became good friends after all. "That man would annoy a saint at times," Edwards wrote, "but he has a fine intellect and I'm fascinated."

In 1915 the province was preparing for a referendum on Prohibition. Hugh Dempsey speculates that

Bob Edwards initially felt that this was the answer, maybe not for him. I think he'd liked to have thought it was for him, but certainly for the people of the West. And he saw the bars as being very, very destructive to the western Canadian family and western Canadian society.

Jennifer Bobrovitz, convinced like many of Edwards' fans that his support of the Prohibition movement was part of his personal struggle, said that his old friends the hotel-keepers decided they could bring him around to a more practical posture.

Foolishly, they went to Bob Edwards and offered him, I think it was, $15,000 — some ridiculous amount of money — to stop supporting prohibition and to come out on their side. And that was their mistake, because Edwards was not the person to be . . . you couldn't buy him; and so the fact that you wanted to, offended him so deeply.

Jennifer Bobrovitz added poignantly, "In many ways, the very poignant narratives that he wrote about [alcohol] were about himself." Edwards wrote, "There is death in the cup, and if this Act [banning the sale of drink] is likely to have the effect of dashing the cup from the drunkard's hand, for God's sake let us vote for it." The Act passed. As in other parts of North America the immediate result was an increase in the criminal purveying of drink and no discernible positive effect. Edwards was dismayed. Perhaps it is a measure of the depth of his own alcoholic anguish that he had expected so much from a simple draconian solution to a profoundly complex social and behavioural problem. But now his journalistic and realistic side came to the fore, and he began to depict bootleggers as monsters, and to rethink the whole Prohibition issue. But he was still publicly scolding drink and drinkers. He wrote, as Calgary was preparing to send a battalion to France, that there should be a battalion of bartenders:

The bartenders have shown such success in killing off men at home, they ought to be able to kill off at least an equal number of the enemy abroad.

But the evidence against Prohibition was too strong to ignore and in the end he came totally around to the other side, and campaigned for its repeal. He also campaigned for votes for women. "Here's to women," he wrote,

once our superiors, now our equals. It is our firm conviction that blending of women's ideas with those of reasonably thoughtful men will someday bring about an era of common sense.

At fifty-four he was a bachelor, and most supposed him to be sexually neutral, or at least indifferent. About marriage he had written,

The saddest and funniest thing on earth is to hear two people promising at the altar with perfectly straight faces . . . to feel, think and believe for the rest of their lives exactly as they do at that minute.

So when a notice appeared one day in the *Eye Opener*, saying that "A certain newspaperman in Calgary got married the other day. . . . When a man is in love for the first time, he thinks he invented it," even his close friends were astounded. His bride, Kate Penman, was twenty years old. He published another cartoon of himself leaning back in the famous armchair, puffing cigar smoke at the ceiling, and thinking up the next surprise, with a caption that read, "Ho Hum! I wonder how they'll like the second reel."

The second reel turned out to be another surprise. Having sensed the excitement of campaigning for social reform, he finally gave in to the persuasion of some Conservative Party friends, including R.B. Bennett, and ran for a seat in the provincial legislature. In the end he decided that he would run not as a party man, but as an independent. "I'll go in clean and I'll come out clean," he said. His campaign consisted of a single one-minute speech. He hadn't really needed even that. He was ahead in the polls from the moment he announced, and he won handily. To nobody's surprise, while he served diligently and advanced some of the social justice issues that were dear to him, the disciplines of party politics he found burdensome, and at the end of only one session of conscientious attendance in the legislature, he stepped down.

There was still no shortage of issues to be addressed. His scope had become more national. He advocated old age pensions, minimum wage laws, public hospitals, schoolbooks with Canadian stories, and the abolition of the Senate. He applauded the earnest courage and humility of social activists like Nellie McClung. By now the *Eye Opener* was being read from Halifax to Vancouver, but there would be only a few more issues. Just about a year after he resigned from the legislature, a lifetime of neglecting his health caught up with him. A nasty flu laid him low, and his heart could not take the stress. On November 14th, 1922, the wire services flashed the word across Canada: "Bob Edwards is dead."

But his spirit is not. For example, until about thirty-five years ago, parliamentary reporting in the nation's capital tended to be deferential, most correspondents allying themselves to one or the other of the major parties, and very few seriously challenging the statements of Important People like Ministers of the Crown — at least not in person. My colleague Douglas Leiterman, a Press Gallery reporter for Southam Press before he came to CBC Television, used to laugh about the times when he would challenge a minister during a press conference, saying something like, "But Mr. Minister that's a contradiction of what you said two weeks ago," whereupon his Press Gallery colleagues would frown and nudge him and suggest that he should cool it or they might lose access. This seems absurd now, given the aggressiveness of the "scrum" in the halls of Parliament. But that aggressiveness represents a relatively recent change of style in parliamentary journalism, one that Bob Edwards would have admired.

About fifty years after his death, a group of Calgarians decided to revive the memory of his puncturing the pompous, and created a foundation that presents a Bob Edwards award for journalism at an annual Bob Edwards luncheon. Here the premier of the day can expect to be skewered ("Neither Mr. Klein nor Mr. Woloshyn could be here today. They didn't want to lose their place in line for their MRIs," said the actor playing Bob Edwards at a recent Edwards lunch). The Bob Edwards award is for uncompromising journalism or commentary, and a succession of well-known reporters and commentators have been so honoured. The recipients treasure the accolade sufficiently that many of them reconvened in Calgary, from all over the country, when the twenty-fifth anniversary lunch was celebrated two years ago.

It is appropriate to give the last word to Edwards himself:

> *Lord, let me keep a straight face in the presence of solemn asses. Keep me sane but not too sane. Let me condemn no man because of his grammar and no woman on account of her morals, neither being responsible for either. Let me be healthy while I live, but not live too long. Which is about all for today, Lord. Amen.*

The recipients of the Eye Opener Award, since its inception in 1977, have been the following:

Grant MacEwan 1977
W.O. Mitchell 1978
James Gray 1979
Jack Peach 1980
James MacGregor 1981
Hugh Dempsey 1982
Pierre Berton 1983
Andy Russell 1984

Margaret Atwood 1985

René Lévesque 1986

David Suzuki 1987

Patrick Watson 1988

Peter C. Newman 1989

Allan Fotheringham 1990

June Callwood 1991

Jack Webster 1992

Knowlton Nash 1993

Mordecai Richler 1994

Lise Bissonnette 1995

John Ralston Saul 1996

Peter Gzowski 1997

Carol Shields 1998

Guy Vanderhaeghe 2000

Timothy Findley 2001

◆　◆　◆

The original documentary was written and directed by Brian Dooley. It was photographed by Dwayne Dorland, with sound by Roger Southgate, Larry MacDonald, Carey Opper, and Mike Beley, and edited by Marke Slipp.

Part Eleven

BILLY HUNT
THE GREAT FARINI

A drive down the main street of Port Hope, Ontario, leaves
the visitor little doubt as to what part of Canada this is. The
solid brick public buildings, the side streets with a mix of
frame and brick houses, spreading trees, a touch of the old
United Empire Loyalist architecture here and there, and
you sense: Southern Ontario. No Question. You would
have to dig a little deeper to find the extraordinary number
of distinguished and creative people associated with what
looks on the surface to be a good solid commercial and
slightly touristy town — a small city technically — with its
yacht and tennis clubs, a retirement town for a fair number
of Toronto folk (it's just over an hour east of Metro), busy
but not driven, easy-going, you would guess. The author
Farley Mowat has made his home close by for forty years
or so. The pioneer television director R.J. (Paddy) Sampson
retired here. David Lloyd Blackwood, the Newfoundland-
born artist, has been teaching art here at Trinity College
School for almost forty years. Canada's first native-born
governor general, Vincent Massey, was born in Port Hope
in 1887, and Joseph Scriven, who wrote the words to the
world's best-known and most sung Christian hymn,
"What a Friend We Have in Jesus," preached in its streets
and died by drowning in a local stream.

It was a town that seemed secure, stable, conservative,
to its nineteenth-century immigrants, which is what

Thomas Hunt was looking for when he arrived from England in the early 1830s to take up farming and start a family. In Port Hope he met Hannah Soper. They married in 1835 in St. Mark's Anglican Church, and three years later, on their farm not far from town, she gave birth to William, an infant whose energy was astounding from the moment he opened his lungs for that first breath and first ear-splitting yell.

Playwright and theatrical producer Shane Peacock, author of a biography of William Hunt, concluded that the boy made life difficult for his rather stern and inflexible father, because from his earliest days he demonstrated a reckless adventurousness that seemed alien to the father, as if this were a child out of a different nest.[14] Young Billy was not only a daring and successful athlete from his first days in school, but also a brilliant student. When a circus came to town, parading down the then dusty and unpaved main street with eight Indian elephants leading the way, young Billy Hunt had been told in no uncertain terms that he would not be attending the event under the Big Top. We have to suppose that there was a blind spot somewhere in Thomas Hunt's understanding of his wilful son — or that he knew very well there was no way of keeping Billy out of the circus, but that he had to attach at least a modicum of guilt to this unseemly entertainment.

It was 1852. Bill Hunt had just turned fourteen. The travelling troupe was Pentland's Equestrian Circus. It was

14. For Shane Peacock's prolific work on Farini and other southern Ontario figures, check the various web sites that turn up by entering the name Farini in any good search engine.

a classical three-ring, big tent affair with wild animals, clowns and acrobats; William Hunt, years later, would claim that before the day was over he knew what he wanted to do with his life.

He went home and set up a short tight wire near the barn, just a few inches off the ground to begin with. He discovered to his delight that walking on it, without even a balancing pole to steady him, was surprisingly easy. He made a little trapeze as well, and practised on it until he felt he had it under control. But it was the image of a slim young man in tights, seemingly hundreds of feet up in the air above the crowd, that he could not get out of his mind, and he simply had to find a way to put up a high wire.

When Thomas Hunt drove his buggy into the yard and saw Bill walking on a wire fixed to the roof of the barn, a line so thin it almost looked as though the boy were suspended in mid-air, the dour farmer was outraged. This was no way for an intelligent young man to behave; it was sheer folly. There were words. But young Bill had a way with words too. Before long Thomas Hunt found himself agreeing to a compromise. The boy would be allowed to continue fooling around with this high-wire nonsense if he would also commit to completing school and then apprentice to the local doctor and work towards becoming a professional physician. A deal was struck. The father may have supposed that ambition and good sense would prevail in time. This seems to be further evidence that he did not understand his son as well as he thought he did, but he was doing his duty as he understood, trying to give the boy a respectable way to make a living.

In the summer of 1859 Bill Hunt was twenty-one. He had kept the high wire rigged up on the barn, and practised on it diligently, but he had kept his word about the medical career too — so far — and would soon write his first formal medical examinations. Thomas Hunt felt that things were sufficiently settled for him to turn his attention to other matters, and left for England on a business trip. He was scarcely out of sight when the young man was approached by a committee from Port Hope who were busy organizing the coming agricultural fair. They had heard about the aerial adventures, and thought that something like that might add a bit of thrill to the usual strawberry jam contests and cattle judging. So out they went to the Hunt farm to see what he could do. They found more than they had expected. The rope angling up from the ground became almost invisible at the point where it stretched along the peak of the barn roof, so that it was like a man walking in the sky. Author Shane Peacock said:

I don't think they were quite prepared for what they saw the day that they went out to the Hunt barn in Hope Township and watched him, because he got on his little rope and went up from the ground to the top of the barn, carried a friend of his on his back, stood on his head and they were just astounded at what they saw.

They proposed that he walk across the Ganaraska River in the centre of Port Hope. He had read about an Italian daredevil named Signor Farini, and decided to adopt that name for the stunt. He put up his rope at night from one four-storey building to another seventy feet above the Ganaraska River. A fall would be crippling, even fatal. *The Tri-Weekly Guide* announced the event in the October 1st edition.

> *This afternoon at 4 o'clock, Signor Farini will make a grand ascension, as the phrase runs, on a tightrope, stretched across the creek from the brick buildings on either side of the stream, north of Walton Street Bridge.*

To give the documentary viewer a concrete example of what this meant, the producers went with a contemporary high-wire man, Jay Cochrane, and videotaped his successful attempt to duplicate that long-ago performance of "Signor Farini." Cochrane says that his own career as an aerialist began in much the same way as his predecessor's.

> *When I was about seven or eight years old, my mother took me to my first circus and I saw a man by the name of Helldosana. It was in Sudbury, Ontario. He did a somersault on a wire about twenty-five feet high, a backward somersault, and I said to my mother, I said, "Mother, that's what I'm gonna do when I grow up." And she said, "Oh no, you're not." I said, "Yes, I am, that's what I'm gonna do." I think it's a God-given talent, I do, but it also takes hard work. If you have the love for it, that is part of the talent and it'll follow, you know you just follow your dream. It's what I've always wanted to do and I'm living out a little boy's dream.*

Our television director mounted a tiny pencil-camera on Cochrane's chest, so that we could see what the Great Farini would have seen, looking down as he made the crossing reported next day in the *Tri-Weekly Guide*:

> *Pursuant to announcement, Signor Farini, on Saturday*

afternoon, walked on a tight rope stretched across the creek. The ascension was advertised to take place at 4 o'clock but so great was public curiosity, that as early as 3 o'clock, a crowd began to collect on the Walton Street Bridge and in every place from which a view of the rope could be obtained. At five minutes to 4 o'clock, Signor Farini made his appearance at the western end of his rope. He was attired in silk tights and the other usual clothing of acrobats. Grasping his balancing pole firmly in his hands, he stepped confidently out upon the rope and commenced his journey. He walked slowly, but steadily, reaching the building on the east side in safety and amid the cheers of the assembled crowds.

The members of the agricultural fair committee were more than satisfied. Farini had stood on his head, hung by his heels, and walked the high wire with and without his balancing pole. It was the largest crowd in the town's history. While most of the crowd believed they had been visited by a famous Italian daredevil, the aerialist's real identity was somehow conveyed to his father in England, and when Thomas stepped off the train at the Port Hope station a few weeks later, the son met him, hoping that the spectacular success of his adventure might win him paternal approval at last. It did not. Farini wrote about it later:

My father said, "I am grieved by what you had done. The news was a great shock to me and now, instead of being penitent for the shameful manner in which you have repaid my kindness and care, you delight in having disgraced your family by becoming a low common mountebank!" Scalding tears of anger started from my eyes as I went forth

*into the open air. I would not darken my father's doors
again. Mountebank though I was, the world lay before me.*[15]

The young man must have had superb self-confidence. A few months later, learning that the famed French acrobat Blondin was going to string a wire across the gorge at Niagara Falls, Bill Hunt, now and for the rest of his life Farini, decided to turn it into a contest. He arrived at the Falls in July, 1860. Blondin promoted himself by saying that nobody else in the world could ever perform such a stupendous feat as walking a wire across the Niagara Gorge. Farini was offended by the hyperbole. He knew, as all tightrope walkers do, that the actual physical skill is something that most healthy young people can master. If you string a line thirty centimetres off the ground you can very soon learn to walk along it quite smoothly, even without a pole. A century and a quarter later, when she discovered who her famous forebear was, Farini's great-great-great-grandniece, Rashmi Baird of Port Hope, got *her* father to set up a line for her, in the garage. She speaks of the sport as if it were, well, something pretty well *anyone* could do.

*The first time I realized I, I had maybe a chance or that
maybe it was in the blood or something, was when I was
probably about nine. So, that's when the research started
for me and I became interested. I was — wanted to do
what he did. I love it and that's one of those things that
surges up the middle and I'm sure I'm supposed to be*

---

15. Today he might have said "Snake oil salesman." *The Shorter Oxford English Dictionary,* 1933, gives, for *mountebank*: "An itinerant quack who appealed to his audience by means of stories, tricks, juggling and the like, often with the assistance of a professional clown."

doing it. It feels natural.

That 1860 Niagara Falls affair was a return engagement for Blondin, whose crossing point was actually about
a mile downstream where the gorge was 800 feet wide.
Farini believed he could do much better, and chose one of
the widest parts of the gorge, just below the falls, a stretch
of about 1,800 feet. Nobody would ever walk a longer rope
across that gorge. Author Shane Peacock says that the
French acrobat was taken by surprise:

> *[He] was absolutely stunned to see that this guy, this*
> *twenty-two-year-old guy who had been practising on a*
> *high rope for ten months and really was only like a semi-*
> *pro, was actually going to take him on.*

The Niagara Falls historian Bruce Aikin took us to
where Farini's rope was positioned, not far from the site of
Clifton House, and pointed to a clearing on the American
side where he believes the other end, the starting point, was
secured. The two rivals had agreed to do their walks on the
same day, supposing that the double event would draw
bigger crowds. And so the self-taught kid from Port Hope
and the world's most storied acrobat of the age squared off
against each other, on August 15th. At ten minutes to four
in the afternoon Farini got into a horse-drawn carriage at
the American Hotel in Niagara Falls, New York, and was
taken to the wooden platform next to his long, drooping,
1,800-foot cable. Shane Peacock describes the next phase:

> *So he started out holding this enormous balancing pole and*
> *he went down, of course he starts descending immediately*
> *as he went down on his rope, probably a little bit frightened*
> *although he claimed that he wasn't. Now then he went out*

*a little bit further and I think he knew he had to do some-
thing spectacular at this point to really show them that he
was capable, so when he got out about 100 feet . . . he put
his head down to the rope and stood on his head.*

But that was just to get the motor running — and perhaps send some runners over to the Blondin site to lure
audiences back to this spectacular newcomer. He next
hung by his hands, then by one hand, then by his feet, and
of course by one foot. He had carried a separate coil of rope
around his waist, and as he began to work his way back
towards the American side, when he came directly above
the tourist steamer *The Maid of The Mist,* he tied the second
rope onto the main line, lowered it to the boat, climbed
down that line to the deck, drank a ceremonial glass of
wine, and then started back up. The return climb was
almost too much. He was trembling with fatigue — or at
least that is what everyone saw — when he finally pulled
himself, agonizingly slowly, onto the main line.

When he stepped ashore, the applause was deafening,
from both sides of the river. In the meantime, a couple of
miles downstream, Blondin made a flawless crossing on
his taut 800-foot cable. Critics said that Farini was more
terrifying to watch on his unstable slack wire, but reported
that the French aerialist was more elegant. The audiences,
however, voted with their feet and their pocketbooks.
Farini's crowds were substantially bigger than Blondin's
and he made more money when the hat was passed. It was
the greatest slack-wire performance on record, said the
Niagara Falls Gazette: "But we never wish to see another
such performance by any rope walker. For however the

performer may consider himself, there is no pleasure to the beholder." Farini was delighted; now the crowds would have to come. Blondin must have been outraged at the upstart's success.

For the rest of the season they had a high-wire duel. Blondin on his taut 800-foot cable; Farini on his 1,800-foot slack rope. When Blondin carried a stove on his back and cooked eggs, Farini carried out a washing machine and did his laundry. When Blondin took a man on his back, Farini carried a taller and a heavier man. Farini began pushing the duel into truly dangerous territory. Blondin made a crossing with a sack over his head. Farini cut armholes in a full-length glazed cambric bag and started down the initial sloping part of his slack wire, slipped, almost went into the gorge, recovered, made it to the centre, and did a head-stand with the sack blowing in the wind. A reporter wrote, "He looked like a small sail spread to the breeze."

In September, the Prince of Wales visited the Falls, saw a Blondin performance, and was quoted as saying, "Thank God, it's over," when it ended. He did not see Farini. As they drove by the Canadian end of the slack wire, it is said that he asked the head of his party, the Duke of Newcastle, what that was, *that* the duke replied, "A pathway for another fool." Farini supporters said that was pretty unfair to Farini — he was, after all, a Canadian and the prince should have taken the time to see him too. But fools or not, Prince of Wales or no Prince of Wales, while Blondin had again proved himself a legendary performer, Farini had consistently drawn larger crowds and made more money.

He went back to Port Hope for a visit. He offended his

father once again by going around in the clothes of a dandy
— the "mountebank." He met a young woman and fell in
love. Her name was Mary Osborne. She is cryptically
referred to as "an unconventional woman," and that could
simply refer to her decision to run off with the mountebank,
and marry him, or could also reflect the fact that before long
she was part of the mountebank's act. The following summer they both turn up in Niagara Falls, Farini announcing
that he will carry his bride across the falls and back. It never
happened. Niagara Falls was having a dreadful season; a
depression was keeping tourists away; *The Maid of the Mist*
was not operating. Clearly there was no money to be made
there that season. Why they chose their next destination is
not known, but they headed for Cuba.

Havana then had a bullring that seated 30,000, an
ideal venue for the wire-walker. They stretched the rope
between masts, over the heads of the crowd and all the
way across the stadium. Biographer Shane Peacock
described what happened next:

> *Mary was on his back. They started to cross, they per-*
> *formed all their routines and when he got to the end, for*
> *some reason, Mary Osborne acknowledged the applause of*
> *the audience and turned and waved to them. And that is a*
> *cardinal sin for somebody being carried on a high-wire*
> *walker's back. And at that instant, she slipped and fell*
> *from his back. And as she started to fall, he allowed him-*
> *self to go with her and he hooked one of his legs around the*
> *wire, reached down and grabbed the hem of her dress,*
> *caught her and was actually at that point, saving her. But*
> *slowly the dress ripped out of his hands and she fell down*

to the seats and he watched her spiral all the way down
and crashed, headfirst, into the seats.

Five days later she died. Farini had her buried in a prominent Catholic cemetery. Her funeral was a major social event. In his grief Farini converted to the Catholic faith, had himself baptized as Guillermo, the Spanish equivalent of his given name. The Cuban who stood in for him as godfather was a man named Antonio; Farini added that name to his new christening.

A rumour began to be whispered about: that he and Mary had had a little son. For a while Farini disappeared from sight, but in the early summer of 1864, he surfaced in New York City and played one of P.T. Barnum's theatres, the Hypotriathon. He added a trapeze number to the act, and some strongman feats. He called himself — his own coinage, perhaps to fit the Greek theme of Barnum's theatre — a "Pangymnastikon Aerostationist." Later that summer he was back at Niagara Falls, trying to walk across the shallow brim of the American falls, just above the cataract, on stilts. On August 8th he climbed up on the stilts, stepped into the rapids, and started out. Less than halfway across, one of the stilts got stuck in an underwater crevice. Farini could not free it. Whether he fell into the water or jumped for it is not clear, but the crowd watched as he was swept towards the brink, reached out for the trailing branch of a tree on one of the tiny outcrop islands, and pulled himself up onto the rocks.

He was marooned on that island long enough for the *New York Times* to print a story about it, and crowds came to see what they thought would be a man starving to

death. There seemed no way to get him ashore, until someone thought to float a rope to him somehow, and he was
pulled safely on land.

He next turns up in London performing with El Niño,
whom he claimed was a street kid he had found in Boston.
The act is now called the Flying Farinis. There was speculation that the child might be the natural son of Farini and
the late Mary Osborne. Farini formally adopted the boy,
gave him his name and a prominent role in his life from
then on. El Niño was beautiful, with silky blond curls. On
stage, he seemed as daring as his adopted father. He flew
forty feet through the air from trapeze to trapeze. His photograph sold by the thousands, and a reporter for the *Daily
Telegraph* was captivated.

> *A boy scarcely eight years old went a height which it
> would be painful to contemplate, takes some astounding
> flights, and plays a remarkable solo on the drum while
> swinging through the air with his head bent back over the
> bar of a trapeze. The gracefulness of the child does much to
> lessen the feeling of peril attached to the performance. But
> there is a general sense of relief in witnessing his descent
> in safety.*

In August, the flying Farinis were booked into the
Royal Alhambra Palace, and their success was sensational.
A popular composer, Robert Coote, put out a new waltz
entitled, "The Farini." The act toured England and Ireland
for the next few years. When they came to the legendary
Crystal Palace in 1867, they played to 22,000 people at a time.

Early in 1870, about to turn thirty-two and financially
very successful, Farini went into seclusion for a few weeks,

to consider whether he should, at that ripe old age, continue with these on-the-edge stunts. He took El Niño with him to Marseilles, grew a theatrically cultured black beard, stayed out of sight, and planned the next incarnation. It was not long in coming.

Lu Lu, "The Eighth Wonder of the World," first appeared on stage on July 29th, 1870, at the 4,000-seat Imperatrice Theatre on the Champs Elysées. When Farini's newest partner, this blond, blue-eyed, allegedly sixteen-year-old beauty, came forward and suddenly leapt twenty-five feet into the air, there was a moment of stunned silence before the house came to its feet applauding. *How had she done it!* She settled lightly onto the carpeted seat of a trapeze. *L'Avenir National* wrote that she was like *un vase de crystal*, that her graceful, inexplicable faërie ascent was something from a dream. Lu Lu had her London debut a few months later at the Royal Holborn Amphitheatre. This time the Prince of Wales did come. The act toured England for a while, then crossed back to North America and played New York, Chicago, Philadelphia — everywhere to the same astonishment and delight as this graceful girl rose so mysteriously into the air. Did she leap? Did she fly? There were no wires, that was clear. And she was so beautiful. Men lined up at the stage door with flowers, but after the performances Lu Lu seemed to disappear.

When they came back to England in 1872, Farini married, in Portsmouth, a grocer's daughter named Alice Carpenter (with whom he would have two sons, William Jr. and Harry). The best man at the wedding was the performer the world had come to know as Lu Lu, who was in fact the same person earlier known to audiences as El Niño. This, however, was a family affair, and the world did not learn the truth about Lu Lu until she was nearly killed in Ireland, in 1876, and had to be examined by doctors at the Trinity College Hospital. That day in Dublin Lu Lu missed the trapeze bar at the zenith of that amazing leap, and crashed to the floor. There was pandemonium in the theatre, and then something of a scandal in the press after the doctor's discovery was reported.

But Lu Lu recovered, and, impudently playing the new gender ambiguity theme, they kept the act going for a few years more. In the 1880s Niño/Lu Lu played a New York date wearing glasses, a moustache, and a fetching female costume. He would later marry and raise a daughter.

The Royal Westminster Aquarium, a huge entertainment palace in the centre of London, had begun as an institution to educate the masses, but ran into financial difficulties. The managers asked Farini to see what could be done to keep it going, and it was here that he tried out his next innovation: the human cannonball. This time his projectile would be a real girl, Rosa Matilda Ricktor. They called her Zazel, and, like Lu Lu before her, she became a reliable audience draw, bursting out of the cloud of smoke as the cannon went off, and soaring across the stadium floor to land safely in a net amid roars from the delighted crowds. Today the act still fools some spectators into thinking that the acrobat has been fired into the air by an explosive charge.

In reality what Farini had invented was an elaboration of the technique that had propelled the Eighth Wonder of the World up to her carpeted trapeze: a powerful spring-activated catapult. In Lu Lu's case, as she walked to her take-off point in the ring she was masked from the knees down by a low curtain wall or skirt that concealed the tiny sprung platform. When Farini released a concealed catch a burst of smoke and a roll of the drums and crashing of cymbals effectively masked the spring's discharge, and what the audience *saw* — and completely believed, was the graceful young acrobat lightly bending her knees, as if for a normal balletic leap of two or three feet, only to keep on her skyward track all the way up to that trapeze. This time it would be a much longer travel — several feet along the inside of the barrel of what looked like a huge cannon — building up enough speed to send the daring Zazel along a parabolic path of more than a hundred feet, wreathed in smoke as a spectacular smoke charge of no propulsive value whatsoever was released just before she emerged from the muzzle of the "cannon."

They began to call Farini the "Father of the Big Thrill Acts." His working drawings for that cannon have survived in the patent office. Zazel became as big a star as Lu Lu; she was even the subject of a comic opera. Soon it was rumoured that the black-bearded Farini had a whole stable of Zazels — in case one lost her nerve or got killed.

Not everyone was delighted by the mysterious signor. In March 1880, a British MP named Edward Jenkins proposed to Parliament the *Dangerous Performances Act*, intended to stop the growing and scandalous evil of Farini's thrilling shows. The Act was never passed, but England began to seem less hospitable. Farini went through a messy divorce from Alice. It seemed a good time to leave. He gathered up his best acts, went to America and joined P.T. Barnum in "The Greatest Show on Earth."

The Greatest Show on Earth was arguably pretty well what it said it was, and Zazel was its star. She packed them in for a long run in New York and then played to as many as 10,000 a night in the big travelling tent.

And then it was time for that restless imagination to try something else. The next stunt seems to suddenly transform him from a showman into a charlatan. He found a young dwarf almost as hirsute as an ape, and billed her as Darwin's Missing Link. He had become a freak-show man. When the Zulu wars became front-page news, he staged Zulu war dances. He seemed to have sunk to the level that his father had feared, but at the same time he became genuinely fascinated with Africa, and it was that continent that generated the last (and some say still unsolved) mystery of Farini's career: the Lost City.

In 1885 Lu Lu/El Niño, was the proprietor of Farini Photographs in Bridgeport, Connecticut, when his father showed up and proposed a trip to the Kalahari Desert. They were there for six months, and Farini produced a book about it, *Through the Kalahari Desert*. In that book he claimed he had found the ruins of an ancient civilization. There are stories about people going out into the desert and falling asleep and waking up and seeing Farini's lost city and falling asleep again, never to see it again. The lost city is probably as fraudulent as Farini's missing link, but an American named Lee Haldeman has tried nineteen times to find it. He told our camera that the lost city is still lost, but that

> *You are always in a situation that you believe it's just over the next sand dune. The area is vast, you're looking at hundreds of thousands of square kilometres that have to be searched and you're trying to translate ox-wagon miles into today's terms, and you're using these vague descriptions of, say, "for three days they travelled west." Now that might be northwest or southwest — and you sort of have to guess in which direction the lost city might be.*

The Kalahari's secrets are (some would say "Alas!") open to the penetrating eye of the satellites today; if there were a walled city there it would have been mapped by now. There is a famous ancient walled city, Great Zimbabwe, a couple of hundred miles north of the Kalahari, which Farini may have heard about and allowed his fancy to play with. But Lee Haldeman is not satisfied with any of the reasonable explanations: He says:

> *Now, if you are the type of showman that Farini appears to have been, you would have made it much more spectacular, maybe pyramids or underground caverns and gold and diamonds and things like that — rather than just a rock wall, which also lends credence to Farini's explanation of the lost city.*

Invention or discovery, Farini returned to England, published his book, and went on to other things. He married again, a German woman of aristocratic bearing, Anna Muller. Fifteen years his junior, and said to be a relative of Wagner and a student of Franz Liszt, she was also alleged to have been raised in the court of the kaiser. Farini began to settle down and to focus on business, investing in railways and other stocks. He bought a genteel house south of London, and became co-owner of one of the world's most successful theatrical agencies, Richard Warners.

The Big Thrill Acts were still a field in which he was as clever and experienced as the best. In 1888 he brought an American aeronaut named Thomas Baldwin to the Alexander Palace, north of London, to jump out of a hot air balloon at 3,000 feet. Baldwin descended to earth wearing a device that, while it had been successfully used in Paris a century earlier, was still little known: the parachute. Baldwin seems to have been the first to use silk for the canopy, and had been demonstrating it in the United States before Farini brought him to London. He made fifteen exhibition jumps that season, and the stunt drew hundreds of thousands of spectators. It is possible that Farini tried to take some credit for the parachute's design, and conceivable that he had in fact made a contribution; he had been inventing things since childhood. In 1890, the profession he gave to the census takers was "inventor." He has been given credit for creating the circus safety net. He actually patented not only the human cannonball, but also the Lu Lu Leap. He invented folding theatre chairs, improvements in firearms, and machines to pack bottles into cartons. He tried botany and developed new strains of begonias. But the Baldwin parachute stunts marked the end of his life as a showman.

Perhaps it was just the passage of time. Harry, one of his two sons with Alice, had died. Britain's charms had run dry. It was time to go home. The Farinis left England for good and moved to Toronto. Here he became involved in one of the strangest inventions in the history of Canadian innovation. He had exchanged notes and design sketches for a revolutionary boat, the roller boat, with a man named Fred Knapp. The idea was that a vessel that rolled along the surface of the water instead of having to plough through it would not have to deal with all that resistance that keeps a displacement hull from exceeding a certain speed. It was — to say the least — a complicated design and engineering challenge, since the passenger and freight compartments of the boat would have to be suspended within the rolling cylinder without themselves rolling. Who actually deserves the credit for this preposterous idea, Knapp or Farini, is a matter of some dispute. Knapp actually built one, and both he and Farini took out patents in 1906. The thing was a dismal failure, although the idea has been revived in various forms since — including an aerial version — but never successfully. On its first sea trials, the Knapp/Farini prototype ran aground not far from Port Hope and lay there until it fell to pieces. Farini probably lost some money on it, and it was his last fling at invention. Now he turned to painting. Port Hope sculptor Ron Baird said that he was pretty bad at it.

The astonishing thing about Farini's painting is that he was a very worldly man. He was sophisticated, and yet he never learned anything about painting. His series of sixty or so paintings based on ethnic costumes — it never gets any better, just one painting after another, after another and they are all the same quality, exactly. I think his painting was pretty well consistently dreadful.

In 1910, the seventy-two-year-old dreadful painter

and his wife moved again, this time to Europe, to be closer to her family. Farini painted and sculpted, soaked up the atmosphere, and somehow managed to weather the war as a Canadian alien living in the kaiser's Germany. In 1920, he and Anna left Germany. Now, after a lifetime of wandering, an aging Billy Hunt really did go home to Hope Township where he still owned some property with a house on it. Moving into it turned out to be difficult. Farini's living niece, Thelma Saunders, told us:

My cousin Lucia was in the house and she wouldn't have Anna and Farini. She said she'd be a servant to them and she didn't want that, so they stayed out in the tent. But of course, with the colder weather coming, they moved into Port Hope.

One of Farini's neighbours in Port Hope was the then ten-year-old Norman Strong, who still remembered, almost eighty years later:

I used to see him ever so many times and I was surprised and astounded. He looked so small and so slight, and he found time, when I would be out cutting grass, to stop and talk to me. And he'd keep complimenting me on doing such a good job. . . . He was a very human being in spite of his notoriety. At my age, we thought it was wonderful, but apparently some of the old people thought that he was too famous.

William Leonard Hunt, *The Great Farini*, Guillermo Antonio Farini, exercised every day and rode his bicycle all around Port Hope. He worked outdoors till he was ninety. They said he was fit as a boy. If he missed the high life and the old times, he didn't show it, although he would tell great tales and always had time for children. In January of

1929, in his ninety-first year, he caught pneumonia and was taken to the Port Hope Hospital. His great-grand-nephew, Ted Hunt, said,

I don't think until Shane [Peacock] started to research, I'd ever heard the story about my uncle Ted and my father going to see him the day before he died and him sitting, you know, bolt upright and steady in his bed reading a newspaper, and saying that an old gypsy woman told him that he would live to be a hundred. And this . . . was the day before he died.

His funeral took place on a rainy winter day. The procession moved up Walton Street, past the place he had first performed on the high wire, three-quarters of a century before. Shane Peacock said,

In those days . . . people around Port Hope believed that children were to be seen and not heard. Farini didn't believe that. . . . He always had time for children. And who could resist an old gentleman who could tell you what it was like to stand on a high wire over Niagara Falls or to be shot out of a cannon. . . . And the story goes that when Farini died in Port Hope in 1929, and the children saw the casket going up Walton Street, they took off their hats as he went by.

◆　◆　◆

The original documentary was written by Shane Peacock and Andy Thompson and directed by Andy Thompson. It was photographed by Douglas Munro and edited by Wes Belair.

Part Twelve

LEON GIGLIO
MANDRAKE THE MAGICIAN

The man on stage appears to be about seventy years old, erect, gracious, lean but not thin, a handsome grey moustache, a twinkle in his eye. He is standing behind a table, on which are a one-gallon glass jug and a white silk handkerchief which has been draped into a cone, with a knot tied at the point of the cone so that it looks vaguely like a tiny dancer in a white robe with her head wrapped in a towel. The distinguished-looking man, who appears quite sane, is speaking to the handkerchief figure. There appears to be some tension between them.

"Come on, Katie. . ."

He pauses. The handkerchief has not responded.

But we now know that it is about to do so.

"Come on."

The handkerchief-figure suddenly 'looks up' at the magician, and then takes a faltering step towards him.

"Ahhh. That's better. You're back with us."

The tiny handkerchief person takes a more few tentative "steps" along the table. The magician picks up a steel hoop, about eight inches in diameter, and dangles it from his right finger, above and to our left of the dancing handkerchief like an acrobat's swinging hoop, and invites the handkerchief to jump through it.

The thing is that we *do know better! We are not children!* But under the charming spell of this lovely man, for a while we are children, and it is more comfortable to believe he is talking to the dancing handkerchief, and she listening to him, than it is to be rational, doubtful adults who know that it is only a trick.

"Come on, Katie. All right. Let's jump through the hoop."

The handkerchief makes a tentative leap towards the dangling hoop, but the steel ring is pretty high, after all, higher than the top of her head, and she doesn't quite make it.

"You're not doing at all well, Katie. Nice big jump now."

The hanky crouches, leaps, sits decorously on the hoop, then begins to swing euphorically on it, we almost think we can see her grinning, she jumps up on down on the hoop, begins to get a little indecorous.

"Well, now, don't knock yourself out, Katie. You're too old for that sort of thing. Come back over the hoop. That's the girl. There."

We are not only watching a fine magic trick, indeed a classic, but also a relationship. For decades now this man has been touring North America out of his homebase in Vancouver, enchanting small groups like this — kids and their parents — with small, intimate, believable little narratives about a princesslike handkerchief who dances and sulks, jumps into the gallon jug when she gets feeling provocative, escapes from it when he stuffs a cork in the neck of the jug to keep her in her place, and finally — the appearance of a conflict or contest between them being, well, you know, just *show* — she comes and sits on his wrist and takes her applause with him. This — for those of us who prefer our magic up-close and intimate — is

Mandrake at his best. And yet this man considered himself a stage magician first and foremost, played the big theatres, had his name in lights on the marquee, swirled onstage in his silk-lined cape and stunned the house with huge illusions and clouds of smoke and scantily clad showgirls vanishing and reappearing.

On the other hand, you could also find him sitting quietly in a senior's home in a small town, one the edge of somebody's chair, with nothing but a few coins and a deck of cards, chatting away as though he were one of the residents, but doing charming, amazing things with his few simple props. His real name was Leon Giglio. His professional name: Mandrake the Magician.

Everyone in North America over sixty will remember the comic strip. For about twenty years Mandrake the Magician was a popular syndicated feature whose hero in dapper evening clothes had a compelling eye and a hypnotic gesture that could compel evil criminals to think that their hands and arms had turned into giant poisonous snakes. The heroic magician travelled with a beautiful assistant named Narda and a gigantic, bald, silent man of colour, Lothar. Lothar, should Mandrake's powers ever fail, would use his prodigious strength to defeat the bad guys and protect his great master. The comic-strip magician had a sharp, narrow moustache and a cloak, and was seldom far from his top hat. He was syndicated in hundreds of newspapers across North America, the brainchild of Lee Falk, who brought the character to life in 1934, and sublet the actual drawing to Phil Davis who drew it for thirty years. Lee Falk died two years ago, but the comic strip is still syndicated by King. An artist named Fred Fredericks now draws Mandrake, and you can see the daily episodes on the King Features Syndicate's web site.

Some of Phil Davis's original artwork for Mandrake is offered for sale via the Internet for as high as $350 (US) per drawing. King Features Syndicate are the people who also brought us Popeye, Prince Valiant, Mary Worth, the Phantom, Rex Morgan M.D., and even the contemporary Sally Forth. King Features Syndicate has played a signal role in the formation of North American fantasy life.

Since the Mandrake comic strip has been in syndication for nearly seventy years, more people know the comic-strip character than ever saw the live magician who took his name. But at the height of his career his billboards advertised this man as America's Greatest Magician, although he grew up and indeed lived much of his life in British Columbia, where he died in 1993. He was born John Arthur Leon Giglio, at Dolphin Bay, Orcas Island, Washington, in 1911. His mother Harriet Jackson took him and his older half-brother brother Carl back to her home-town of New Westminster, BC, when Leon was still an infant. He said that his first great magician, the man who inspired him with a love of the craft, was a candy man at a circus midway who took a coin out of his ear and then made it disappear. The seven-year-old Leon got the bug. He worked for that candy man for a while, and was sent out to the ballpark to sell peanuts. He said that was where he learned to project his voice.

An aunt gave him a boxed set of magic tricks for kids, and he started practising in his room. The records show that he was first hired to perform on the stage of the old Edison Theatre in 1922, when he was eleven. He joked later that he was shaking so much during that first show that his knees were bruised from knocking together. He dropped stuff, and screwed up here and there, but there was a smattering of applause, so he went home moderately encouraged and continued to practise, practise, practise. For a while a rival theatre hired him, clumsiness and all, to compete with the Edison, and he would tell self-deprecating stories — after he was famous — about how the audiences would groan when he came on with the same old patter and the same awkward tricks. There wasn't a living in it, however, and young Leon had to start making a living. He hired on at a shingle mill.

When the carnival came to town that seemed closer than the shingle mill to where he wanted to be in life, so off he went and got a job in the midway. That was where his apprenticeship took place. Thirteen years old, and learning to *work* the crowd, picking up whatever the carnies would teach him, a bit of ventriloquism here, fire-eating there, card tricks, illusions. Among the junk and the trunks he found the wrecked remains of a mirror-based illusion, a "sword box." He dressed an old school chum in a blond wig and a false bosom and high heels (only at night, as the mirrors were in very bad shape) and called her Princess Thora (remember that name). Every once in a while some kid in the audience would call out, "That's not Princess Thora! That's Jackie Giles!"

The important part was that he learned to work the crowd, not lose your nerve, trust your patter. Although he left school after grade six, he used public libraries for the rest of his life, often visiting the local branch in a new town as soon he had checked into his hotel. In later life he sometimes encouraged young magicians to meet him at the library; that was where he had done his research, he told them, and looked for ideas.

He went to every vaudeville show he could find. Years later, in Hollywood's Magic Castle, it was the vaudeville shows that he recalled as being the turning point, the intimation of a way of life that the adolescent found irresistible. This is from a 1972 interview videotaped with Peter Pit, then the programmer at the Magic Castle:

Oh, the polish. Four shows a day every day and oohhh. And you're looking . . . it's a world of wonder and the girls are all beautiful and they're wearing red diamonds. You find out later they're called brilliants and they're a little cheaper than the real, real thing. But it doesn't matter. You know, it was a wonderland. And it's like you went through the looking glass, like Alice. So you sit there in your overalls and you paid a dime to get in, you know, you can sit through two or three shows. You don't see backstage, you don't see the travel, the thing, the business, nothing, you just see it and say, "Gee, that's for me."

Downtown in Vancouver the Orpheum was beginning to attract the really big names in magic, Thurston, Alexander the Man Who Knows, then Blackstone and Dante. Leon would scrape together the busfare and sit there in the dark lusting, lusting to *do that*. To *be those guys*. When he was about sixteen he got backstage at the Orpheum to meet a man named Ralph Richards, who billed himself as the Wizard. This perfomer's name was really Ralph Ennis, and he is said to have been a relative of the actor Sir Ralph Richardson. Leon talked himself into a job and went on the road with the Wizard's show for six months, but then the show folded, and the teenaged boy came home and enrolled in business school. He had realized that being slick on stage with a bunch of billiard balls and a fan was all very well, but you'd better know something about keeping books, paying bills, and setting something aside for emergencies. As wiz of a wiz as you wuz, you wouldn't keep on wizzing very long when the creditors came calling.

Bit by bit Leon Giglio assembled an act, some props, a tuxedo, a line of patter, a style, and enough confidence in the dreary woodwork of road shows that he could book a house, find the accommodations he could afford, get local kids to help on and off stage for free — for the glory — and keep out of trouble. He revelled in what he was getting to be really good at: charming the starch out of people with his apparently unstudied and spontaneous approach to the material, while in reality polishing, polishing, polishing, so that all that memorized patter would sound as spontaneous and natural as though he had only that moment thought of it. He prepared alternatives and attitudes for those moments when things went wrong. That is the test of a fine magician: that he can get himself out of trouble even when a prop has not been loaded or a sleight fails.

In 1935, not long after the first appearance of the Mandrake the Magician comic strip, Leon and a few other local entertainers took over the lease of a little joint on E.

Hastings Street, the Green Lantern, in return for picking up the $6 a month neon sign rental. He did magic, some ventriloquism, even a bit of dancing, and for a while he and his pals were able to pay the rent. Now the twenty-four year old began to feel he was a genuine professional, but he was on the threshold of the first of a series of disasters that would periodically assault his life. About a year after starting at the Green Lantern, he nearly died. He was thrown from a car in a collision, the car rolled over on him. He lost a kidney, and suffered such messy fractures to his left hip and leg that the doctors wanted to amputate. He refused. For a while he had to walk with a brace, and when he recovered he walked with a slight limp for the rest of his life. He had to give up the dancing, but he developed a more elaborate ventriloquist act, which allowed him to work sitting down.

The Green Lantern went broke and closed. Once recovered sufficiently to perform, Leon decided Vancouver was too small a stage, and went out on his own to build a career as a travelling entertainer. Over the next few years he would put together a little show, take it on the road as long as it was earning (and, at first, sometimes too much longer than that) and then come home to Vancouver and get a day job for a while if he had to. Then he would practice and plan some more until he could get another road show together. Getting a road show together and taking it out and making it work became his life. By all accounts he was never happier than when moving out a new show, whether it was one of the enormously elaborate later illusion shows, with tons of props and staging and a troupe of twenty or so

dancers, assistants and roustabouts — or just a little intimate piece, with himself and (later) his wife/assistant, and
Katie the Dancing Hank. If, to make ends meet, he had to
sell soap door to door or bus tables for a while in the hotel
where he was playing the current act, then so be it. Once he
was taken on as a maître d'hotel, not because he had any
experience but because he owned a tuxedo.

A magician friend, Dick Newton, who met him in
those grubby days, said:

*Working in cabarets, beer halls, with audiences that had
been drinking a lot and were even likely to toss something
at you if they didn't like you, was great training. And if
you could do well with those audiences, you could play
anywhere.*

It was a chimerical, unreal kind of life. A different
town every night, perhaps too much to drink, a constant
watchfulness for scoundrels, few people whom you could
trust. He began to feel that his family was disintegrating
His brother had committed suicide and his father died of a
heart attack. He was in need of some stabilizing human
contact, and he found it in the person of another performer

Bernard Abrams who spent years as Mandrake's tour
manager, was a magician playing those same circuits when
they met. They stayed friends for the rest of Leon's life.
When they were working the speakeasies and grubby little
nightclubs together, Abrams says that Leon was

*so versatile that he could take the place of two acts. In
those days when you were working in a nightclub and if
you were the master of ceremonies you went out and
stayed there for a half hour. And he would do master of*

ceremonies and magic and then he would do the ventrilo-
quist act, and then he could go on for hours because he was
sitting down. We got along fine because I was impressed
with his tricks, and he was impressed that I had a rabbit.

Packing along his cards and silks, his billiard balls and ropes, his "vent" dummies, and a couple of small "boxes" (as magicians call the kind of illusion where the girl steps into the closet and vanishes), he built enough confidence working the northwest circuit to start branching out, so he headed south. But then another disaster struck again. In a club in Arizona a fire destroyed his dummies.

Vents can get pretty attached to those articulated dolls. The vent invests the dummy with a personality, and night after night exchanges jokes and insults with this person in what, at its best, is really almost credible. Leon was in grief when his Sammy, Gerry, and Charlie died. He did not have enough money to buy replacements, and he was somewhat impaired in his ability to get work, since part of his act had gone up in smoke.

He needed a "box jumper" (the girl who disappears from the magic chest or closet), and hired a dancer named Lola Wilson. She soon became his general assistant, and, as often happens in this trade, they married. It is not clear how or why he began to think that the comic-strip charac-ter might be his to bring to life on the stage. It is difficult to understand how King Features Syndicate allowed him to get away with it, but sometime before World War II, when vaudeville theatres regularly offered movies as well as stage shows, audiences began to see a short black-and-white animated screen announcement:

Coming on stage in this theatre —-
America's Mandrake the Magician !!

The producers of our documentary found a number of these cinema/vaudeville relics.

Coming . . . on the stage of this theatre . . .
a magical musical, starring in person . . .
America's Mandrake the Magician. Don't Miss It!
It's a Once Seen, Never Forgotten Program!

So now he was coming out in a top hat, with a scarlet-lined cloak, pencilled eyebrows, a pointed moustache, a hypnotic gleam in his eye, a wave of the hand that seemed very familiar to comic-strip readers. A recognizable figure from the Funny Pages had come to life on the stage.

For a while he worked the same circuit under different names, to double his bookings. "So as to work solid," he said in an interview. "I'd go down the coast as Leon the Ventriloquist and come back up as Mandrake the Magician."

Journalists who tried to pin him down about using the comic-strip name had little success. The only occasion we know of that he came close to admitting that he had appropriated the Mandrake name and image with something less than a perfect right to do so was the Peter Pit interview at the Magic Castle in 1972.

Peter Pit: *Where'd you get the name Mandrake? You weren't born with that name were you? Were you born with it?*

Mandrake: *Does it matter?*

Pit: *No, I just wanted to know. How'd you hit upon it? I mean, what was it that fascinated you . . . ?*

Mandrake: *Who am I to explain the accident of fate.*

Pit: *I don't know, tell us.*

Mandrake: *I said who am I? Almost every person that made it in our business started out under one name, didn't do too well, bombed a little, changed their name and went in and said, "Um, Brad just came into town." And they had a different name. And along the line somewhere they went over real well. And somebody said, "I want that act." And that's the name you are stuck with from there on.*

Pit: *That has to do with the cartoon?*

Mandrake: *Got a lot to do with a lot of things.*

Pit: *Got a lot to do with a lot of things? It's one of those things?*

Mandrake: *Peter, everything is a commercial, in a sense, so you make any tie-ups you can and try to get established.*

This is unsatisfactory on two counts, the first being the obvious evasion, and the second that it does not seem to fit the usually generous and open personality of the man as we see him in almost every other environment. Court records in Los Angeles show that in 1944 he legally changed his name to Leon Mandrake. He often gave the impression in interviews that he had taken the name long before he had actually started using it, and that in fact he was the first. According to friends he started to bill himself as Mandrake in late 1941 or 1942. As far as we can tell, the Peter Pit interview is the closest he ever came to talking frankly about it. Artist Phil Davis always said that the comic strip and the live performer were mutually beneficial. If King Features Syndicate ever threatened to sue, the documentary producers could find no record of it. In his publicity he used Leon Mandrake the Magician for a time but then went back to Mandrake the Magician. If you check out the Mandrake web site you may find, in the old strips, a character called Thora, the name young Leon said he gave to his school chum in the carnival sword box illusion.

As Leon and Lola polished the act, they refined and slightly modified an illusion that Harry Houdini and his wife had made famous, the substitution trunk. Lola (now named Narda, after the comic-strip Mandrake's companion) would be tied up in a mail sack and nailed into a large crate. The magician would stand on top of the crate, raise his cloak in front of him until he was concealed, at which point, almost instantly, the cloak would drop, and Narda would be standing there instead of Mandrake. Then, when the crate was laboriously opened (by a committee of audience members who had been on stage with them the whole time) Leon would be in the mail sack, in a different costume from the one we had just seen, smoking a lighted cigarette. It is a great trick, still widely and sometimes superbly performed.[16] Admirers said that Mandrake's "sub trunk" was the fastest ever, and Leon himself claimed to have originated the cigarette and the change of costume.

Peter Pit asked him to explain how it was done.

Pit: *We didn't have Velcro at those times. How did you make such a fast change?*

Mandrake: *That is one of the hardest secrets.*

Pit: *Is it really?*

---

16. Notably by David Copperfield and the Pendragons, among others.

Mandrake: *This is — look, you can go to a public library and find out almost any principle in magic but just try to find out about quick change. Oh, that's a hard one, Peter. Those secrets are not written. If they are I can't . . .*

Pit: *You're not going to tell us?*

Mandrake: *Yes, I'd be happy to explain it.*

Pit: *I'd love to hear.*

Mandrake: *Well, first you take the efferdan and tantifraz then you put them with the fabersham which will collidrig and puzzle. The incandescent frill, if the weather's proper, now you've got to take the phase of the moon into this or you're lost. Then the molidig remains fallified and the . . .*

Pit: *. . . You're not going to tell us are you?*

Mandrake: *I just told you. What do you mean? You answer the man's question right away and he says, "Huh, they never tell you nothing." What do you want me to do? Tell you to practise?*

By 1945 they had a big travelling show with a costly troupe of dancers, assistants, and wagonloads of props and equipment. They played Chicago, Vancouver, Los Angeles, in big theatres for a substantial ticket. The billings said MANDRAKE AND NARDA, but in fact the marriage was winding down, and 1946 was the last year they played together. When the marriage ended the magician lost his highly trained and popular assistant. He let it be known that he was looking for someone to replace her, and another dancer who had worked a number of magic shows applied for the job. Her name was Louise Solarno, a show-business kid who had grown up on the road.

I was in Chicago and I had just come off of a stock compa-

ny so I decided to go to this agent Paul Saunders and I'd never been to him before and Leon was there. When [Paul] heard that I had worked for Blackstone he suggested that I go with Leon and I said, "Gee I was hoping for some small part in a musical or something." So he said, "Well you take this two weeks and I'll find another show for you," and he said to Leon "You take her and I'll find another girl for you." So I signed up for two weeks and stayed forty-seven years.

They agreed on a stage name, Velvet, which she still uses as his widow. They married after six weeks.

It was simple all right, we got married at six o'clock at night and at eight o'clock we were doing the first show. We used to do two shows a night and when we were in the Midwest the clubs were open seven days a week. On closing night we would have to pack as we did the last show, travel all night and then get into the next town, which was usually 200 or 250 miles away and open that same night. You got so much practice because you were always doing your show and you had to get smooth, because you did it all the time.

By now television was making inroads in the American entertainment world. Big theatrical shows like Mandrake's cost too much. Ticket prices were too high for people who could get free entertainment at home. Many magicians turned to the nightclub scene. This was a very different relationship with the audience. In the theatre you had people seated out in front of you and you controlled the lighting. In a club you often had people sitting on three sides of the playing area, your lighting was sometimes rudimentary, people were being served, eating, drinking — often too much. Some magicians hated it, among them Blackstone. Mandrake seemed to thrive on it. It was in that environment that he took the classic Dancing Hank, combined with another classic, The Spook in the Bottle, and developed the enchanting presentation with which this chapter opens.

Leon and Velvet had three children, all the while touring, the South, the West Coast, and the Midwest. Their first son, Lon, was born in Chicago, Ron in Miami, and Kimball in Dayton, Ohio. Bernard Abrams says he knew that Leon was worried about keeping bread on the table, but that he never shared those worries with the troupe, that he seldom fired anybody. "You have to spread the blanket," he would say. But it was getting tougher all the time, despite his established reputation. "The real magic," says Bernard Abrams, "was that he kept the show on the road when all the rest of them folded up. The real magic the audience never saw."

Although Leon never stopped performing, for a while the audience stopped seeing Mandrake altogether. Charles Dunninger's mind-reading act had moved from the stage to radio and then to network television after 1944, and had made "Mind Reading" hugely popular. Another mentalist billed himself as Alexander: The Man Who Knows, and had enjoyed a successful touring career. Alexander died, and Leon bought his props, methods, and the rights to his show. "I'm not a mind-reader," he said. "I'm a people reader." Good magicians, those who work an intimate show, must be people readers. Many, like Alexander, combine mentalism and conventional magic. Leon had done a bit of the former, and now decided his career might get a boost from Alexander's reputation and that Mandrake might take a strategic vacation.

It is conceivable that there was some pressure from King Features Syndicate at this time (1951) about the use of the name Mandrake, and that the new identity was partly a way of riding out the storm. The strategy does not seem to have worked very well. Television had become an immense rival. A few TV impresarios — notably Ed Sullivan — booked magic acts from time to time, but the competition was fierce. Leon went back to being Mandrake and got a few bookings on TV, where he looks ill at ease with the illusions. He kept on touring. In 1955 their daughter Geelia ("Jill") was born in Portland, Oregon. It became more and more difficult to keep the family together. For a while they packed the kids off to their grandmother in Chicago. Lon says he woke up one night after a nightmare and told his grandmother that there had been a terrible fire, whereupon the phone rang from Anchorage where a club that Velvet and Leon had worked many times, and loved, had burned to the ground with all their props and costumes. The catalogue of disasters in the magician's life kept growing.

For a while they lived in Hawaii, and then came home to Vancouver, bought a house, and put the children into school, which Lon says they hated. Leon and Velvet did their best to book shows that involved less travel. They played fairs in the summer, including the British Columbia Provincial Exposition, home shows, conventions, gradually easing out of the nightclubs. Velvet got cut in half with a buzz saw and shot through the chest with an arrow on a ribbon.

On the surface Mandrake's career looks like the life of a journeyman who is doing what he is good at because that is how you earn a living. But the testimony of Mandrake himself, and of Velvet and the children, makes it clear that there was a conscious sacrifice in being a professional magician. He could have done better in real estate, he was a hell of a salesman, a people-reader like all good sales-men. Talk to a hundred magicians; at least fifty will tell you a similar story. Few are as diligent or adroit with the busi-ness side of their business as they are with the endless practice you have to maintain if your sleight of hand is going to be flawless, or with the people-reading and other elements of the performing scene. The great Dai Vernon (see *The Canadians: Biographies of a Nation*, Volume I, Part Four), acknowledged worldwide as an all-time master, was never able to save any money and was, to all intents and purposes, supported by the Magic Castle and friends and admirers for the last quarter-century of his hugely produc-tive life. Performing magic is a consuming, obsessive craft for many. Leon Mandrake at least seems to have found it a source of deep and continuing joy. "You don't care if you have to eat beans," he said,

and sleep in the car because you know what you want and you're going to do it and nobody's going to stop you. But if you expect luxury, if you expect the arts to keep you like . . . after all, we're very dispensable you know. We are a luxury, we're easy to do without. You can't expect to be — play and

have fun and have everything else showered on you too —
you've got to give up something to get what you like.

As Ron moved into his teens he began to replace
Velvet on the road from time to time, so that she could stay
home with the kids. They all remember their father as a
man who was full of surprises, not just new magic
(although he seems to have constantly been learning and
trying out new tricks). "He came up to my room one day
when I was practising," Kim said,

and he took my guitar and played some really hip little
finger picking thing. I never knew that he could play at
all, and that was the one and only time he did that. He
never played it again.

Mandrake had, in fact, composed complex orchestra-
tions of his own original themes for some of his more elaborate stage shows, but it is not clear whether he ever formally studied music.

He began to do a little more steady television in the
1970s on a CBC series called *The Manipulators*, and played
himself in a dramatic role on the long-running Vancouver
CBC production *The Beachcombers*, with Bruno Gerussi. The
Magic Castle recognized his contribution with their presti-
gious Performing Fellowship. He was generous with his
time to institutions for old people and children. Velvet says
that he never really gave up the dream of going on the road
again with a big show and a real troupe and, now well into
his seventies, in 1985 he did mount a major show. But he
discovered a very compelling reason for it to be his last.
His son Lon was backstage. "He came out and he did a
wonderful thirty minutes," Lon told us.

Then he said, "Thank you very much, ladies and gentle-
man, for coming" and he closed the show after [only] thir-
ty minutes. And I think now he might have had a little bit
of a stroke, because, you know, afterwards I said, "What
happened?" And he said, "You know, I thought that we'd
completed the show." That was the last show.

"He couldn't not work," his son Ron said.

If he . . . thought his career was over or when he thought
his career was over he ah . . . he became much older. . . .
My Dad's whole life was a show, and I think . . . his whole
life, he was the entertainer and he wouldn't allow anybody
to, to not be happy, you know. He wouldn't allow them not
to be happy.

Bernard Abrams said that right up to the end his
friend kept talking as though he might get a new show
together, take it on the road next spring. When Mandrake
died in 1993, his friends went back to the place where he
had got his start as a stage performer, seventy-one years
earlier: the old Edison Theatre in New Westminster. They
say he would have got a laugh out of the fact that it's now
a strip club. And that during that very last Mandrake show,
the funeral, things didn't quite go according to plan. "The
furnace went off," Velvet said.

And I said, "Leon would have loved this." No matter how
much you planned, something always goes wrong, and it
was the furnace, he would have really laughed. He's prob-
ably up there or down here laughing at the whole thing.
Anyway, that was that.

As an epilogue, on a slightly personal note from this
writer, who has from time to time sailed close enough to

the wind of that obsession with performing magic to think he knows something about magicians: There is something odd about Canada and magicians — Dai Vernon, Stewart James, Doug Henning, Mandrake — names that resonate among magicians around the world. But not one of them turns up in *The Canadian Encyclopaedia*. That's what I mean when I say there is something odd about Canada and magicians. But maybe there is just something odd about magicians.

◆　◆　◆

The original documentary was written by Lynn Booth and MaryUngerleider and produced by Lynn Booth. It was directed and edited by Mary Ungerleider, photographed by Kirk Tougas, with sound by Jon Ritchie and Dennis Burke.

Part Thirteen

JAY SILVERHEELS
The Man Beside the Mask

The first native North American to star in a television series was a Mohawk from the Six Nations Reserve at Brantford, Ontario. His name was Harry Jay Smith, but the film world remembers him as Jay Silverheels, and so do millions of fans of *The Lone Ranger*.

The Lone Ranger made its way into the legends and language of North American kids with the radio series that first went to air in 1933 and was broadcast continually for twenty-one years.

In all media the Lone Ranger story starts with the same fictional events. A man named John Reid, born in 1850, was the only survivor of a group of Texas Rangers who were ambushed by outlaws. Five rangers were killed, including Reid's older brother, Daniel. The Indian Tonto found him and nursed him to health. Reid then donned a black mask made from his dead brother's vest, mounted his stallion, Silver, and roamed the West as the Lone Ranger to aid those in need, to fight evil, and to fight for justice.

The character was created in the Lone Ranger radio program written and produced by George W. Trendle and Fran Striker. It began on a single radio station, WXYZ in Detroit, Michigan, on January 30th, 1933. In less than ten years, more than four hundred stations were carrying it. It is probably fair to say that more people think The *Lone*

Ranger's theme music was created for that program than know it as Rossini's *William Tell Overture*.

The radio programs got off to a rough start, with three different actors in the title role during the first three months. The original Ranger was a man named George Stenius who left after two and a half months to pursue a career as a writer in New York. As George Seaton, he would go on to a career in Hollywood as a screenwriter-director-producer, winning two Academy Awards for his screenplays along the way. He was replaced by one Jack Deeds, who was fired within days. The station's dramatic director played one show, and then they found Earle Graser, who became the Lone Ranger on April 18th, 1933.

Graser found the voice and the manner that raised the Lone Ranger from a character in a radio serial to something close to archetype. He played the part for the next eight years, until the morning of April 8th, 1941, when he fell asleep at the wheel of his car and was killed when it slammed into a parked trailer. Graser's death presented two immediate problems to the Lone Ranger's producers: a new actor had to be found fast (the show was broadcast live three days a week; no reruns and no pre-recorded broadcasts) and the transition had to be handled smoothly without an abrupt and obvious change in actors. Moreover, the many adolescents in the listening audience had to be reassured that it was not the Lone Ranger himself who had died.

The part was filled by Brace Beemer, an announcer and studio manager who had at times narrated *The Lone Ranger* program, had been making personal appearances as the Lone Ranger (because he was much more physically impressive than Graser), and was currently playing the lead in *Challenge of the Yukon*, a popular television series later renamed *Sgt. Preston of the Yukon*. Beemer's voice was noticeably deeper than Graser's. They had to find a gimmick to ease him into the role. The gimmick used was to have the Lone Ranger shot and wounded at the beginning of the next script, an injury that left him unable to speak for several days as he struggled to recover. The transition helped convince children that, despite what they may have heard on the news, the Lone Ranger was not dead, as well as providing a bridge to Beemer's deep-voiced playing of the hero.

Brace Beemer was the Lone Ranger for the next thirteen years, until the radio series ended with its last live broadcast on September 3rd, 1954.

This may seem a long road to travel on the way to a story about the life of Jay Silverheels, but that life itself cannot be fully appreciated without understanding that *The Lone Ranger* was not just another radio serial; it was an extended morality play that worked out simplistic but powerfully presented issues of good and evil and was listened to by millions and millions of American and Canadian kids. Millions of them are still alive, to whom the image of a great white stallion rising up on its hind legs as its masked rider pointed off towards the next adventure is still vivid. That image and the characters connected to it became cultural icons so *present* that it is difficult for the people who lived through that period to realize that the Masked Man and Tonto, and "Hi-Yo, Silver, Away" (the hero's call to the white stallion as they set off to vanquish evil) . . . to realize that they are gone. *The Seinfeld* and *This Hour Has 22 Minutes* generation — who may know of the Masked Man and Tonto as quaint symbols — never had the experience of being enthralled by them, and of believing that they were real.

The moral centre to the Lone Ranger stories makes the subservient, illiterate Tonto role played by Jay Silverheels seem ironic to us today. It did to Silverheels then — both ironic and demeaning. Nonetheless it did move the Mohawk actor into the Hollywood mainstream. Once there, he diligently used his reputation to advance First Nations actors out of their largely wordless stereotypical roles — howling, raiding white settlers, and getting shot and dying. Jay Silverheels prepared the ground for artists such as Chief Dan George, Graham Greene, Tom Jackson, Tantoo Cardinal, and Tina Keeper, who have been able to build serious careers and soar far above the clichéd confines of their Native predecessors.

Harry Jay Smith was born on Canada's largest reserve, the Six Nations, near Brantford, Ontario, on May 26th, 1912. He was the third in a family of eleven children, eight boys and three girls. The large family grew up in a rambling Victorian house, on land that was given to the Six Nations in 1784. The house was a tall, imposing brick structure with an eccentric central section that towered above the ridge of the main roof, and decorative brickwork up the corners and on the valances. Harry's father went off to World War I and came back with a commission and a chest full of medals. Major George Smith had more decorations on his tunic than any other Native Canadian soldier in that war. He also came back deaf from a shell that exploded in a nearby trench and nearly killed him. And so young Harry had little conversation with his father as he helped him work the 100-acre farm near the reserve. Most of his instruction, encouragement, and guidance in life came from his mother.

He went to a racially mixed school in Brantford, but there was little mixing between the kids from the reserve and the kids from town. His brothers Steve and Cecil remember him as a slight kid who was fascinated with the bodybuilding ads in *Popular Mechanics* and *Liberty* and the other five-cent magazines. Charles Atlas offered to turn every "97 pound weakling" into a muscular, confident giant who could reduce the nasty bullies on the beach to snivelling wrecks. Jay Silverheel's brother Steve Smith says:

My dad bought him these wrestling books on holds and all that, and the other people would be out mowing hay or cutting wood, and he'd be in the barn punching a punching bag. He used to get these magazines that were on bodybuilding. He used to look at all the barbells but he could never afford them. And so he would make his own out of steel rods and cement blocks and he would weight lift.

Then he started playing lacrosse and discovered that he was a natural. When he was sixteen he joined the Mohawk Stars, a field lacrosse team, and soon became one of their best players. The team's goalie was a man named Judy — Judy "Punch" Garlow. Garlow says he was there when Harry got the name "Silverheels."

When we played a good game, so our manager says, "I'm

gonna buy all you guys new running shoes." So he bought us all white running shoes. And then after a while we started playing and Tonto would run down the field. All you could see is white feet flying. Says that we can't call him "White Heels" cause he's an Indian so we says "Silverheels." So that's how they call him Jay Silverheels.

A lot of the young men from Six Nations went down to Buffalo, NY, during the Depression to look for work, and Jay went too. He played semipro lacrosse there, and photographs in the sports sections from that period sometimes call him H. Smith, and sometimes Jay Silverheels. He heard that some of the other guys were winning modest amounts of money at amateur boxing events. So he joined a local gym — you could become a club member for a quarter — and met a really good boxer at his club, a young man named Jack Donovan. Donovan invited the penniless Mohawk kid from Canada to come home with him and get a good feed. There is a photo of Donovan's mother serving out a huge platter of bacon and eggs to the two boys, Jay grinning broadly as he digs in. His grin and his demeanour evidently charmed the Donovan family; Jay moved in and lived with them for some time. The Buffalo Boxing Museum has an extensive collection of records from that period. Ed Cudney, the curator, showed us photographs of Jay in the ring in those days, and talked about the Donovan relationship.

And she did all the cooking for him and put him up for the three or four weeks he was training for the New York State Championships. And they [Jack Donovan and Jay] both went to New York City to fight and they both won the

Championships. And after winning it, they took them to Jack Dempsey's restaurant and they took pictures with Jack Dempsey. I don't think boxing was his primary love but he took it up and he just . . . he won at everything, I guess, that he ever played in.

The Dempsey/Silverheels/Donovan photographs are now in Cudney's collection at the Buffalo Boxing Museum.

Jay Silverheels was building a reputation. He began a relationship with Edna Lickers, a sixteen year old from the Six Nations reserve. Edna became pregnant. Her son Ron was born in Buffalo and took the name Smith. But Edna and Jay were both too young to really know what they were doing and the relationship did not last. Jay went back to lacrosse and was soon playing with a popular "All-Indian" team. It seems from some of the photographs and the memories of the players that part of the fun for the white spectators was to get tanked up on beer and yell "Kill the Indians!" But the team was very successful, and in the midst of the Depression Jay was beginning to earn a decent living, which he supplemented by modelling for local advertisers. He was still working with the barbells and the punching bag. A beefcake photograph that survives bears this caption:

He's one of those V-man jobs — broad of shoulder, narrow at the hips and with rippling muscles. He's a perfect specimen — wavy, jet black hair and sharply chiselled features set off the frame magnificently, and qualify him for matinee idol honors should he ever take a whirl at that industry.

That was from the *Buffalo Evening News*, December 14th, 1936; he was now twenty-four. He married a woman named Bobbi, and they had a daughter, Sharon. When Jay's team played an exhibition game in Los Angeles, the comedian Joe E. Brown (*Some Like It Hot*) was in the crowd, and came back to the dressing rooms to meet the team. Brown took a liking to Jay. Like the *Buffalo Evening News*, Joe E. Brown wondered if the good-looking athletic kid shouldn't have a career in the movies. He arranged for Jay to get an extra's acting card. Bobbi did not like the idea of leaving home for California, but she liked even less being left alone in Buffalo with a new baby; so she came west with Jay and got a job as a waitress. They needed her small salary; the acting jobs at first were few and far between. When he began to do better, Bobbi was able to quit wait-ressing. But she was uncomfortable watching him being photographed with starlets. Perhaps she was right to be suspicious. His daughter Sharon says that he became very self-centred, that there were affairs outside the marriage, that she seldom saw him.

Before long Bobbie had had enough. She went back to Buffalo, sued for divorce, and remarried. Sharon would not see her father again for fourteen years. Jay's brother Cecil says the divorce made Jay stand back and take a more thoughtful look at things than he had before. It was too late for his marriage with Bobbi, but it may have helped him set-tle down to a more professional and more disciplined life.

Better roles began to come his way. He got a Screen Actors' Guild "A" card, and played an Inca prince in *Captain from Castille*. Then they cast him as the Osceola brother in Humphrey Bogart's *Key Largo*. Before he was finished he would play in fifty-five feature films, including

The Man Who Loved Cat Dancing and *Cat Ballou*. He was always an Indian: that had not changed. In fact, for a long time Indian actors were not given principal roles even when the lead character was an Indian. Actor Peter Kelly Gaudreault, of the successful Canadian series *North of Sixty*, says, "The . . . parts which had reputations which transcended generations . . . characters like Geronimo and Crazy Horse from American Native history, they were always played by white actors."

Jay later starred in *Santee*, a thoughtful, articulate, sophisticated role as a breeder of quarter horses. Horses were a great love. When Jay was about fifteen, his brothers remember him on his father's farm gracefully riding a difficult black stallion, a stallion that nobody else had been able to stay on. Later in his career he would have a ranch of his own, take up driving a sulky in trotting races, and marry a Los Angeles woman who shared his love of horses and the track. But it was another kind of involvement with riding horses that was about to turn him from a successful actor into a star, shortly after he finished his film with Bogart in 1948. It was a movie called *The Cowboy and the Indians*. There he met an actor named Clayton Moore, who played the cowboy. They became friends, and Moore admired Jay's work enough to suggest that he audition for a television series that Moore would star in. This was, of course, *The Lone Ranger*.

Jay Silverheels had to compete with thirty-five other actors for the Tonto role. We don't know the names of all the others, but probably many of them were not Indians. The first Tonto on radio had been a white man, Jack Todd, who dressed in Native costume for publicity photographs. There was a 1937 movie serial of the Lone Ranger that played in the Saturday afternoon double features in ten-minute (one-reel) instalments. Its Tonto was also a white man, Victor Daniels. There had never been an Indian star; Jay was breaking a colour barrier. He and Clayton Moore became a partnership. He had steady work now, and within months he was famous.

The actual making of the television series sounds like a nightmare. Each episode was shot in two days. Much of the work was done in studio, but from time to time they would take a week out in the desert, at some of the spectacular rocky mesa sites that Hollywood has made so familiar. In that week they'd shoot all the exterior action scenes needed for a whole season.

Film historian Frank Thompson says that the company would rent a stagecoach for one day and use it from dawn to dark:

> *All day long they would have a bunch of bad guys chasing the stagecoach, the Lone Ranger and Tonto intercepting the stagecoach. And those scenes would be interspersed among five, six different episodes of the film. But they would have to do it all in one day. They worked very, very hard for very low pay. No star of a TV show would work for what they worked for.*

The actor John Hart, who played the Lone Ranger for one season, replacing Clayton Moore during a contract dispute, said:

> *Guild minimum in those days was $125 a week — and that's a six-day week. And I didn't get much more than*

*that, and I think he'd got a bit more than that because he'd
done all those previous shows. If he had any kind of an
agent, they'd have bumped him up. Because he was just as
valuable an asset to the show as the Lone Ranger. And you
couldn't be bringing in a new Tonto all the time.*

Frank Thompson recounts an episode that seems to
show a dawning political and social sense, which would
later become directly focused on the status of First Nations
actors in the movie capital. John Hart had finished out his
one season as the Masked Man. Clayton Moore had settled
his contract differences and was back in the saddle on the
big white stallion.

*When they shot up here at Iverson's Ranch, they would
have to stop at a gas station down at the bottom of the hill
and change their clothes in the men's room. One day Jay
Silverheels refused to change his clothes. And they got to
the set, everybody was set up and Jay Silverheels was
nowhere to be seen. And Clayton knew that he would often
come out to a big rock, perhaps that rock. He followed him
up and said, "What's wrong?" And Jay said, "We're the
leading actors in a hit TV show and we don't even have
dressing rooms. They shouldn't be treating us this way. We
have to change in a men's room. This is not right." Clayton
said, "Yeah, you're right, but we do have the whole crew
waiting for us and we should probably get back to work." I
think it's . . . to Jay Silverheels' credit that he did get back
to work. And the next day they had dressing rooms.*

And there was another aspect to the daily grind as
Tonto that Silverheels knew he had to swallow, but also
knew that he had to do something about, someday.

Here is some sample dialogue.

TONTO

Him sent men to ambush me, but me take care of him. You find Cavendish?

LONE RANGER

Tonto, what happened?

TONTO

Nelson, he hit me. But me all right now. That not make sense. Me not understand.

Even his adoring relatives back at the reserve, who would gather at a neighbour's house to watch Cousin Jay star on the box, were embarrassed to hear the literate, intelligent man they knew talk in grunting monosyllables. John Hart, who had played that one season of *The Lone Ranger* and stayed close to Jay for the rest of his life, recalled his own unease when Jay talked about trying to get more challenging roles.

He thought he was being a dumb Indian a lot of the time, creeping around and someone hitting him on the head, and he'd fall over. He wasn't too happy with that. But it was a job and he did it, you know gracefully, with good spirit. He was [actually] capable of doing all kinds of things, but he was just Tonto to all these dumb producers that wouldn't see him any other way. He got that one part in Santee and it was a nice part, he was a wonderful, very good in it. Well, I think it really frustrated Jay a lot to be Tonto to everybody, trying to get other jobs with other producers and they'd say, "Oh yeah, he's great, he's Tonto!" Well, so he's Tonto but he's a good actor, too. He can do other things.

Always proud of his physical strength and agility, Jay insisted on doing his own stunts. But in 1955, after a rough brawl, something went terribly wrong. A sharp pain brought him to his knees. He was taken to the hospital with a heart attack. He was off the set for two months, replaced by the Lone Ranger's nephew. He came back to work with nitroglycerine tablets, a low-fat diet, and doctor's orders to stop the stunts.

Soon *The Lone Ranger* was cancelled, overtaken by more sophisticated Western series with more complex characters and situations: *Gunsmoke, The Rifleman, Bonanza*. Although he played in two more Lone Ranger movies, in 1956 and 1959, things were slowing down. He and Mary di Roma had married in 1954. With her love of horses and his new "career" as a sulky driver, it seemed to make sense that they start raising racehorses themselves on the ranch they shared. He went back to Brantford once, in 1957, to a hero's welcome and a slightly uneasy but excited reunion with his daughter Sharon, then seventeen. But the connection with Six Nations and family was now more symbolic than real. His ties were to Mary, the ranch, the horses, the track, and the community of Native actors in California.

The Lone Ranger had vanished from all but the Saturday morning rerun screens, but Jay and Clayton Moore occasionally still went on well-paid tours for advertisers who knew very well which generation would remember the Masked Man and his Faithful Sidekick.

They were able to keep this up well into the sixties.

A joke entered the culture about then. Tonto and the Lone Ranger are cornered in the arroyo by a crowd of Sioux warriors who are galloping in for the kill. The Lone Ranger says, "Tonto, we're in serious trouble." Tonto rejoins, "What do you mean 'We,' Paleface!"

Jay was spending time with younger Native actors in Hollywood. In the mid-sixties, amid the social ferment that was activating —and perhaps creating — radicals all over the Western world, Jay Silverheels' political awareness matured. With the veteran actor Will Sampson he formed the Indian Actors' Workshop.

It would be difficult for a bright kid growing up Mohawk to avoid being at least slightly affected by the bug of First Nations politics. Of all the Iroquois nations, the Mohawks have the reputation for being the most determined. It was Warriors from the Caughnawagha community who met Laura Secord after her famous walk during the War of 1812; they were a fighting unit under the command of Colonel Fitzgibbon and turned the tide in the subsequent battle with the invading American forces. When the Iroquois nations (five at first and a sixth later) were united in confederacy by a Huron prophet remembered as Dekanawidha, it was the Mohawk leader Ayonwhatha who spoke to the once warring nations on behalf of this speech-impaired visionary. Ayonwhatha is remembered in later retellings of the story as "Hiawatha."

Dekanawidha declared the Mohawk chiefs to be Heads of the Confederacy and the Great Lords of the Peace. Dekanawidha had paddled across Lake Ontario in a magical stone canoe and demonstrated his prophetic role by surviving a leap or fall from a tall pine — the Tree of Peace — into a deep river gorge below. The Iroquois confederacy was assembled out of a group of linguistically related but traditionally warring separate cultures — Mohawk, Onandaga, Oneida, Cayuga, Seneca (and later the Tuscarora). It was a triumph of civilizing politics over tribal rivalries. The constitution, symbolically embedded in a superb belt of wampum, may date from as far back as the fifteenth century. It is almost certainly the first example of a code of laws in North America. It recognized women as persons and as a special repository of political wisdom. The version published by the University of Oklahoma's law school declares in its article 44:

Lineal descent shall run in the female line. Women shall be considered the progenitors of the Nations. They shall own the land and the soil. Men and women shall follow the status of the mother.

It is said that Benjamin Franklin, as he considered the challenge of putting together a constitution for the newly independent United States of America, studied the constitution of the Iroquois confederacy. Every kid raised in a Six Nations community hears these stories, and it seems to be the Mohawks who carry them with the most aggressive pride.

So when Jay Silverheels helped put together the Workshop, he was acting like a Mohawk. Although he had made a reputation and a modest fortune playing a sidekick, now it was time to help Native performers escape the racist clichés.

Actors Frank Salsedo and Michael Horse talk with affection of how Jay brought the young First Nations hopefuls in California together, trained them, watched out for parts for them, and kept arguing with producers. These talented people *must* be considered for non-stereotyped roles, for roles outside the racially determined ones that had been their only venue since the beginning of movies. Michael Horse said, "He fought a lot of the fight for us. I didn't realize again until I got into the movie business, talking to a few of the Indian actors who were around at that time, what a hard time they had, what trailblazers they were, what battles." The Workshop was a cheery, companionable place. It did find work for the members, but still always playing Indians. For a while it seemed as though those hidebound racist attitudes of the producers were immutable.

When he was not at the Workshop Jay spent a lot of time at the track. He was recognized as an outstanding harness racer. When he won at the Meadows in 1974 it was a national racing event, and suddenly he was in demand for television interviews. Perhaps it was that new prominence that allowed some Hollywood producers to see the actor in a new light. In any case it was shortly afterwards that his agent brought Jay number of offers, and suggested that he had better convince the producers that he was physically up to a major commitment — it would be in the contracts anyway — and get a thorough set of medicals even before the negotiations began. It was then that calamity struck, just as he was on the threshold of yet another breakthrough.

He went in for an angiogram. This was a routine and mandatory part of an exhaustive medical examination, and nobody told him that there was any risk entailed (perhaps there was not). But during the procedure he was stricken with massive pain. It was a stroke, and when the pain receded he could hardly speak, his left leg trailed when he walked, his face was badly twisted, and his mind was far from clear.

Jay Silverheels was nothing if not courageous. He tried to fight that stroke, but it was bigger than he was. He sued the angiogram doctors for malpractice on the grounds that he had not been adequately advised of the dangers in the procedure, but it is likely that he was even less well advised in the bringing of the suit, which he could not have won. He sat stiffly in the courtroom, tears rolling down his face as he listened to witness after witness describe how he was merely a shadow of the physical man he'd so recently been. His defeat there discouraged him painfully. He tried one race in the sulky, but it was clearly too dangerous for a person as severely disabled as he had become. He had to give up the Indian Actors' Workshop. Without him at the helm it soon disintegrated. Now none of the old roads was there for him to walk down. In the film and photographs of those last five years he appears to shrink, bit by bit, day by day. There was a celebration when his star was laid down in the Hollywood Walk of Fame, but he was unable to even speak to reporters that day, and in the news clips of the event he looks sad, lost and helpless.

Not long after that he vanished. John Hart, who had done that one season as the Lone Ranger and stayed friends with Jay, says that he found him in "a dinky little hospital in South Pasadena. How in hell he got there, I don't know. He was down to a hundred pounds. I cared about him a lot." Hart's eyes welled with tears remembering Jay Silverheels, who died in hospital in 1980, at the age of sixty-eight.

The distinguished Cree actor Tom Jackson, born on the One Arrow Reserve near Batoche, said,

I don't remember the guy who said, "Hey Silver, come here." What was that guy's name? I don't remember him. I do remember the guy who went, "Get 'um up, Scout. Uhm. Kemo Sabe. Uhm." I remember him.

His name was Jay Silverheels.

◆　◆　◆

The original documentary was written by Maureen Marovitch, and directed by David Finch and Maureen Marovitch. It was photographed by Andrei Khabad, with sound by David Finch, and edited by Jason Levy.

Part Fourteen

WILF CARTER AND MONTANA SLIM
THE YODELLING COWBOY

When they have a Wilf Carter night in Canning, Nova Scotia, the Annapolis Valley town where the singer used to haul apples as a boy, there isn't an empty seat in the house, and most of those seats are filled with senior citizens. Wilf was born over in Port Hilford on December 18th, 1904, and even though he became identified with the Prairies and the Rockies and Western cowboys, his fellow Nova Scotians still know where he really hailed from. But singers also come from as far away as Alberta to "do" Wilf Carter here, in his hometown. In the opening scene of Tom Radford's documentary life of Carter, as the yodelling Carter imitators stand up on that little stage in Canning, and wind out the old familiar prairie laments, ("Oh how my lonely heart is aching tonight, for a home I long to see . . .") you can see lips moving all over the hall as the fans silently mouth the words to the songs they know so well.

Wilf was one of seven kids. The family photographs show a lean, good-looking gang of lookalikes, all contemplating the camera with the same appraising expression. The father was a Baptist minister. It seems likely that the tall, handsome, presentable boy was intended to follow in the reverend's footsteps. Emotionally powerful hymns are an important part of Baptist worship. Wilf knew and sang them with gusto every Sunday at the compulsory services.

There are echoes of them in his own music. Back in about 1916, after a Saturday night concert in that same Canning community centre had featured somebody called the Yodelling Fool, young Wilf took to yodelling his way through his barnyard chores and probably up and down the echoing valley roads. His father the preacher was not pleased. "That was not a very nice noise for a minister's son to be making."

This was a strict traditional Protestant minister's home. Reverend Carter gathered the children each morning, had them kneel on the floor as he prayed for them, and then made each of them read aloud a chapter of the Bible before they set out on the long walk to school. Young Wilf started working for local farmers when he was twelve, harvesting, packing, and hauling to market the potatoes and apples that were the mainstay crops. If the father, as the legend has it, let him know that yodelling was an unseemly practice for a minister's son, Wilf wouldn't give it up. It is not difficult to imagine the tension in the Baptist home if the boy was slipping out of his early baritone into the yodeller's falsetto hour after hour, in house and out. Whatever the accumulated reasons for it were, when he was fifteen the conflicts became intolerable and the boy was asked, or told, to leave.

He walked the roads for a while, sleeping in ditches at first, until he found a job on John Tingley's dairy farm, milking cows and cleaning stables for twenty-five cents a day. That first winter he started to work the New Brunswick lumber camps. He later said that this was where he first encountered ten-cent paperback cowboy novels, which built a romantic image of the Prairies in his adolescent mind. When he saw a poster in the Canning railway station offering free transportation west for young men willing to work on the grain harvest, the lure of the prairie was irresistible, and off he went.

A boy from the Annapolis Valley would have been amazed by his first sight of an Alberta wheat farm. In the valley there were trees and hills everywhere, and until you went down to the shore and gazed out to sea — a vista that somehow never caught this boy's imagination — you wouldn't have seen anything like these endless miles of waving grain. Before long he began to work with horses, and the horse and Carter seemed made for each other. People will still tell you that Wilf Carter was a horse-whisperer long before anyone thought of the name, and it began here on the Alberta grain farms as the tall, long-boned, good-looking kid showed an aptitude for driving the horse-drawn machinery and looking after the big animals as if he had always lived among them. If the sound of the falsetto yodel bouncing off the hills of the Annapolis Valley or the walls of the parental parsonage had been irritating at home, it seems to have been at least tolerated out here on the prairies. Maybe it was even welcomed when the kid with the big, capable hands got his first guitar and began to twang away on it. He would croon the traditional "Come-all-ya's" to the guys at night, and soon put together his own rudimentary more-or-less original variants. Almost always with a refrain that let loose the gurgling high-pitched yodel that would become his trademark.

Soon he was living in a bunkhouse and riding the

range on cattle farms, the wheat fields abandoned for something closer to his dime novel imaginings. Riding cattle did not pay as much as wheat farming, but it was closer to the dream. The songs he made began to tell the stories and yearn the yearnings of the guys he worked and bunked with. They were probably Alberta's very first own cowboy songs.

Tommy Hunter, who much later would build an impressive television audience for his weekly country music show on the CBC, got to know Wilf Carter well, and talks about him with a kind of affectionate reverence, well-salted with humorous observations on some of the pioneer country singer's idiosyncrasies. Hunter says,

He had the heart of a cowboy and the heart of a westerner. [But] he never forgot his roots. He had a tremendous love of the East Coast, but he was . . . a cowboy. Wilf used to have the old thumb pick. Like I said, he had powerful hands. You'd hear Wilf getting ready there, and he would start a song: "Now here's one that goes back to the early days of my recording career," and he would give a couple whacks on the strings. And he'd hit this and if it got out of tune, boy! You'd hear that. You'd see that thumb whomping those strings. And I'm not sure whether it was to blame the guitar for going out of tune, or see if he could hit it hard enough to bring it back. . . .

When he started going to the Calgary stampeded in 1927, it was both to ride broncos and to sing. This was a performer here who, while he loved his music and loved to sing and to play the guitar, but did not set his sights on a performing career until fairly late in the game. Unlike, say, a Bob Dylan, who seems to have wanted to be a star from the time he began to think about anything, and bent all his efforts in that direction, Wilf Carter's songwriting and his ultimate move to the professional stage grew out of the working contours and paths of his life. As he wandered from one job to another, the idea formed gradually that he might actually earn money by singing about this itinerant life with its joys and its loneliness.

Edmonton is home to the first ever public broadcaster in Canada, radio station CKUA, which went on the air from a studio at the University of Alberta in 1927 (and was privatized by the Alberta government in 1994). Its veteran programmer Brian Dunsmore said in the documentary:

I think it is significant that Wilf Carter the entertainer didn't come about for a number of years after he hit Alberta. It took him a few years of becoming himself, becoming this man that we talk about. He's sleeping in a bunkhouse with a bunch of rough and ready men, and he's up at the crack of dawn riding horses, this Wilf Carter who was very deeply grounded in his own being. And then he starts to think about doing other things. And one of these other things is becoming an entertainer.

He would go into town on weekends and sing at community dances, just trying it out. Now it was time to test himself in a larger venue, the Stampede. He would get himself thrown off a bronc a few times, sometimes collect a modest amount of prize money, sometimes break a bone, and then, evenings, if he was in shape for it, he would seek out a dance or a beer hall, get out the guitar, give it a few whacks with that great big thumb, and sing them one of his new creations. There were lots of guys trying out their cowboy songs on the Stampede crowd. Few if any of them were really cowboys. This tall, big-boned guy was real. Even the love songs seemed real.

> *Ay – yii yii yii,*
> *Beautiful girl on the prairies*
> *With Eyes so blue*
> *And a heart so true*
> *She's the girl I'm going to marry.*

Both the lyrics and the tunes were often pretty derivative, a characteristic of country songs that doesn't bother its fans. It was not just the songs they were coming to hear: it was the man. The Alberta disk jockey Jack Fox told us that this particular song somehow rang a bell for him when he was just a kid. "My introduction to Wilf Carter was at the age of five. That song just turned me on to country music. I've never forgotten the song. I can [still] recite . . . the first verse of it." (Which he does: *Ay – yii yii yii . . .*)

Wilf Carter began to record the stories of the living legends of Alberta. Pete Knight was a world champion bronc rider. There are dramatic photographs of him lifting off the horse as if he was being shot into outer space, one hand high in the air for balance, the other gripping the reins, the mouth wide open in a triumphant yell, the wide leather chaps ballooning out from the calves of his legs, with the word P E T E in huge white leather appliqué on each side. Knight watched Wilf doing his best in the bronco ring, and then came to hear him sing at night. He told Wilf to give up riding the broncs and concentrate on his songs, which would not kill you, after all. When Pete

Knight was killed, by a horse called Duster, his funeral was one of the biggest Calgary had ever seen. Wilf Carter put it all into a song.

The musician David Wilkie, who travelled the country with Wilf years later, when he was making his "Last Roundup Tour," says, "He was singing songs about Crossfield, Pete Knight, the Calgary Stampede, and the Yoho Valley. Wilf was really putting all of that down on record. I think someday people are going to realize that is really our only Alberta folk music."

> *Come all ya young boys and lean over the rail*
> *I'll tell you the story of the dynamite trail.*
> *In Calgary Alberta . . .*

The song might become a panoramic portrait of the Stampede, with a catalogue of all the familiar elements of that annual event making up the texture of a narrative song about danger and daring. Gordon Lightfoot says that Carter had a strong influence on his own work as a balladeer, telling the mythic stories of his own land. And as Calgary theatres began to pay Carter five dollars a week to come and sing on their stages between movies, an interesting new device called the microphone began to show up. Radio was making its way across the land, perhaps nowhere more effectively than on the Prairies. Vast distances electronically disappeared when people gathered around the huge battery-powered black-boxed ponderously dialled early sets and made their way through the squeals and static of what sounded like the whole universe clashing out there in the cosmic waves, until they found a human voice or the sound of fiddles. One of the voices,

Wilf Carter's, made its way not just across the prairie spaces but also right across Canada, where the romantic idea of the cowboy was almost a universal.

There's a love knot in my lariat

And it's waiting for a blue-eyed gal you bet. . . .

When I swing my lasso

You'll hear my yodel-ay-ee-whoo!

There's a love knot in my lariat.

When he got a regular Friday night spot on CFCN radio the pay was now five dollars a show. CFCN advertised itself on billboards, celebrating its amazing ten-thousand-watt signal and the fact that it was "Locally made, Nationally known."

David Leonard, the official historian for Alberta Historic Sites, sees that as a turning point both for Carter and also for Canada's sense of itself.

It was the biggest radio and most powerful broadcast station on the prairies. And when Wilf Carter began to broadcast over FCN this was one of our own. This was a western Canadian cowboy singing music that relates to us, about us, to us. . . . Western Canadians . . . saying to Eastern Canadians, "We aren't a pale imitation of you. We are Western Canadians. With our own . . . culture and our own music. And . . . the ethos of the cowboy became the most dramatic symbol of that.

The Trail Riders of the Canadian Rockies was a tourist organization operating out of Banff. Adventurous and well-off Americans would pay twenty dollars a day to ride the breathtaking mountain trails, bathe in icy streams, eat camp meals around a campfire, and sleep in tents. Early film footage of those rides through the spectacular scenery shows the excited, wide-eyed faces of these visitors. The Trail Riders had heard him on the radio. Dennis Orr is a past president of that company. He told us,

The original sponsorship of the Trail Riders . . . was done by the CPR. They needed people both to entertain and to be cowboys, and Wilf Carter fit both those categories. . . . A tremendous number of his original songs (the only ones that he did) were actually written in those trail ride camps, to entertain the people.

Photographs from the 1930 season, taken around the campfire in the evening, show many of those people holding song sheets and singing along with a tall good-looking guy in a cowboy hat, a guitar in his big, spreading hands.

Oh how my lonely heart is aching tonight
For a home I long to see . . .
In my Blue — OOO Canadian Rockies . . .

People who are too young to have heard the long, yearning wail of a steam train whistle in the night as they drift off to sleep in a sleeping bag are missing a sound remembered in many of the Carter songs. The painful longing for home and loving arms, always central to country music, is the theme of dozens of songs.

He was bo-o-orn in Crawwwssfield Alberta
And he rode on a strawberry Roan.

I remember my own older brother John, sometime in the late 1930s, bringing home a ukulele and sitting on his bed with mournful eyes, twanging away and crooning out cowboy songs, and trying a yodel or too. I did not know it then but I do now; they were the songs of Wilf Carter.

There was only one summer of that Trail Riders idyll for Wilf. By the time he was back in town and the snow began to dust the foothills, the Depression had made itself cruelly felt all across the Prairies. David Leonard said that grain prices were down to thirty-five cents a bushel

for number one wheat! Too low to make it viable for most western farmers to ship their grain to the Lakehead. The railway was seen to be maybe the culprit in all this, as the freight rates were just a little too high. By the same token the railways seemed to be a sort of lifeline to freedom. You knew things were terrible where you were right now, they may not be much better in the next community, but it couldn't be any worse.

But it did get worse. Suddenly there was no work for Wilf in Alberta. He tried fishing on the west coast and farming in Saskatchewan. He learned that his father had died, and if he had dreamed of reconciliation, as the songs sometimes suggest, now it was too late. His daughter Sheila Dukarm says that he just sat on the street corner in Calgary and sang with his hat out on the pavement. Like Woody Guthrie and Jimmie Rogers in the United States, he was singing of the lost generation, the lost dreams. People who only had a few cents for a cup of coffee were putting five or ten of those desperate cents into Wilf Carter's hat. He said he would go into a restaurant and get some crackers and a cup of hot water and put ketchup into the cup to make a free soup. Foxy John at Radio D says he thinks that tough as things were, Carter may have been better off than a bricklayer or a carpenter, because "people would always throw a nickel in your hat."

In 1933 you could buy a hamburger on a bun for ten cents.

Somebody at RCA Victor Records in Montreal heard Wilf on the radio, tracked him down where he was doing odd jobs on a ranch somewhere in the foothills, and asked him to come to Montreal for a meeting. There was a first-class ticket, the meals were paid for, the beds were warm and comfortable. He had probably — like so many out-of-work men all over the continent — ridden trains by climbing up to the roof of a cattle car somewhere out in the yards, or hanging on underneath "riding the rods." Now he was going in style. When he got to Montreal they showed him into a recording studio. This would be Canada's first cowboy song on disk. He recorded "Swiss Moonlight Lullaby," and "The Capture of Albert Johnson," a narrative ballad about the "Mad Trapper" who had recently been shot to death in the snow by the Mounties.[17] Then Canadian Pacific sent him to New York to perform on a two-week inaugural cruise of their huge new liner the *Empress of Britain*. Wilf cracked that the ship was so big it took him three days to find his stateroom, and he had to camp out in the dining hall. While he was at sea "Swiss Moonlight Lullaby" was released in the United States as well as Canada and was an instant hit. Tommy Hunter's eyes crinkled with delight when he recounted what happened next.

This record was so popular, somebody from RCA ran down to meet the boat and they had this great big limou-

17. For an account of the manhunt and shooting of the "Mad Trapper" see *The Canadians: Biographies of a Nation*, Volume I, Part Eleven, "Distant Skies." It's the story of pioneer bush pilot Wop May who found the fleeing killer from the air.

sine for him. Wilf kept looking at him and he said, "Get in,"
and Wilf looked back at him and walked away. . . . "We're
from RCA!" And he said, "I don't care where you're from,
get out of here," and kept right on walking by them.

RCA signed him to a contract and told him to go back
to the Rockies *and* keep on writing songs. Now both those
brittle ten-inch wax 78-RPM disks, and the increasingly
popular and necessary radio were bringing Wilf Carter's
voice into the lives of Canadians from coast to coast. In
1937 CBS radio called from New York. They signed him up
with Lucky Strike Cigarettes, and the newspaper ads for
the regular morning radio program show him puffing a
Lucky, something he did only for the photographer.
Something else he did, and does not seem to have been
troubled by, was to change his name. Why some CBS executive would think that Montana Slim would play any better than Wilf Carter who had already made a continental
hit with "Swiss Moonlight Lullaby" is not clear, but Wilf
went along with it, and so there are millions of Americans
who know that haunting tenor twang as the voice of
Montana Slim while the same songs for Canadians are
unmistakeably Wilf Carter's.

> *Oh what I'd give if I could be home tonight*
> *With the sweetheart who's waiting for me.*

Tommy Hunter says he believes that it was Carter
records that kept RCA Victor's Canadian company from
going broke during the Depression. Important as recording
had become for him, David Wilkie, who played with
Carter's road show towards the end, says that Wilf refused
to fuss over the process.

Nowadays they spend millions of dollars and they have overdubs and thirty-four tracks where they have the banjo player come in at noon and the steel guitar player at three. Wilf . . . just hated that. He didn't like to rehearse. He'd just go in and say, "I got twelve songs, turn on the tape machine. I'm gonna be here for as long as it takes me to do them once, and you'd better get them down 'cause that's my new album." So it was like bronc riding for Wilf, recording was. Like getting it on for eight seconds and riding it . . . and going home. That's the way he was.

Recording had made Wilf Carter prosperous in the midst of a Depression that had dropped land prices to the floor. He came back to Alberta in 1939 and bought a substantial ranch to bring his new wife to, a New Yorker named Bobbie Bryan. They agreed that it was time to start a family and settle down, but it must have been a shock for a professional woman from Manhattan (Bobbie was a registered nurse) to suddenly find herself helping to run a grain farm, with the thrashing team showing up at five o'clock in the morning ready for the big breakfast that would send them out to the fields. Wilf got a broadcasting contract that would take him into Calgary once a week for a show; Bobbie could get her hair done, take in a movie, get at least a faint touch of the city life that she missed.

But the worst thing was the car crash. Driving in Montana they had a head-on collision with a truck that had crossed the centre line, and after several operations Wilf still had to walk with a brace and live with constant pain. For years he couldn't face up to recording. But there were two new elements in his life that seem to have been the determining factors in getting him and Bobbie through that rough period — their daughters Sheila and Carol. The Carters were in good shape financially. Even though Wilf was not recording, his records kept selling. In 1947 they hit two million. Wilf began to feel well enough to think about going back on the road. The girls were learning the songs around the fireplace at night. A handsome pair of bright-eyed blond kids, they could belt out the lines with gusto as their dad's big thumb whacked the guitar. In 1949, when it was time to let the world know that Montana Slim and Wilf Carter were both back on stage, he took the girls with him as part of the show.

They started with a cross-Canada tour, playing towns of any size, from Vancouver Island, up to Whitehorse and Yellowknife, back down through Alberta, across the prairies and the woodlands, right out to the east coast and then by boat over to the newest province, Newfoundland, which had joined Confederation just that year.

Carol Cooper, Wilf's younger daughter, said,

I must have been maybe five or six years old and we were on the stage. Daddy was singing a song and I pulled at his pant leg. He stopped singing and said, "What's the matter?" I said, "You made a mistake." He said, "Okay. We'll just have to start right over again." So we started from the beginning, and . . . everybody laughed, and of course I didn't realize that I was causing a commotion, but that was part of us being together as a family on the stage.

There are plenty of showbusiness stories about the terrible tensions of being on the road with the family in tow, but from the geniality of the photographs and the chuckled memories of the surviving members of what Wilf Carter called "The Family Show With Folks You Know," it appears that this was as happy and productive a time — for all of them — as they would ever have.

They played some stops that looked like a crossroads in the middle of nowhere. Ken Reynolds, the Ottawa promoter who put the tour together, talked about pulling into Minden, in the Haliburton Highlands of Ontario:

Wilf noticed a sign, "Population 260." And he [said] what was I trying to do to him! Even if everybody came there wouldn't be enough — even though I was paying, it was coming out of my pocket.

They needn't have worried. The rural population for miles around turned up that night in Minden, as they did in similar small towns across the country. Ken Reynolds said that they had to stop the show several times as the people kept crowding in by the hundreds, to reposition the loudspeakers so that everyone could hear. Wilf's daughter Sheila Dukarm said,

By six o'clock at night this town had thousands of people coming in and you were just wondering where do all these people hide! I can remember Mom is trying to take tickets, tear off tickets and take money, and there's money every-where, and she looks up at these Mounties and says, "I've got to have some help down here." And he says, "You don't ever have to worry here, nobody will ever touch one of those dollar bills." He says, "Let them fall on the floor. No one will ever pick them up." And nobody ever did.

Singer Bobby Wright, who toured with the family, said,

*I always looked forward to it because it was like working
with an encyclopaedia. He had . . . stories about every
town you would go into. One place in Ontario, we'd pull
in there and he said, "I remember working a rodeo here
once. They didn't have a stage set up. There was so many
people . . . I had to climb up the telephone pole and hook a
belt around of me and hang off of the pole and sing to the
people"*

He tried a few other things. Perhaps it was Bobbie
who said, after a few years of this touring, Look, you're
getting on. Maybe we could settle down — but to something a little less demanding than a ranch. They bought
property in a Florida orange grove and built a big motel,
with TV in the rooms and a huge sign across the building,
THE WILF CARTER MOTOR HOTEL. Not Montana Slim;
there were lots of retired Canadians in Florida.

Television had come to Canada, and Tommy Hunter
soon had a regular show of his own. Wilf was one of the
first of the early performers to make a guest appearance.
For the hip young television producers, he was already
somewhere back there in the past — even though the
Hunter production team was turning out a country music
show. "None of the producers, frankly, wanted him on the
show," Hunter says now, with a puzzled look. Had he gone
on too long?

"He never became . . . hip," says musicologist Richard
Flohil:

*Wilf was the old geezer, you know, who came on and
smiled and sang the old songs. . . . The young kids never
got onto him in the way they got on to Stompin' Tom*

Connors. Who would tell you to your face that Wilf Carter was the greatest thing that ever happened to country music. . . . Maybe [Wilf's] music was just what it was for its time.

Another famous country and folk singer, Ian Tyson, suggested to us that Wilf had, in fact, gone on too long. "As a senior citizen," Tyson said, "I'm allowed to voice that." But the reality is that wherever he went, they came. The people. As he got older, so did they. They were coming to hear a man who had sung to them when they didn't have enough to eat and didn't know how they were going to clothe the kids. But if they were coming to hear a memory, they stayed to listen to a friend. How could he stop doing that? It was nourishment for him. It is clear from the bits of film and video that survive, and from the thousands of photographs, that going among the crowd and shaking hands, and signing autographs, was not a chore. He is beaming in those photographs. He answered all his mail by hand. We found people who had written to him regularly, over the years, and said they could always count on a reply. In 1985, when he was eighty-one, the CBC broadcast his inauguration into the Canadian Music Hall of Fame. At the awards shows they were introducing him as a surprising survivor out of the past, almost as if a dinosaur had unexpectedly come to life and was still among us. There is a video clip of him performing in a seniors' home. Like those Nova Scotian oldtimers listening to Wilf Carter imitators in the community hall in Canning, Nova Scotia, the audience knows the words. Wilf tells them a story. He had been playing at another seniors' home:

I looks over and there's this little guy in a wheelchair. "Come here," he says. So I got up real close to him, and he says, "How long have you been in here?" And I said, "Not very long." And he says, "I ain't seen you around." I said, "No." He says, "I don't like your singing." And I said, "I'm sorry sir." "I don't like it," he says. "I'll tell you something. I don't know if you know him or not, but that Wilf Carter can sing." I looked at him and I said, "You know him?" And he said, "No, but I've got lots of his records and we play the dickens out of them. You never met him?" And I said, "No." And he said, "I don't think you're going to go far in singing."

Tommy Hunter went to see him do some of those seniors' shows, when he was now past eighty.

He was getting very hard of hearing. That bothered him. . . . . There were people that . . . just loved to come and sit and talk to him. They would be . . . pouring out their soul, about the first time I met you, you were so kind to me, you signed my autograph and I've carried it around with me. And they'd pull out an autograph signature. And it used to bother Wilf because he couldn't hear.

There had to be an end. He decided on a final concert. He chose Alberta, of course. Trochu, Alberta, population 907. It was May 30th, 1994. Wilf Carter would be ninety later that year. He had never learned to read a note of music, but he had written the words and music to six hundred songs and sold most of them. He was in the Music Hall of Fame in both Canada and the United States. He had sold millions and millions of records. There were people all over the continent who knew his songs, often without knowing they were his, they had always been there, they were part of the country music landscape. At Trochu he introduced his daughter Carol's daughter Bobbie, his youngest grandchild, who had never seen him in concert. He brought her up on the stage with him. People who were there say that while the applause was deafening and never seemed to stop, the tears in everyone's eyes are what they remember most vividly.

Brian Edwards, tour manager for that last concert, said he sobbed along with everyone else. "He put his hands up on the guitar, like this, and he said, 'Well folks. Me and the old girl are gonna have one last tune. And here it is.' It was called 'Have a Nice Day.'"

And at the end Wilf said, "I'm gonna unstring my guitar." He never played it again.

The Calgary Herald. *December 17, 1996*
Wilf Carter, the yodelling cowboy, who was Canada's first cowboy star, died Thursday night in Scottsdale, Arizona, at the age of 91.

◆　◆　◆

The original documentary was written and directed by Tom Radford. It was photographed by Mike Beley, with sound by Larry MacDonald, and edited by Michel Lalonde.

Part Fifteen

GRANT MACEWAN
A People's Prince

It was one night sometime in the mid 1970s. Henry the vice-regal chauffeur was driving the lieutenant governor back to Edmonton from an official ceremony somewhere or other, he doesn't remember *that* detail any more, when his honour said, "Henry, pull over." He wanted to get out and look at the stars. They were spectacular that night, as they so often are in a clear Alberta sky.

The lieutenant governor and the official chauffeur stood there in the cool summer night and looked at the display together. After a while his honour asked the chauffeur to get the sleeping bags out of the trunk, he wanted to lie down and *really* look at those brilliant lights in the sky. And that night the queen's representative in Alberta, and his official chauffeur, slept on the open ground under the stars.

What kind of man, wearing the official trappings of vice-regal office, would do that? Not new to public office and public note, he had been an alderman for the city of Calgary, and later mayor of that city. He'd been head of the Alberta Liberal Party, an unsuccessful candidate for the federal Parliament, a professor of agronomy, and a broadcaster. Before he died, he would have published fifty-five books, novels, biographies, textbooks on agriculture, and histories of a dozen different aspects of his beloved West. Where did he come from?

His name was Grant MacEwan, and he began and

ended almost precisely with the beginning and end of the twentieth century, a farm boy, from Brandon Manitoba. A farm boy who kept a diary. Almost from the beginning words and the making of them on paper began to take him into orbits away out beyond the fence lines. But his feet and his hands never lost the feel of the soil, and his spirit never left it for a moment. Animals great and small, plants of every kind and especially trees, were a spiritual necessity. He started a conservation movement on the Canadian prairies at a time when many laughed at the idea. He planted trees where they were not supposed to grow. There are people today who will show you a tree that came out of the trunk of Grant MacEwan's car one day, not much more than a seedling, and they will say, as they stand in the shade of its spreading branches, "This is Dr. MacEwan."

He was born before the first airplane flew, and he died long after the computer had become entrenched as a way of life. He grew up amongst cattle and hogs and fields of grain; before he died he would preside over the deliberations of governments, teach generations of university students, and softly leave a world that scarcely resembled the one he had been born into it. His dazzlingly beautiful and mischievously humorous granddaughter, Fiona Foran, chuckled at the camera as she said of her beloved grandfather in those last years (and in saying it set the tone for this biographical documentary), "A lot of those [new technological] things he found . . . incomprehensible. Things he couldn't really understand, and why should he? You know, when he was nearly 100, at the turn of . . . the millennium, [well, he'd say] 'Bugger it!'"

His mother Bertha Grant was a serious Presbyterian from Brandon, in fact from six generations of hard, determined Nova Scotia Scots lately arrived in Manitoba. She was strong-willed, judgmental, radiantly beautiful. She had just graduated from Brandon Nursing College the year before she met Alex MacEwan, a tall rangy hired hand with big ideas who had come to work on her father's farm. This was also a determined, confident man. *His* granddaughter — and there is a remarkable sense of cohesive family about this clan — Alex MacEwan's granddaughter Heather MacEwan Foran, tells a story about Alex, a "family story" which you know, as you hear it, is a MacEwan way of telling you what the family values are based on.

"He was coming back across the country by train," she said. "And the train was stuck . . . in the snow, and they didn't know when they were going to . . . get out of this snowbank. And my grandfather walked the hundred miles home. . . . He had only the clothes on his back . . . dress-up clothes and his little satchel . . . I think he had a sandwich . . . in the satchel."

So Alex and Bertha got married, Grant was born, and Alex got a farm of his own. Times were good and he liked to experiment. His son grew up in a universe that prized risk and innovation. It seems that Grant caught his love of animals from his father, and learned that how you cared for a horse was as important (because of the relationship) as was the labour the animal provided. They had prize Clydesdale horses and Black Angus cattle. Every year they would show at the Winnipeg Fair, and check out the amazing new machinery, *some of it actually self-powered — by gasoline-burning engines!!* — that was changing the face of agriculture.

Alex MacEwan had a business drive in him, and when the Great War in Europe began to drive grain prices up, he seized the financial moment, took his unexpected profits, invested them in a fire-extinguisher business in Brandon, and left the farm.

Bad call, as it turned out. During a demonstration of the new products, the building that housed his business and his inventory caught fire, and for all the dozens of fire extinguishers lying around Alex could not get the blaze under control. The building and its contents were destroyed, and so was the business. There was no insurance.

There were still homesteads in Saskatchewan to be picked up just for the asking. The MacEwans took up an empty piece of land near Melfort, dug a well, lived in a neighbour's barn while they built their own place, and started all over again. Grant would later recall how his mother frugally turned down the flame in the lamp when the family knelt for their evening devotions. There was no point burning up kerosene when everyone's eyes were closed in prayer. That's what things were like in those early days in Saskatchewan. The frugality was a characteristic Grant MacEwan would inherit, and later be accused of penny pinching. When he was mayor of Calgary he walked or took the bus to work, leaving the official car in the official garage because it was just, well, *extravagant*, to use a car when the bus service was good and walking was good.

But that was much later.

They did rebuild a life on that Melfort farm, but there

was a painful sacrifice in it for the bright, inquisitive, book-hungry boy. Needed in the barns and on the fields, Grant had to quit school at the end of grade eight. About then he started keeping a diary.

We still have some of those early journals. They record the weight of cattle he took to the fair or the auctions; the breeding of a prize steer; the sinking of a great ocean liner; the boy's craving for a dish of ice cream; the barn-raising bees where the whole neighbourhood would gather to pole up into position the sides of a huge barn and get the roof on, all in a single weekend; the time when a neighbour was so sick he had to be taken to hospital, and the neighbours carried him the whole way (Grant said it was fifty miles) in a litter.

Now he was well into his teens. He began to discover girls. He told his biographer, Donna van Hauff, about Mamie Argyll, whom he met at a box lunch social. The boys would prospect the box lunches on display and bid on them. The lunch you bought brought with it the girl who had made it, and she became your date for the evening. Grant and Mamie went for a sleigh ride that night under the buffalo skins. Grant would later say with a grin, according to Donna van Hauff, "Everything I needed to know about women I learned from Mamie Argyll."

Another young woman, his cousin Willa from Ontario, came for a visit and changed his life in a different way. Willa was from Guelph. There was a new institution of learning there, the Ontario Agricultual College (OAC), and they were teaching a new kind of science called agronomy. Grant did not want to leave the farm, exactly, says his son-in-law Alberta historian Max Foran, "But [he wanted] to go beyond the farm." He sensed that farming was just as susceptible to the great advances wrought by science as were the more spectacular fields of weapons, transportation, and energy, and became convinced his future lay in bringing science and farming together.

It was the fall of 1921. The country was relatively tranquil, prosperous, and optimistic with the Great War nearly three years behind it, the boys back from the front, the myth of permanent peace very much in the air, and a widespread assumption of new possibilities and horizons. Grant MacEwan emptied out his small bank account, took the $63 the college required for registration (several thousand dollars in today's money), and enrolled in the Bachelor of Science program at Guelph. The amiable idiosyncrasies for which he is fondly remembered produced at least one story about the train trip east. Grant slept in the nude, did not own the pyjamas he would later need for a college initiation parade, and often walked in his sleep. You can see it coming. The story says that partway to Toronto he woke up in the middle of the sleeping car corridor, naked as a jaybird, the object of inquisitive glances from behind the curtains of neighbouring bunks. He was obliged to climb the awkward little ladder in front of all this scrutiny to regain his upper bunk. If it is true it seems likely, from what we learn of Grant MacEwan as his life story unfolds, that he would have been as amused by it as everyone else. It is also conceivable that he made it up to entertain his friends, although he was known to be a truthful man. But the most significant thing about the story is that his friends and relatives love to tell it, and tell it with affection, not derision.

He was a striking kid, six and a half feet tall, a glistening head of rich dark hair, lots of it, and blue eyes, people said, that "cut through a room." He was in love with horses and they said he could drive a team with scarcely a tug on the reins. He was a quick student. He thought for himself and spoke his mind. This may have irritated some of his teachers but seems to have won the respect of most because there was no hint of hypocrisy or falseness. The cockiness and self-assurance were authentic, not, as in many young men, a mask for insecurities and inadequacies. He played an outstanding game of basketball. Years later the basketball coach, by then an old man, came to visit him in Edmonton, and said to Grant's son-in-law Max Foran, "Did you know that 'Shorty' here was the best centre in Canada?"

In the summers during his long stay at the Ontario Agricultural College he went down to Toronto in the summer breaks and sold farm produce out of the back of an old Model T Ford. He began to understand the demands of the small entrepreneur and to respect that trade. In 1925 he was awarded a position on the college livestock judging team, and that winter, at the Royal Winter Fair in Toronto, his team won the Canadian intercollegiate championship.

Another young man might have been lured to stay close to the lights and the excitement of the big city. He loved theatre and acted in comedies, and found the cultural life of the city very attractive. But the Manitoba boy had become a son of Saskatchewan, and Saskatchewan for all its severity and challenge — or perhaps because of it — seems to inspire unquenchable loyalties in many of its children. When he got his Master of Science degree — the first degree of any kind in seven generations of farm families — he headed for home.

The next few years were hard work and career building. He took up a post in the University of Saskatchewan's extension department, and set about establishing and spreading scientific and verifiable agricultural methods in a society built on old traditions and not inclined to experiment. This is not a kid any more. He was twenty-six when he started the university job, and while he was far from socially inept or withdrawn, he seems not to have felt any pressing interest in marriage or starting a family. But after a few years he met Phyllis Klein, from Churchbridge, who was in the cast with him in a goofy slapstick show called The Pickle King. Grant played the eponymous lead. When they were married in Saskatoon in June of 1935, the federal minister of agriculture was a guest at the wedding. This was thought to be a mark of distinction.

As he went around the province spreading ideas and offering counsel, he built a reputation for intolerance of sloppy or careless husbandry. Son-in-law Max Foran recalls going with Grant to visit a farmer friend "and the hay was on the ground, and the guy was inside watching a baseball game. . . . 'That hay is on the ground, it's not raining . . . how dare he!' . . . 'Well,' I said, 'maybe there's a good game on.' He said that didn't matter. This guy had no *right* to leave the hay on the ground!"

This illustrates some of the attitudes, not untouched

by the Presbyterian part of his background, that Grant MacEwan brought to his profession. The farmer was not just taking a living out of the land, he was a *custodian*, a *warder*. He had rights as an individual, but they were balanced by obligations, not just towards other citizens and the law, but also to the land and to what it produced. Anyone who did not respect those rights and act accordingly lost the respect of Grant MacEwan. He knew that the university was seen as an elitist institution, and the farmers distrusted it because of the academic disdain for the judgment and opinions of the hands-on guy in the barn. He believed that by beating up and down the province month after month, bringing to farmers ideas they could use, ideas that would improve their production (and their custodial roles) that he could build a bridge between science and tradition. And he felt that he gained ground in that respect. The farmers began to listen to the scientific ideas, his colleagues' respect for the knowledge of the working farmer rose substantially, and the university was able to learn from their experience. Each side was listening to the other more openly.

In the mid 1930s the heady prosperity of the postwar decade was forgotten. The Depression that was crushing North America and the world was literally terrifying in Saskatchewan where a sustained drought was causing whole farms to blow away in clouds of dust. Livestock was starving to death, farmers were dying of despair, and there was year after year of crop failure, with wheat yields averaging less than three bushels an acre. Grant put his agronomical research training to work and researched drought-

resistant wild plants. Russian thistle not only survived, but
it had also helped hold the soil in place. This weed (*salsola
pestifera* or *s. tragi* or *s. iberni*) is popularly known as tum-
bleweed because it breaks off at ground level and rolls in
the wind, sometimes for miles. Farmers and ranchers hate
it, as it sharply reduces crop yields. But in this cropless
landscape it was surviving, and, amazingly, hungry cattle
could eat it, metabolize it. The Russian thistle program was
a lifesaver.

A second experiment was less so. Grant MacEwan
loved horses, but horses were dying and being slaughtered
compassionately — and the people were out of meat.
Grant knew that there would be terrific resistance from
horse-loving Saskatchewanians to the very idea of eating
horsemeat, so he concocted an uncharacteristically devious
scheme. He brought sandwiches to a university cocktail
party, and did not tell anyone that half of them were made
with horsemeat. He kept this quiet until the sandwiches
had all been consumed. Then, still without saying why, he
took a poll as to which sandwiches people liked best. It is
not recorded how he distinguished between the two, but
when the poll declared the two types of sandwich to be
equally popular, he revealed the secret. And, says Calgary
history librarian Jennifer Bobrovitz, "There were people
who never, ever forgave him for that."

He began diligently to preach the interaction and
interdependence of living things, the way in which vegetation secured the soil, bacteria fed the plants, decayed matter fed the bacteria, trees cleansed the air. Even "noxious"
animals were dear to him. His daughter Heather said that

when she was a kid her parents acquired a pair of baby skunks: someone had killed the mother and brought her two babies to Grant out of curiosity. Grant got out his scalpel and some anaesthetic from his veterinarian studies kit, descented the kits, and named them This and That.

"Grant adored trees." He loved tiny things," Heather's daughter Fiona says, her eyes gleaming. "Guinea pigs, gerbils, mice . . . animals like that are often maligned, you know . . . they're vermin, they're pests. . . . Little creatures were . . . the underdogs of the animal world; so Grant was their special friend. . . . [And he] adored trees. There was the romantic aspect of trees and how lovely they were; but then there was the very practical . . . you know, on a farm you plant trees for windbreaks . . . for food, apples, berries. . . Trees were necessary for oxygen exchange. . . . So Grant was always a voice for animals and for trees and the environment, long before it was in vogue to be that way."

It was right in the blackest part of this prairie disaster period that he became poignantly aware that not only were land and farms and livelihoods being ruined, but also that the preoccupation with disaster was leading people to forget their stories, their legacy. On June 10th, 1937, he went to Eaton's and bought a typewriter. He would write the story of the Canadian West as he knew and loved it. He went to the CBC and sold pieces to the old radio Department of Talks and Public Affairs. His first one was called "How Horses Came to Western Canada." Then he did a very popular series of essays, "Sodbusters," very personal pieces about his boyhood on the homesteading

frontier. One of the most heroic characters in these sketches was his father, Alex MacEwan.

But Alex and Bertha were dead now; within a year of
leaving the farm they were both gone.

By the end of World War II he had a prairie-wide reputation, and his daughter Heather had just started to
school when he got a call from Winnipeg. They offered him
the position of dean of agriculture at the University of
Manitoba. It was too good to resist, and even if he was
leaving Saskatchewan, well, he *had* been born in the adjoin-
ing province, so in a way he was going home. Not long
after he took up his new post, the worst flood in Canadian
history hit Winnipeg. There are photographs in the papers
of Grant MacEwan saving the university's pigs and sheep.
He spent night after night up on the dikes with the citizens,
piling up sandbags, patrolling for breaks, taking the midnight to 6 a.m. shift and then putting in a day's work before
he caught a short nap and headed back to the floodwaters
for the midnight watch.

A man whose view of his own integrity and rightness
is as serene and confident as this man's appears to have
been does not escape envy and even hostility. The citizens
may have admired Grant's pictures in the papers during
the flood, but some eyebrows at the university were raised,
not with admiration. Some colleagues thought that it looked
as though MacEwan was actually *seeking* the publicity.

He began to realize that he had better watch his back,
and it was probably at that point that he began to think of
the importance of politics, negotiation, compromise, and
the need to take time, to plod, to not expect everyone to

instantly see your truth. Now he was better known than
the president of the University of Manitoba. He recognized
that there was a risky imbalance of reputations. But if these
rumblings of disapproval were sharpening his political
sensibility, they may also have caused him enough unrest
and dissatisfaction with the university authorities to start
him thinking about alternatives to an academic career.
When a by-election came up in his old hometown of
Brandon, he somewhat imprudently dived in.
Imprudently because his opponent was a native son and a
skilled campaigner, Walter Dinsdale, later to be a prominent and popular minister in the Diefenbaker
Conservative governments of 1957 to 1963. Walter
Dinsdale just ploughed poor MacEwan into the dirt.

So it was another turning point. The university had let
him know that his political candidacy was not acceptable.
There was no career protection then for parliamentary can-
didates, as there is now. Even before the election they
brusquely told him he would not be welcome back in the
dean's office. And so the day after he was defeated he
packed his bags, headed out to Alberta, and took a public
relations job with the Canadian Beef Producers'
Association. A bit ironic for a vegetarian whose motto was
"You don't eat your friends."

He and Phyllis bought land along the slopes rising to
the Rockies, at Priddis. He would say that he intended to
farm there, but Phyllis knew better; she knew he had
caught the disease called Public Life, endemic wherever
democracy is practised, and that he couldn't keep away
from that public, from the attention, the limelight, the

society, the argument, the turmoil, the chance to make a difference.

She was right. In 1953 Grant went after a seat on the Calgary city council, as alderman, and won it. He was almost immediately a source of confusion and dismay to many of his new colleagues at city hall. When a petition came around to ban prostitutes in the neighbourhood where he lived, he said, "These people are my friends!" He would meet them late at night when he walked home from the office and they were working the streets. He had no difficulty with the profession they pursued. They were citizens. He thought the petitioners stuffy and constipated. What they thought of him is not difficult to guess.

Now the provincial Liberals came after him. They supposed he was one of them, at least in spirit; he had after all run as a Liberal in the Brandon by-election. Would he consider leading the not very healthy party? It had long been in the Alberta political shade of the Social Credit Party, the bizarrely successful invention of the evangelist William Aberhart.[18] Founded ostensibly to carry out the economic fantasies of a British fascist named Major C.W. Douglas, the party had somehow survived the hostility of the local press (which it had tried to legislate into silence), and its failure to deliver anything resembling rational policies. It had grasped the anxiety of prairie Albertans in those dark days of the thirties, appealing to their superstitions and promising divine intervention. Aberhart's successor as party leader and premier, Ernest Manning, a balanced and

18. See Part Three, "Bible Bill," in *The Canadians: Biographies of a Nation*, Volume I.

far more attractive politician, was still seen by some Albertans as having a pipeline to the Lord. The Social Credit Party had brought great prosperity to Alberta said one farmer. New Liberal leader Grant MacEwan asked if it weren't possible that the discovery of oil and gas had a lot to do with that prosperity. To which the farmer is said to have rejoined that the Good Lord put the oil and gas in the ground in answer to Mr. Manning's prayers. Once again there is some difficulty in distinguishing between legend and reality when Grant MacEwan's friends and family are talking about this extraordinary teacher, writer, and politician. Max Foran says that MacEwan, when he began to write the stories of The West, consciously and deliberately began to build myth. Myth was needed; there was not enough Canadian myth. Myths were what held a people together, said MacEwan.

"We as a nation are not myth builders," Foran said to us. "And that's part of our problem with identity, I think. See, he built the myth, the Western Canada myth . . . through his writings and his love of the land. . . . He built the myth . . . and he *was* the myth."

For all the human encounter and bustle and attention of the political game in mid-century Alberta, it is possible that during this period (and perhaps even constitutionally) Grant MacEwan was a lonely man. His biographer Donna van Hauff says so. She attributes it to his being out there in public, responding to groups and pressures and policies eighteen hours a day instead of playing with his daughters or spending time with Phyllis. His son-in-law and adoring granddaughters don't talk that way, however; and it will not be possible to write or talk objectively about a man of such presence until those personal connections and memories have receded a bit.

And perhaps it does not matter. Lonely or not, he gave of himself, hugely. In return he was loved and hated, admired and despised. When Harry Hayes relinquished the mayor's chain of office to go into federal politics in 1963, he campaigned successfully to move Grant into the empty office. "Hayseed Wins Mayoralty" is what the *Calgary Herald* wrote, and when the official press release described the new chief magistrate as "lean and lanky," one reporter said it should have read "mean and cranky." They said he was a penny pincher. He left the city's black Chrysler limousine in the garage and walked to work or took the bus. Walking into town before sunrise one day he was stopped by a suspicious cop, who looked at the ID and gasped something like "Holy God, I've just pinched the mayor!" The thrift of the bus appealed to him, and so did the company. He talked to everyone, and reported on his gleanings to his colleagues.

And he started writing again. Out of this period came books on the Blood Chief Tatanga Manni, Louis Riel's pioneering grandmother Maria Ann Gaboury, Nigger John Ware the Black Cowboy, *Eye Opener* Bob Edwards the journalist,[19] a clutch of characters whose individuality and slightly contrary Alberta spirits he found companionable and worthy of recounting. He loved to read aloud. Fiona talks about his reading poetry with tears streaming down

19 See Part Ten of this text.

his cheeks. It was not just the myths of his own making that moved him deeply.

Heather went off to Australia to teach, and came back with Max Foran in tow, and in the spring of 1963 they married. Soon Fiona and then Lynwynn were born, and the Gramp doted on them. He still worked dawn to dusk. A few years later, at the age of seventy, he decided that the house needed an addition, and that he would build it himself, by hand.

"Of course he had done this," Heather told the camera, "many times, on the prairie, with his dad. So we started by digging the foundation with a shovel, putting all the dirt in the back of my truck, hauling the dirt up into the field, dumping it, coming back for another load. And this went on, of course, for months. Because this was a big . . . eight hundred square feet . . . and we were eight feet down!"

Soon after this there came a phone call came that would, in a way, bring us back to the start of this chapter. In 1963 the Progressive Conservatives under Prime Minister John Diefenbaker lost their grip on the national confidence, and the Liberal leader Lester B. Pearson squeaked into power with a fragile minority government. Alberta has always been a tough sell for the Liberals. Pearson needed a popular and attention-getting appointment. He phoned Grant MacEwan. Be our lieutenant governor, he proposed. It was a pretty surprising appointment to most; but probably not to the appointee, who always took everything in his stride.

So now this stoic-looking tall Scots Canadian with the stiff little bit of a moustache and the straight back and the thrifty habits is the queen's representative. How would he be? The stories began to circulate. He was soon going around switching off lights in government house to save money, and Phyllis went around after him turning them on again. People outside saw this processional dance of lights in the windows of the official residence.

"He pushed the office to the limit," Max Foran told us in his engaging Aussie twang. "He set a pace that no one [could] keep up . . . he showed how an elitist position that is window dressing could be translated into a viable political function. . . . He does for the lieutenant governorship what he had done for the university. He takes that bloody thing to the people like no one ever could."

He opened the New Year's levy to women. It is hard to believe that in the second half of the twentieth century there was a public function like this, in the populist province of Alberta, from which women were excluded. But Grant MacEwan put an end to that absurdity. When Phyllis was not well enough to attend public functions, he took Heather with him instead. He brought his grand-daughters into the legislative building's cafeteria and bought them every cake and goodie they pointed to. He kept cookies in a jar on his desk and pressed them on people, including Pat Halligan-Baker, his new secretary.

As she remembers it, "He would say, 'Now Miss Pat, have a cookie.' And I would say, 'Your honour, I can't spend [all] day coming into your office having two or three cookies.' And he would say, 'Woman! Have a cookie!'"

Party leader Peter Lougheed's Alberta Conservatives finally beat out the long-reigning Social Credit government in 1971, but the new young premier forgot that he had an obligation to the vice-regal office.

"I heard his voice as he came into my office. He said, 'Is he in?' And . . . I thought, Oh my gosh, I've forgotten. It's my responsibility . . . to review the cabinet with . . . the representative of Her Majesty. He said, 'You know, I'm supposed to see your list before tomorrow.' And I said, 'Oh I know, your honour, and I'm really embarrassed about that.' And he looked at the list."

Remember this is a Tory premier meeting a long-committed Liberal, who by one of the elegant quirks of our parliamentary tradition stays in office at the pleasure of the federal government, and has the power to name a new premier should death or any other misadventure remove the existing premier.

"He didn't make any suggestions for change," Premier Lougheed told us. "But he made comments about it that were helpful to me then and in the future. . . . He was a good mentor . . . we would have our periodic meetings where the leader of the government can go down the hall and consult with the representative of Her Majesty, and I was very very fortunate to have a Grant MacEwan down the hall."

The graciousness and wisdom went hand in hand with the idiosyncrasies, and perhaps, in that tall personality, they were the same thing. He still loved to work with his hands, especially in wood. For the librarian, Jennifer Bobrovitz, he carved a beaver and a maple leaf out of a piece of a beavered log complete with the tooth marks where the animal had felled the tree. He offered to build coffins for Heather and Max, and when Max expostulated, "What do we do with them in the meantime!" the practical-minded lieutenant governor said, "Use 'em as blanket boxes."

He carried a shovel in the trunk of the official car and planted trees at many schools, hospitals, and other institutions.

When the queen invited him, as her official representative, to fly to the coast and dine with her on the royal yacht *Brittania*, he turned it down because he had already accepted an invitation to a Boy Scout supper on the same day and he wouldn't let them down for royalty. When he finished his term in 1981, the province gave him a high-end Jeep as a farewell gift. MacEwan traded the glossy machine in on a smaller, more efficient model, and gave the difference back to the provincial treasury. A new community college in Edmonton was named after him, and he agreed to conduct informal seminars with the students. He was still doing that at the age of ninety, taking the bus into Edmonton, often to be greeted by the drivers with, "Well, Grant, you going to drive the bus to Edmonton for us today?" to the consternation of those passengers who didn't know the joke and feared perhaps the bus driver meant to turn the wheel over to this ancient, blinking creature.

Grant MacEwan's century was drawing to a close. Phyllis was gone now. He moved into a seniors' home. He needed care most of the time.

"Bugger it," he said sometimes, when he fell off a chair or suddenly found that there was some once simple task he could no longer perform. His family tried to tell him that he should stop trying to do everything, but "you could not tell Father not to do anything," Heather said.

"You could tell him, but he wouldn't listen."

Fiona went to see him in the hospital after he had broken a hip. "I smuggled my guinea pig into the hospital to show him, and . . . I'm blithely walking into the room in the hospital and I could hear this 'oink, oink, oink' from . . . my purse. . . . I opened my purse and out came that little black head, and Gramp was just overjoyed. . . . There was a sort of childlike quality that never left him. Never."

He decided to make one last trip to see the students.

"We thought, well, he can't; he's slowed so much," his granddaughter Lynwynn said. "He's tired if he makes the trip to the dining room and back, you know? That's a long haul for him. And if he has a visitor for half an hour he's tired at the end. How can he possibly make the trip?"

Paul Byrne, the college president, went to the seniors' home to see if the old man was really fit for a trip. Grant was not in his room and the roommate didn't know where he had gone. He was not in the bathroom. Somebody at the nursing station said, "Oh, he's decided to take lunch in the cafeteria." That was a long haul. "It was during the walk back that I knew, Now he *is* serious," Paul Byrne told us. "Just as an Olympic competitor, he was in training, and wanted to make sure he had the strength and the stamina to take on a day of visiting our campuses and speaking to our students."

Greyhound had named a bus the Grant MacEwan. They brought it back from the coast for this last trip. It had to be the bus; Grant would not agree to go in a car. When they lifted his wheelchair down from that bus, he was surrounded; some were weeping, some were laughing, and

335

many came to kiss him and shake his hand. Grant MacEwan just grinned and said, "Let's go." He made it to every event they had planned for him.

When Grant MacEwan died, Max Foran delivered the eulogy in his rangy, compelling Australian voice.

When I went to say good-bye, and I saw those hands, those big gentle hands that had written a million words, hands that had assisted in a birth of many an animal, hands that had reached across three provinces to touch people, hands that could carve wood beautifully, that could use an axe like you and I would use a toothpick. Yet hands that had never raised in anger and never raised in threat to any human being or animal.

And I could see those great big hands. And I kind of lost it. And I said, "Good-bye, Mate."

Director Tom Radford, who made the documentary biography on which this chapter is based, chose one more image with which to follow that farewell. It is a wide shot of the prairie, with foothills in the distance, an empty shot: and into the frame there comes a lone fox, its ears up. It stops briefly, in the middle of the frame, and looks towards us. And then it turns and lopes off, easily, confidently, gracefully. It seems tall, somehow. And then it is gone.

◆　◆　◆

The original documentary was written and directed by Tom Radford. It was photographed by Dwayne Dorland, with sound by Roger Southgate and Larry MacDonald, and edited by Paul Smart.

◆ Part Sixteen ◆

RUTH LOWE

I'LL NEVER SMILE AGAIN

Between the one-hour biographical documentaries in the History Television series on which this book is based, and many of the Historica Foundation's *Heritage Minutes*, there is a natural affinity. I opened the Mona Parsons chapter of this book with its related *Heritage Minute*, and it seems appropriate to do this again for Ruth Lowe. Here is the script of a *Minute* that, at the time of writing this chapter, is in the queue waiting for production.

◆　◆　◆

LOMBARDI

A Heritage Minute

EXT. NIGHT. A stretch of war-torn battlefield on the edge of a Normandy beach, a day or two after the D-Day Landings of June 6th, 1944. Close-ups of Canadian soldiers in battle gear, dug into slit trenches in the sandy soil. Distant flares as artillery shells go off. SUPER: NOR-MANDY, 1944

In a lull in the distant gunfire, a very British voice, considerably exaggerated in its pompous formality:

VOICE
This is the BBC. . .

We see that it is actually a helmeted Canadian SOLDIER,

his face blackened, crouching in his foxhole, speaking with exaggerated tones into an imaginary microphone.

SOLDIER

Dauntless Canadian troops beat back hitherto invincible German forces on their Normandy beachhead today.

Other soldiers' faces in other slit trenches grin nervously, all look up as two Pathfinder Mosquito bombers roar overhead and fade off rapidly to the east. Now another "radio voice" is heard.

LOMBARDI

And this is Canadian Armed Forces Radio . . .

We see this other soldier, also speaking into an imaginary microphone, his free hand digging a battered, tarnished old cornet out of his pack. His nametag says LOMBARDI.

LOMBARDI (cont.)

*. . . with sump'n that **really** matters, that great, great hit, "I'll Never Cry Again," by Toronto's own Ruth Lowe.*

He puts the cornet to his lips and plays the familiar first four bars. As he hits the last note another pair of Pathfinders roar by, and LOMBARDI instinctively ducks, pauses in his playing. As the noise of the Mosquito bombers fades we hear a spattering of applause, see a few hands, faces, in foxholes, as a voice calls out,

VOICE

Play it again, Johnny!

Other voices echo, *"Yeah! Encore!"* etc. with spatterings of applause, as the cornet picks up again, this time with "Put Your Dreams Away."

NARRATOR

Musician and broadcaster Johnny Lombardi would continue to play a prominent role in our popular culture for another half century, and . . .

DISSOLVE

STILL PHOTO: RUTH LOWE, PULL BACK INTO THE HERITAGE MINUTE GRAPHIC. LOON CALL.

NARRATOR (cont.)

. . . his Toronto composer friend, Ruth Lowe, would be named to the American Music Hall of Fame.

◆ ◆ ◆

This chapter is about that same Ruth Lowe. Her song was indeed "a great big hit," a sensational hit. All the radio stations were playing it. I vividly recall my sister Mary bringing home the sheet music, spreading it out on the piano, and singing the words. That was probably in 1940. I remember my brother John saying, "Did you know that song was written by a Toronto girl?" That seemed very special, a song that was being heard all over the continent, written by a Toronto girl? We knew nothing about her, but we all felt proud anyway.

She was born in 1914, and left us twenty years ago, in 1981. But as the production crew began to prepare this biography, they found no shortage of people who wanted to talk about "Ruthie." First among them, Ruth's younger sister Micky Cohen.

My mother was born in England, my father was New York born, where they met I don't know. . . . We were born in Toronto actually, Ruth and I, and then we moved to California when I was about two years old.

Bert Lowe, Ruth's and Micky's father, was a butcher who had been brought up in an orphanage in New York. After a few successful years in Toronto he yielded to the luxurious descriptions of California life in letters from his two brothers there, and decided to try his luck in his native country. Photographs of Bert show a ready smile and an outgoing personality, plump, genial, a touch of playfulness around the eyes and mouth.

"He had a wonderful sense of humour," Micky Cohen says. "He liked to entertain a lot at family gatherings. He sang. He could always improvise and make everybody laugh."

In his butcher shops, it is said, Bert was likely to be singing when a customer came in, would start up again as he made up the order, and break off in the middle of "Gee But It's Great After Being Out Late," and hand over the string-wrapped parcel with "Pound and a half of veal, Mrs. Green, twenty-five cents, thank you" and go right on with "Walkin' My Baby Back Home." He was seriously overweight.

There was always a piano in the house. In middle- and working-class homes of the pre-television age a piano was often the entertainment centre of gravity. Tens of thousands of unwilling kids were forced into piano lessons. To get a teaching certificate in Ontario schools, a candidate had to have a certificate of proficiency in piano from the Royal Ontario Conservatory of Music. There was a piano in almost every classroom, and music was a fundamental component of the public education system. By grade three kids were being taught to read music by what was called the Sol Fa system (*do, re, mi, fa, so, la, ti, do*); long green-and-beige charts hung from windowblind rollers on every blackboard in the junior grades.

Micky Lowe was one of those kids who did not find the piano lessons very rewarding, and soon gave them up. But Ruth loved the piano from the start, and her Los Angeles teacher ("Professor Zimmerman" he called himself) predicted a future for her as a classical concert artist. Ruth had other plans: jazz and popular songs had taken over her creative imagination, and would never leave.

"Ruthie's jazz was really of her own invention. She was never *taught* jazz," Micky says.

We always had a piano. We could be poor as church mice but we had a piano, always. Family days were picnic days, going to a big park on a Sunday afternoon, taking big picnic lunches. . . . There was always a lovely bandstand with music playing, and that was our Sunday afternoons. Ruth and I got along extremely well. We didn't quarrel although there was six years' difference. [But then] due to bad circumstances things go really tough and my father decided to come back to Toronto to my mother's family. And the only thing he shipped [back to Toronto] was the piano.

This was the Depression that followed the stock market crash in October 1929. And if Bert Lowe was determined to keep music alive in his house, he certainly was not alone. Songs kept pouring out of America. "If You Knew Susie," "Don't Bring Lulu," "These Foolish Things Remind Me of You," the whole Al Jolson canon because Jolson was everybody's favourite, "Mammy," "Alabammy Bound," and a seemingly endless stream of love songs, most of them soppy, some of them sublime. Irving Berlin and the Gershwins were as well known in Canada as they were in the States.

In the dozens of family photographs that have survived you can see the affection Micky speaks of. The two girls always seem to be together, more often than not hugging each other or holding hands or looking affectionately at each other as the parents beam at them, Depression or no Depression. The Lowe family came back to a Toronto that pretty well ended at St. Clair Avenue to the north. Nobody in downtown Toronto had even heard the word Mississauga, and a kid could get on a bike and be out in the country within ten minutes from just about anywhere in the city you cared to name. A fine new building was going up on King Street, the Canadian Bank of Commerce, and Torontonians boasted (correctly) that it would be the tallest building in the British Empire. The Royal Ontario Museum, which had opened on Bloor Street just before Ruth was born, was now overflowing with visitors who could afford little other entertainment but would spend a happy family afternoon browsing the mummy cases, the arms and armour, and the dramatic glass-cased First Nations and wildlife dioramas.

There were lots of cars left over from the pre-

Depression days, the early Chevrolets, the Model T Fords, and a long spoke-wheeled monster called a Hupmobile with two spare wheels tucked into wells in the front mud-guards and a real steel and leather-strapped trunk mount-ed on the back end. Horses were still everywhere, drawing the milk and bread and ice wagons and delivering for Eaton's and Simpsons, the two big rival department stores. On the east side of Yonge Street near Shuter there was an archway that opened into a tunnel running right through to Victoria Street. It was called the Yonge Street Arcade. As you strolled through on the sidewalk level, looking in the windows of Doc Jones' Clothing and Furnishings, or Harry Smith's ARCADE MAGIC AND NOVELTY SHOP, you could also look skyward towards the arched glass roof and see the second and third levels with their cast-iron bal-conies and staircases running up from the ground level. A few doors further along you would come to Anne Foster's Song Shop, the *Song Shop* for short. Within a few years after the Lowe family returned to Toronto that's where you would find Ruth Lowe almost every afternoon.

Bandleader Johnny Lombardi went into the Song Shop all the time. "Our band would play one parish hall after another." He says. "We were very popular because we played for less than anybody else. We found our material . . . on Yonge Street . . . and particularly in the Arcade. . . . It seemed to be the Tin Pan Alley of Toronto."

When she was about sixteen, Micky says, Ruth quit school to work full-time at the Song Shop. There were sheet music shops like that all over the continent. That was what George Gershwin did for a living before he became famous as a composer. Good young sight-readers would sit at the piano all day. You came in and said "What've you got that I'd like?" or "Gee, I heard a new Irving Berlin song on the radio today, something about dancing cheek to cheek? Have you got it yet?" and the song-plugger would pull it down off the shelf and put it on the music rack on the piano and play it by sight. And if she played it well and you liked it you took it home for the Saturday night party and started to learn it. Ruth was a superb sight-reader.

"She had to be," says conductor Howard Cable, who was long a mainstay of CBC Radio in the days when radio concerts were still a big programming item. "Because the music would come up from New York and it would be lined up in the shop and she'd have to play it by sight if she hadn't seen it before. . . . I always understood that she was pretty well self-taught. But she was certainly an exceptional pianist and she could . . . also personify the song. She didn't actually sing the song, she wouldn't sing it but she would say, "This is the way the song goes and these are the lyrics . . ." Of course, the idea was to sell the [sheet music.] We got almost all of our repertoire, our library, from Anne Foster's Song Shop."

And Johnny Lombardi adds, "When we talked about certain hits of the day . . . we would always mention, "This is what Ruthie Lowe suggested. . . . And she was always giving you advice, especially newcomers in the business, people like myself that were just starting up a band. Musicians are a hard sell. They just don't buy anything. They've got to be sold on the idea. And she sold everybody that listened to her piano playing."

段1

In addition to plugging sheet music for Anne Foster, Ruth got some work at a local radio station. She was playing and listening to songs all day long. It was inevitable that she start creating some of her own. One of her early pieces, which appears to come from that period, when she was about nineteen, is "My Dreams Will Soon Be Gathering Dust, But I'll Get Along." It is a mature, well-thought-out and quietly witty romantic lyric with a comfortable and original tune.

Ruth's family was dealt a heavy blow at about this time. Maybe it was the overweight problem or maybe it was just bad luck, but Bert Lowe died of a sudden heart attack, and didn't leave much of anything. Now Ruth would have to be the family breadwinner. She was working close to full-time as a studio accompanist at CKCL radio. That paid more than the Song Shop, but she kept on part-time at the Song Shop too, and so the family kept going.

In the famous Marilyn Monroe movie *Some Like It Hot*, there is an all-woman dance band. It is, in fact, modelled after a real band, led by a dynamic blond conductor and arranger named Ina Rae Hutton. Toronto was an important venue for all the big American bands. Duke Ellington, Cab Calloway, Tommy Dorsey, Glenn Miller: they all played Toronto. Sometimes they performed at the Casino Theatre on Queen west of Bay, which was a vaudeville and striptease theatre that booked good swing and big band jazz from time to time, sometimes at the huge Shea's Hippodrome on Bay Street just north of Queen. The Shea's stage could accommodate the biggest of the big bands. Ina Rae Hutton was playing Shea's. When the pianist got sick someone told Ina Rae Hutton to check out this young girl name Ruth Lowe, at the Song Shop.

Not only was Ruth a fine sight-reader able to learn new music by heart in the beat of an eyelid, but she also could write out arrangements on the suggestions of the conductor-arranger. Ina Rae Hutton was dazzled. By the end of that week at Shea's Ruth was invited to join the band and go on the road.

"I think the sales of music sheets went down considerably when Ruthie Lowe left town," says Johnny Lombardi.

It was 1934, so Ruth was about twenty. And when this natural brunette turns up in her first photograph with the Hutton band, she is suddenly a blond. They toured by bus. They would sometimes strike the setup at one town and get on the bus to the next, find a hotel, stretch out for a few hours, and then be on the bandstand again for two or even three shows the next night. If the band stayed in town for several days there could be up to five shows a day. Ruth loved it. The photographs show a very happy woman who is maturing rapidly, has put on a modest and healthy few pounds, and seems to have found her place in the universe. She is sending home a substantial amount of her salary to her mother and sister, and she is seeing New York and Pittsburgh, Minneapolis/Saint Paul, Kokomo Indiana, St. Louis Missouri, San Francisco, Boston, and all roads in between. And Chicago, where she met Harold.

In every city there was no shortage of good-looking men who wanted to rub shoulders or better with the women in Ina Rae Hutton's glamorous band. Harold

Cohen was a song-plugger in Chicago, so he and Ruth had a lot to talk about. Although she was soon on the road again and a long way from Chicago, Harold burned up the telephone lines night after night, and Ruthie wrote home to Momma about this great guy she had met. Before long they were married.

But it didn't last. By all accounts, and from his photographs, Harold Cohen was a strong, optimistic, capable, athletic, extremely good-looking man. But Micky recalls a very difficult moment, not two years after Ruth and Harold married. The phone rang; it was Ruth. Harold had gone in for a routine operation, and had died.

Ruth came home to Toronto. Her photograph from that period shows a pinched face, exhausted eyes, the comfortable roundness of her figure from the pictures of only a year earlier now gone, the frame thin, the shoulders stooped.

Seeking consolation in her music, she began to work on a song that would become, almost overnight, part of the repertoire of just about every band and singer on the continent, the song that Johnny Lombardi plays in the *Heritage Minute* script at the beginning of this chapter, the song that she addressed to her dead husband, "I'll Never Smile Again (Until I Smile at You)." It is melodically and harmonically sophisticated, three different chords for each of the three notes on "I'll ne-ver," right at the beginning, with a yearning and even slightly sexy augmented fifth on the last of those three, and a clear and authoritative melodic line all the way through the piece.

Ruth soon found her way back into the radio studios

as an accompanist. One day, she was playing her new composition in the then only six-year-old CBC station in the Canada Carbon Building at Davenport and Bathurst. The CBC's elegant and famous composer-conductor-arranger Percy Faith stopped by, listened to the plaintive melody and lyric, and asked if he could use it in his big-band live CBC concert. He did a rich arrangement with lush strings and brass polish. In those days there were no tape recorders, but whole shows were sometimes recorded for archive purposes on big fourteen-inch disks called "soft cuts." These were cut directly into an acetate plastic that would not survive more than a few plays with a phonograph needle. Percy Faith gave Ruth a soft cut of her song from that show. The family still has a copy of it, with a faded typewritten label dated November 22, 1939, and marked "Dub." So it is not the original, which must have been made not later than August of that year. We know that because in August the Tommy Dorsey Band was booked to play the Canadian National Exhibition in the huge tent where ten thousand people could dance to the visiting orchestras. Ruth decided to take the big acetate disk down to the musician's entrance at the tent and wait until Tommy Dorsey showed up, and then give it to him.

"You see," she said much later, in a radio interview, "I knew his guitar player very well. And Tommy Dorsey thought it was a marvellous song. He asked if he could publish it. He also thought Percy Faith was . . . wonderful . . . and wanted to hire both of us at the time!"

It is not surprising that Dorsey was impressed. Big name bandleaders were flooded with manuscripts of new songs from hopefuls, but here was a recording, with a big band (and strings, no less!) and a name conductor, by a virtually unknown composer-lyricist, and a young girl at that, a girl with a real romantic tragedy behind the song. He apparently thought it was a song worthy of a well-strategized launch. In 1940 a promising young singer joined the Dorsey band, a kid named Frank Sinatra, and Tommy Dorsey gave him "I'll Never Smile Again" to work on. Howard Cable speculates that Dorsey believed that America was soon going to war and the song was meant for those going away and for those who were left behind, "I'll never smile again, until I smile at you."

"And I think in 1940 [Sinatra] left Harry James and he went over to Dorsey, and I think Dorsey's idea was that . . . this . . . would be part of that whole nostalgic emotional aspect of wartime music."

Johnny Lombardi adds, "They'd hear Sinatra singing that song, and they'd say, 'Gee . . . I'm thinking about my girlfriend and my family, and that's the song I remember more than any.'"

Dorsey used the song to launch his new singer. Sinatra's brilliant technique, with phrasing which mined out of those simple, straightforward words the maximum impact they could convey, turned it into an instant hit. Glen Miller was one of the first of the other big bandleaders to pick it up, and then pretty soon it was everywhere. Dorsey recognized the marketing power of Ruth's personal story, the story behind the song. He brought her to New York and made sure she was interviewed by newspapers and radio at every opportunity. Photographs of the

Paramount Theatre, where the band was presenting the song, show RUTH LOWE in two-foot-high letters, bigger than Sinatra and bigger than Dorsey himself.

Before long Ruth felt overwhelmed by the demand for public appearances, and brought Micky down from Toronto to act as her secretary. "Frank [Sinatra] was performing with . . . the band at the Paramount" Micky remembers. "That was when all the people were lined up outside and screaming and screaming. And after the performance that night Frank came back to our room in the Astor to say Hi and everything, and I . . . I just about died. . . . I *met him!!!*"

When Frank Sinatra got his first network radio show he called Ruth and said, "I need a closing theme." She was thrilled, and agreed to start on it right away. Sinatra said that was good, because he needed it tomorrow morning. Ruth said that she had a melody shaping up in her mind almost before the phone call was over, but she had trouble with the lyrics. So she called two songwriting friends, and the three of them stayed up all night and delivered the song on time, the next morning. It was "Put your Dreams Away for Another Day."

For a while Ruth had been half of a double-piano act in New York with a popular and gifted pianist and singer named Sair Lee. Sair and Ruth had met in the Ina Rae Hutton days. There is a recording extant of a goofy song they sent Harold in Chicago during the courtship period. Sair and Ruth had stayed friends, and now they became very close again, playing New York clubs, according to Howard Cable, until Ruth went back to Toronto. Sair Lee died very young. Ruth had lost two of the people with whom she was closest. Her songs often reflect a dreamy and slightly sad sense, and Ruth herself used to say, "Audiences enjoy a good cry sometimes."

But a blind date brought new sunshine to Ruth's life. Her brother-in-law, Mickey with an "e," had arranged for her to go dancing with a businessman named Nat Sandler, and Nat Sandler kept putting it off. Perhaps he felt he was being set up with a nice widow, but that wasn't exactly on *his* road map, and so he would say yes and then change his mind. The first time he actually agreed to meet Ruth he did not show. So when they finally met and Ruth realized that this was the rude man who had stood her up she was pretty cold at first.

But not Nat Sandler. He was, it seems, smitten.

"He just couldn't keep his eyes off her, and from that moment on," said Johnny Lombardi, "he just knocked on her door until they married."

They were married two months later and soon had a son, Stephen, followed not long after by Tommy. From the photographs of those first days, photographs in which someone is always embracing someone else, much like the albums of Ruth and Micky and Momma and Poppa, it looks as though all the threads had come together at last.

Nat was probably a little uncertain about the entertainment world from which Ruth had come, but he was fascinated at the same time — sufficiently so that one night after a few too many whiskies with an old friend he actually agreed to buy an old Toronto nightclub. At around that time the film director Vincent Minelli approached them about making a movie based on Ruth's life, to star Minelli's wife Judy Garland. It was a pretty heady proposition: both Minelli and Garland were names you saw in lights at that time. But Nat Sandler was very cautious about the business side of the entertainment world. When he had finished examining the terms of the Minelli deal he advised Ruth to turn it down, and she turned it down.

The nightclub at 12 Adelaide Street West had been operating as the Club Norman. Nat and his partner changed the name to the Club One Two, and Johnny Lombardi remembers it as " the nicest club in Toronto."

Stephen Sandler remembers going there. "It was black tie. They had live dancing, live bands. I don't know how he got out of that, the transition between that and the brokerage business . . . [but] when he started his own firm in 1962 or 1963 . . . he was probably the first or second Jewish member of the Toronto Stock Exchange."

It seems strange, in 2001, to think that anti-Semitism was still such a functional part of Toronto society only forty years ago. But for the most part Ruth's life had taken on a social and familial tranquillity and stability that was welcome and comforting; restful after all those years of travel and glamour and the excitement and demands of the band circuit. Tom Sandler describes it from the child's point of view.

> It was . . . a typical 1950s kind of an upbringing where that's basically what the roles were, the man would go out and work, and the woman, the wife, stayed home sort of thing. But she really didn't stay home, and do baking and cooking, kind of. She did that too, but, she had a lot of fun,

she liked to have nice things and she would like to go shopping, she was involved with a lot of charity work and stuff like that. And then of course she was always writing or re-writing or playing music or, you know, speaking to somebody, going somewhere like New York to talk to somebody about her music.

I remember her playing every day. She would sit down at the piano, and play, and she had a number of songs that she really loved. The music was . . . totally powerful, all-encompassing.

And Cookie Sandler, Stephen's wife, adds, "Whenever there was a party we'd always get her to sit at the piano and play. We used to do May long weekends at the cottage, and we'd have fireworks and I can just remember her sitting there pounding away at the piano and everybody singing. . . . Everybody loved her."

She was an avid card player. The room service bills and other notes all scribbled over with game scores on the back — which Ruth saved from her honeymoon with Nat — show that even at the beginning of their marriage they were spending hours playing gin rummy. One of her great pleasures was to go off to Buffalo with some women friends, hole up in a suite in a hotel, and play cards non-stop, for money, for a whole weekend. She went to the races and bet on them too. Tom Sandler remembers the all-day card parties at the house at 1 Manitou Boulevard.

And I would come home from school sometimes and the house would be like . . . you needed a gas mask to walk into the house because there was so much smoke in the air you couldn't breathe, they were all smoking cigarettes, they were all screaming at each other, there was no booze, nobody drank, thank God, or they would have burned the house to the ground probably. The card games [were] always in the basement There were at least twelve to fifteen women, all my "aunts." My sister-in law Cookie reminded me that as well as the smoking and the screaming, some of them would be sitting playing in their brassieres. Mom would aways make me her partner, but only if she was winning.

Life had settled into comfortable patterns. Ruth may have thought that the world was beginning to forget about her, although in Toronto, whenever they went to a clubby restaurant like the Imperial Room at the Royal York Hotel, where there was an orchestra, they would always strike up "I'll Never Smile Again" when she walked into the room. The Mills Brothers played that room and would come and sit at Ruth's table between sets. Oscar Peterson was a friend. Lena Horne brought a show to town and Ruth took the family backstage to meet her afterwards and they all sat around the dressing room and talked about the old days.

There was a woman songwriters' convention of some kind in New York to which Ruth invited her daughter-in-law Cookie.

We stayed at the Waldorf Astoria. And as we were walking around the corner to the hotel . . . she yelled, "There's Frank!" She started moving very quickly forward to catch him, and we walked into the lobby and she yelled, "Frankie!" and he turned around and said "Ruthie!" And I kind of stood there . . . and she introduced me, and we chatted for a while, and . . . I mean . . . it was as if he'd seen her the day before!. . . . She did tell me that she [had thrown] Frank Sinatra out of her room [once, and that] she kind of regretted it at times. She'd say, Maybe she shouldn't have. . . . It would have been a nice story for her.

It is clear that the life of family and friends completely overshadowed her showbusiness career. Of course there would be moments when the stage beckoned, and sometimes in a club Ruth would begin to make signs that she might like to go up there and maybe do a number or two at the piano, the bandleaders would have loved it. But Nat valued his privacy and discouraged that. Ruth was really happy with Nat; so she complied for the sake of the marriage: that was where the real values lay.

One day in 1955 she was asked to go to California, to discuss the possible publication of one of her older songs. She did not for a moment suspect that she was being set up. Her sister Micky had been enlisted to help ensure her unwitting compliance. It would be fun to spend a few days in Los Angeles, maybe look up some of the old music pals, maybe have a drink with Frank Sinatra, take in a show. She had no idea what was really in store.

It is difficult now for people of the cable and satellite era to sense what the television world was like when there were only four or five channels, and the most popular programs were known to virtually everybody in North America. One of those shows was called *This Is Your Life*, and its smooth and charming host, Ralph Edwards, was as well known in America as the president of the United States. The program brought both celebrities and relatively unknown local heroes (a street cop beloved in his town, for example) out to Los Angeles on some pretext or other. Their secrecy was almost watertight. They were very inventive in helping a conspiring friend or relative devise reasons why the unsuspecting Guest of the Week should suddenly pick up and get on a plane or the train for the West Coast. Very few of the subjects ever guessed the real reason behind the sudden suggestion from the kid brother or the cousin in Milwaukee that they take a few days and go have some fun in LA. In the meantime the program's research staff would have contacted as many relatives and close friends as they could manage and invited them to the live broadcast, sworn to secrecy. In the case of media celebrities they would secure some film footage or sound recordings to play during the show. And then, expecting that you were going to the theatre for an afternoon's entertainment, you would be led out onto the stage, and told "Joe Smith, This Is Your Life!" And there would be people you might not have seen for decades, the evidence and footprints of your life across the years, your accomplishments, your loves, sometimes your losses and dismays. Tears were a necessary part of the emotional armamentarium of that experience. Millions tuned in every week.

Micky Cohen was the prime conspirator this time, and says that she easily persuaded Ruth that the fake cover story was true. There was to be a press conference — still not that unusual when Ruth made one of her visits to the States — in a downtown theatre, which was also fairly ordinary.

Ralph Edwards is seen in the old kinescope recording of that show (no videotape in those days) whispering conspiratorially to the live audience in the theatre, "She's a Canadian. So she doesn't know anything about *This Is Your Life* being from this theatre."[20] Ruth was suitably emotional. The boys, then five and ten years old, were flown out and brought on for their hugs and kisses. Ruth is seen saying, "If I'd known I'd've had a bleach!" People who remember the television of that period will know that, even for a mature and already well-recognized artist such as Ruth Lowe, appearing on that program was tantamount to having some kind of Global Seal of Approval stamped on your life. Ruth took it in stride; the family still light up with smiles and excitement when they talk about it. You had arrived, if you were on *This Is Your Life*.

The American Academy of Recording Arts, the people who organize the Grammy Awards, sponsor an American Music Hall of Fame. When they learned of Ruth's death in 1981, Tommy Dorsey and Frank Sinatra signed the nomination for her inclusion in the Hall of Fame, and the same year saw her awarded a Grammy posthumously. There is, to this writer's knowledge, no such honour for the prophet in her native land, nothing for the brilliant composer and lyricist who sent a song into the hearts of millions, and stayed home in Toronto to play poker with the girls.

If Ruth Lowe's head had been turned by her success, if celebrity had been the driving force in her life, she could,

20. The kinescope recording was a sixteen-millimetre-film camera focused on a television screen, with a shutter adapted to eliminate the problems caused by the difference between film's twenty-four frames per second and television's thirty frames. It was really just a black-and-white motion picture of the television image as it appeared on the screen. It was low on contrast and resolution, but a perfectly useable archive or analysis recording, and still employed as late as 1966, six or seven years after videotape was in common use. It is the only format in which many programs from as recently as the late 1960s were recorded.

like many a "star," have put together a publicity machine to make sure her name was always in print and up for nomination to every award going. Celebrity is a well-understood business, and most of its practitioners are obsessed with it. But this was a creative artist whose authentic life currents were as rooted in the core values of family and friends as they were in her music. She was too wise in the joys of simple human intercourse over a dinner table or a hand of gin rummy among the laughter and affection of old friends — too wise to be taken in by the glitter. Agreeable and entertaining though it was — to be sought after by the columnists and hailed as a friend by the great and famous — it never became a need for Ruth Lowe, and so it never threatened to destroy her as it has destroyed so many.

When Frank Sinatra died in 1998, his family chose one song to be played at the funeral. It was "Put Your Dreams Away for Another Day," the piece Sinatra had commissioned from Ruth Lowe for his radio series so many years before. The stories about Ruth Lowe just keep on coming. My favourite is Johnny Lombardi's, who said that as he lay in a slit trench under the artillery barrages during the invasion of Normandy, he reached into his kit and pulled out a battered German soldier's cornet he had "captured," and put it to his lips, and inspired the brief drama with which I opened this chapter.

And the boys called out from the other trenches, amid the clamour of war, *"Play it again, Johnny. Play it again."*

◆ ◆ ◆

The original documentary was written and directed by Martin Harbury. It was photographed by Andrew Binnington, with sound by Tom Bilenky and Gary Oppenheimer, and edited by Peter Shatalow.